Praise for TXT ME (646) 759-1837

"Bonin Bough is one of the most important change agents in marketing; his knowledge of mobile marketing is second to none. One of America's most energetic mobile believers and a true friend, Bonin brings his unique sermon on mobile from the pulpit to the page."

—Carolyn Everson, VP of Global Marketing Solutions at Facebook

"Insightful, in-the-trenches look at how businesses can transform themselves with digital and how individuals are having their lives transformed by mobile."

—Gary Vaynerchuk, entrepreneur and marketing leader

"Surprising and insightful. . . . Bonin reveals the many different ways in which mobile technology can impact our lives. A powerful message that affects us all."

—Peter Guber, CEO of Mandalay Entertainment, owner of the Golden State Warriors & LA Dodgers, and #1 *New York Times* bestselling author

"Bonin is a scientist in marketer's clothing, studying the nature of communication between people through networks the way a biologist would observe ants touching antennae. His insights are not mere intuitions, but rigorous, workable, and applicable lessons in the transmission and dissemination of ideas. In the wrong hands, these tools are dangerous. In the right ones, well, let's see what you come up with."

—Douglas Rushkoff, author and media expert

TXT ME
(646) 759-1837

TXT ME
(646) 759-1837

Your Phone Has Changed
Your Life. Let's Talk about It.

B. BONIN BOUGH

BenBella Books, Inc.
Dallas, Texas

Participating in the *Txt Me* experience may unlock exclusive deals and special offers. As your contribution is important, please keep in mind that standard carrier rates regarding SMS or data may apply, and you can opt out whenever you wish by texting "STOP" to (646) 759-1837.

OREO, TRIDENT, PHILADELPHIA, CADBURY, CHIPS AHOY, HONEY MAID, RITZ, TRISCUIT, WHEAT THINS, and TANG are trademarks of Mondelēz International group, used with permission.

 BenBella Books, Inc.
PO Box 572028
BenBella Dallas, TX 75357-2028
www.benbellabooks.com
Send feedback to feedback@benbellabooks.com

Printed in the United States of America

Library of Congress Cataloging-in-Publication Data
Names: Bough, B. Bonin, author.
   Title: Txt Me : Your phone has changed your life. Let's talk about it. / B. Bonin Bough.
   Other titles: Text Me
   Description: Dallas, Texas : BenBella Books, Inc., [2016] | Includes bibliographical references and index.
   Identifiers: LCCN 2015039214| ISBN 9781942952374 (trade cloth : alk. paper) | ISBN 9781942952367 (electronic : alk. paper)
   Subjects: LCSH: Cell phones—Social aspects. | Information technology—Social aspects. | Information technology—Economic aspects. | Telecommunication. | Mobile communication systems. | Internet industry.
   Classification: LCC HE9713 .B68 2016 | DDC 303.48/33—dc23 LC record available at http://lccn.loc.gov/2015039214

Editing by Leah Wilson
Copyediting by Eric Wechter
Proofreading by Brittney Martinez
   and Lisa Story
Indexing by Debra Bowman
Full cover design by
   The Participation Agency
Cover photos by Lizzy Snaps Sullivan

Cover logos courtesy of Twitter, Inc.;
   Tinder, Inc.; Pandora Media, Inc.;
   AOL, Inc.; BuzzFeed; Facebook; and
   Uber Technologies, Inc.
Text design and composition by
   Publishers' Design and Production
   Services, Inc.
Printed by Lake Book Manufacturing

Distributed by Perseus Distribution
www.perseusdistribution.com

To place orders through Perseus Distribution:
Tel: (800) 343-4499
Fax: (800) 351-5073
Email: orderentry@perseusbooks.com

Special discounts for bulk sales (minimum of 25 copies) are available.
Please contact Aida Herrera at aida@benbellabooks.com.

contents

acknowledgments

F ROM MANUSCRIPT TO MOVEMENT, it was a three-year journey to bring this book project to life. Taking my thoughts on mobile from the pulpit (of the numerous global conferences I speak at) to the page started off as a "fun-to-do" project, but it became more challenging than I could have imagined. I can't express how excited I am to share this book with you.

There were many people who made this book what it is. One of the earliest was Luke Robert Mason, the researcher and one of the strongest believers on the project and also the person responsible for this book's title. Completing the manuscript was only the first half of the journey; it was not until two years into the project, when Luke and I sat at a coffee shop two blocks from my house, that we came up with "Txt Me." I knew all along that we wanted to do something different and it was that title that was the inspiration to turn the book into a conversation: to start a movement. A movement to understand the impact your phone is having on your life.

This book would have not been possible were it not for the unique talents of Peter Smith, who was able to both carry my voice and craft this book into a compelling read. His ability to mold complex ideas around provoking narratives is unparalleled. We were truly lucky to have him agree to be part of our team.

This book was truly a team effort, and I am so grateful of every single person who has been on this journey. One of the most important is Cheryl Kuchel Joseph—the love of my life. She has been there for every call (even when I wasn't), and was copied onto every email and every text that was sent on the project. It would have never happened without her love and dedication.

Special mention goes to Mickey McManus and Bant Breen—the smartest people I know. They were there for me whenever I thought the book had lost its direction or needed to be inspired. They are both dangerous armed with white-boards and marker pens.

Jonathan Cohen was the one who helped to start the spark that gave rise to the flame. Together with his team from Agency of Trillions, he was able to help us find our agent, writer, and publisher and shaped the development of the project during the early days.

However, without our agent Jeff Kleinman in our corner we might have never met the amazing people at BenBella, who have been pivotal.

The involvement of BenBella might be the single largest reason this book is happening. Their belief in this book has been unprecedented. I want to thank everyone there; they have been been amazing, and I could not have asked for a more dedicated publisher. Special thanks go to Leah Wilson for her tireless editing. It is because of her that the book is 1,000 times better than I could have ever imagined. And it is because of their entire team that I know we are going to crush it. Big shout-outs go to The Participation Agency of Jessica Resler and Ruthie Schulder for their creative genius and Josh Cocktail for his inspiration and excitement.

Then there are all of the people who shared their opinions, stories, and perspectives for the book. It is impossible to count the number of conversations with various folks over the last three years but these names stick in my mind (in alphabetical order): Raj Amin, Dana Anderson, Chrys Bader-Wechseler, Adam Bain, Trudy Barber, Katherine Bell, Brad Berens, Gary Bunt, Hedi Campbell, Gotham Chopra, Nigel Clarkson, Josh Cocktail, Susan Cole, Matthew Collier, Louis Cona, Ron Conway, Frank Cooper, Dick Costolo, Doug Davis, Laura Desmond, David Droga, Marc Ecko, Carolyn Everson, Brian Felsen, Chris Fralic, Cindy Gallop, Mike Germano, Alexis Ginas, Renny Gleeson, Daniel Gluck, Peter Greenberger, Bobby Grunewald, Peter Guber, Mark Hatch, Gail Heimann, Guy Horrocks, Lacey Hulsey, Tim Hutchings, Alex Johnston, Dan Jones, Jeffery Jones, Jesse Kirschbaum, Elliott Klein, Daniel Kraft, Kevin Lee, Ben Lerer, Ken Lerer, Bex Lewis, Brian Logan Dales, Jeff Lucas, Marc Monseau, Amanda Mork, Mahesh Murphy, Kate Nocera, Ogi Ogas, Thomas Otton, Amanda Palmer, Shelly Palmer, Rosette Pambakian, Eva Pascoe, Antonio Peronance, Simon Perry, Steve Phelps, Pete Philips, Jim Plante, Jane Pratt, Sean Rad, Sarah Robb O'Hagan, Douglas Rushkoff, David Sable, Karen Salama, Gary Schwartz, David Shing, Bob Sillerman, Mark Silva, Joel Simkhai, Redg Snodgrass, Jamie Soper, Ivo Stivoric, Jesse Stollak, Steve Stoute, Volker Sydow, Chris Tamara, Sue Thomas, Andrew Thompson, Joe Tripodi, Gary Vaynerchuk, Natacha Volpini, Belisa Vranich, Stefan Weitz, Bryan Wiener, Rodney Williams, Brett Wilson, Ian Wolfman, Brian Wong, and Shayan Zadeh.

This book is dedicated to my mom Monica Evans and my dad Martin Luther Bough. They are the people I thank the most for all the opportunities I've had in my life. With their love and guidance, they made it possible for me to share this book with the world.

Finally, and most important, a special thank you to everyone who spends time texting with me about the way their phone has changed their life.

So text me and I'll see you on the other side.

introduction

I N MARCH 2014 I stood underneath a white-canopied out-door terrace at the ten-day-long South-by-Southwest conference as a line of people approached a machine that in less than two minutes spat out a free customized Oreo cookie whose color, taste, and design were inspired by the topics trending in real time on Twitter.

One of the highlights of my work year is when I fly from New York down to Austin, Texas, for the festival. Founded in 1986 by four journalists with the modest goal of showcasing the city's music scene to local audiences, South by Southwest (SxSW) quickly grew in size, ambition, and popularity. The festival drew in 700 attendees its first year; last year it attracted nearly 30,000 people to Austin. Barenaked Ladies, John Mayer, James Blunt, and Fred Armisen are some of the musicians and performers whose careers were launched there. SxSW, whose name riffs on the 1959 Hitchcock film *North by Northwest*, also hosts Hollywood world premieres, such as *The Hurt Locker* in 2008 and *Bridesmaids* in 2011. When emerging technology and gaming joined the event at the start of the millennium, SxSW officially became a music, film, and "interactive" festival.

It was the best possible place to launch our latest global partnership with Twitter.

By "our," I mean Mondelēz International, previously the snack division of Kraft Foods, where I work as the chief media and e-commerce officer. As a digital marketer and longtime mobile evangelist, my job is to help come up with unusual, provocative ways to advertise and sell to consumers online, or via their mobile phones, and otherwise bring attention to our portfolio of brands, which include Oreo, Trident gum, Philadelphia cream cheese, Cadbury, Chips Ahoy, Honey Maid, Ritz, Triscuits, Wheat Thins, and even Tang. More importantly, I live to identify new business models.

At 2014's SxSW I led our company to install a pair of 3D printers inside two "Trending Vending" machines—an attempt to put an Oreo factory inside a box about the size of your average vending machine. A touchscreen display scrolled off that day's most popular Twitter trends and conversations, including #GrumpyCat, #PenguinSweaters, and Ellen DeGeneres's #OscarSelfie, in which Jennifer Lawrence, Meryl Streep, Lupita Nyong'o, Brad Pitt, and assorted celebrities leaned in for a famous-persons' huddle during the 2014 Academy Awards. One after another SxSW attendees queued, some for almost two hours, to create custom cookies, each with a unique flavor combination and pattern, and watch as the machine robotically assembled them using 3D printing technology and a pneumatic pump system. The algorithm that translated the live Twitter trends into custom cookies allowed for around 10,000-plus taste and design combinations in all, using a chocolate or vanilla wafer and flavors including banana, mint, lime, peppermint, chocolate, vanilla, lemon, and birthday cake, in assorted colors and designs.

Users could even "mash up" two Twitter trends to make the cookie their own. By giving them the ability to "snack" on what was happening in American culture that moment via a cookie, the Trending Vending machines were an experiment in synesthesia and connectivity that we called #eatthetweet.

Why bother, a few of my colleagues had wondered. Some doubted that a Fortune 500 company could ever produce customized cookies, much less any individually tailored food or drink, at mass scale. But that wasn't the point. The point was to try something new. The point was to take a risk. The point was to push past static, worn-down grooves of thinking, and maybe even give others in the industry *permission* to try something similarly offbeat. What if in the future we could customize cookies with a person's initials on them? In an industry where it can take up to three years to create and test a single flavor, could our company start to imagine doing something like that at scale? What if someday you and I sitting at home watching the Super Bowl could watch an Oreo commercial, comment on it on Twitter, and the next day, at our local supermarket, buy a cookie customized based on the outcome of the game? If nothing else, our SxSW experiment might help us reimagine the relationship we have with the things we eat and drink.

As I stood there, phone in hand, I pondered the words everyone, myself included, had used as we brought this project to life over the previous six weeks—*Twitter, tweet, 3D, trending*. These words weren't around ten years ago, or at least not in the context of technology. *Twitter* wasn't a company; *tweet* and *trend* weren't verbs; *3D* mostly referred to throwaway glasses moviegoers wore, not printers, which currently a lot of people believe will someday revolutionize manufacturing. The sight of the two machines pumping out one Oreo after another under a savage springtime Austin sun showed that the changes brought on by mobile technology affect far more than business. These changes, in fact, have transformed every relationship in our lives.

THAT MOBILE PHONE USAGE is reinventing almost every aspect of society is not exactly what you would call breaking news. Among the industries and areas of life that the digital, and now mobile phone, revolution is obliging us to reimagine are healthcare, education, home entertainment, friendship, sociability, love affairs, cash registers, clothes buying, photo taking, taxicab rental, note taking, map reading, picture drawing, diary keeping, video watching, sports data, game playing, home repair, travel planning, flight data, hotel and rental car reservations, encyclopedias, dictionaries, fast food, mail delivery, and music listening.

Everywhere you go, no matter where in the world you live, people are bent, coiled, or crouched studiously, prayerfully, over a small, glowing rectangular screen. They're scanning, reading, playing, "txting," commenting, reviewing, "liking," disagreeing, banging on, or checking in. They're eavesdropping, auditing, and window-shopping; they're traveling without tickets, chattering without talking, and at their desks while in transit.

A hundred years ago, humans came into possession of a life-changing functionality known as electricity. This century's life-changer is digital connectivity. It's the fastest disseminating utility in history, more accessible globally today than electricity or water. It took the company General Electric 100 years to reach a market worth of $400 billion dollars. Today, another company, Google, only thirteen years old, is already worth $100 billion more than General Electric is now. Pinterest, the online bulletin board, was founded in 2009, and by 2015 was worth $11 billion. That same year,

two five-year-old companies, Dropbox and Square, had market caps of $10 billion and $5 billion, respectively. Whether
or not these companies are overvalued, their worth reflects
an exciting business landscape that shows no signs of slow-
ing down or reversing itself. Some of the youngest, smartest
minds in America are forgoing college for entrepreneurship,
one of the best-known being David Karp, born in 1986, who
founded Tumblr at age twenty-one. Will.i.am, a founding
member of the Black Eyed Peas and a technology entrepreneur, was quoted once as saying that coders are today's rock
stars, an observation obvious to anyone who's passed by a
newsstand over the past few years to see Steve Jobs on the
cover of *Rolling Stone*, Twitter cofounder Biz Stone on *Billboard*, or Facebook's Sheryl Sandberg on *Cosmopolitan*. Even
Stephen Colbert's opening lineup for his new *Late Show* in
2015 included the likes of Uber CEO Travis Kalanick and
PayPal cofounder and real-life Tony Stark Elon Musk.

Less than a decade after the first iPhones came to market,
there is no point in arguing whether the mobile revolution is
good, bad, or in-between. It just is. It's not going anywhere
either; the influence and ubiquity of mobile phones are only
going to increase.

Of the roughly 7 billion people on earth today, 5.1 billion
of them own a cell phone—which, I might add, is more than
the number of people who own toothbrushes. Over half of
all Americans own a smart phone, and 29 percent of us own
either a tablet or an e-reader, up from only 2 percent three
years ago. In 2014, *CNN Money* reported that for the first time
ever, Americans used smart phone and tablet apps more than
laptops to get onto the internet. In terms of numbers, this
means that 55 percent of all US internet usage comes from
mobile devices, with apps making up 47 percent and mobile
browsers making up the rest.[1] A friend of mine once joked

that the US Constitution may someday be reworded, with the libertarian hard-liners exclaiming, "You'll have to pry my mobile phone out of my cold dead hands."

As everyone who has one knows, mobile phone use has also become unconscious, a reflex no different from yawning or blinking. Our phones are annexes of our brains and bodies—add-ons, bump-outs, wings, virtual limbs. Few things feel more personal, more nakedly "us." Without them, something tugs at us, some ghostly vibe pesters. Something is missing, wrong. Only when we have them back in our hands do we feel like "ourselves" again, whole, resolved. Our phones console us. They strengthen us. They authorize us. They cover over our shyness, our self-consciousness. We use them to occupy and distract ourselves, as well as to *look* busy and in demand. We reach for them when we feel anxious, or in limbo, or as a gesture of comfort, the same way we clutched a blanket or a stuffed animal when we were children to make sure the familiar world was intact. We leave the table in restaurants, saying we're just going to use the bathroom, not adding that more than anything, these visits are opportunities to check back in with our *real* lives, to see what news we've missed, who's texted or called us, and who didn't, and to reply, or not reply, or pretend we never saw the message in the first place. By driving old and new fears and anxieties—that we're not sought after, or liked, or loved; that without our phones in our hands others might see us as alone, or friendless, or living lives that have no buzz, no urgency; that the people we love may be at risk unless we monitor them at all times—and then giving us any number of instantaneous solutions to these anxieties, smart phones are, arguably, among the most perfect products ever made.

Have you ever felt phantom phone vibrations? #NA

Someday we'll probably look back on this period as the Era of Mobile Immoderation. Humans often overdo things in the days, weeks, and months that follow new discoveries. The first glass of wine or first cigarette often leads to drinking and smoking to excess. We discover sex and we don't leave our bedrooms for months. We are still in the early days of figuring out what mobile phones can do or solve. We're learning how they are changing us and whether those changes are permanent or not. We're discovering who we are with and without them, and what we may be running away from, or coming up against, when we use them. Just as growing up and finding out who we are involves a series of negotiations carried out in private, each of us will have to figure out our own baseline of technological restraint and balance. For most of us, it won't happen for a while, because right now we are in love with our phones, and love, as everyone knows, makes people spellbound.

The digital world has been a passion of mine since I was a boy growing up in New York City. In my teens and in college I worked as a programmer and website builder, and today I'm fortunate that whatever talents I bring to my industry have intersected with a genuinely transformative moment in human history. I'm something of a mobile missionary, a true believer, an un-shy proponent all things digital and handheld. But I'm not only an advocate of the mobile revolution, I'm also a consumer and an observer who spends most of his days pondering the roles and effects technology has on our lives. Much of what I do for a living involves a close-up, ongoing study of how people of all ages interact with the internet and with their phones. I study behavior models. I oversee media consumption patterns. I look at why mothers and children buy things, what appeals to teenaged boys and grown men, and what the future of mobility looks like. I wouldn't be able to do any of this without staying constantly aware of, and switched on to, what is happening in technology both in the United States and overseas.

In the course of an average month, I'll fly to India, or China, or Russia, or London. There, I'll give presentations and speeches to my colleagues, work alongside local brands and advertisers, visit stores, and plan and track advertising campaigns. I might fly to Australia to launch our "Mobile Futures" program, where my company brings in a dozen start-ups to fire up our organization's thinking. In San Francisco I'll spend a week in meetings with Twitter, Facebook, or Google. Then it's on to Los Angeles to try to set up an alliance with, say, Pharrell Williams, or the house DJ and producer David Guetta. In LA, I might also spend time with a start-up incubator devoted to the wearables industry, or attend the Milken Global Conference to hear from music artist Akon about how digital phone technology in Africa is improving the overall quality of life in a rural village in Burkina Faso. A week later, I'll find myself at Singularity University, talking to the employees of a new company called Made In Space, which has manufactured the first and only 3D printer designed for use on the International Space Station.

One reason I love giving speeches and presentations across the world is that afterward I get to talk to the members of the audience. If someone wants to have a word with me, I'll always make the time—hold me to that. Thirty seconds, a minute, five minutes, ten. It doesn't matter who they are, how good their ideas are, whether they're pushing me to advertise with them or if they just want to talk about what's going on in their lives or industries. As Fast Company said about me in 2014, the best way for folks to track me down is often at digital-savvy events. My experience and expertise may be inside organizations, but my job is also a platform that allows me to get a lot of input, inspiration, and new ideas from all across the world. My goal as I see it is to listen, think, ponder, explore, and maybe even inspire, while remaining open to *any* kind of new thinking.

Along with everything else, digital and mobile phones have done two obvious things: They have quickened, and they have flattened. The quickening part we all have an ambient awareness of: We want things now, and we don't want to wait for them. The flattened part is somewhat less well-known. Others have remarked how the internet, and mobile phones, have also "equalized" or "democratized" traditional master-servant, command-and-control relationships. As evidence, they point to a specific industry, say, real estate, or car buying. Or they cite the ability you and I now have to hunt down our medical symptoms, research an orange juice brand, or find out the name of that actress on a search engine. Less has been written about how this democratization has transformed areas of life that might not be immediately apparent to most people.

Here's an example: The word *dude* dates back to the late 1880s, maybe even earlier. In the first half of the twentieth century, "dude" was a noun used to make fun of a fashionable or dandyish male who dressed in an overly fancy way in an informal setting. In the 1970s, "dude" reentered the thesaurus as an ingredient of West Coast surfer, stoner, and skateboarder cultures. In the mid-1980s, "dude" featured prominently in a song by the rock band Aerosmith, in the slacker film *Bill and Ted's Excellent Adventure*, and in Bret Easton Ellis's novel *Less than Zero*, as well as in the late '90s film *The Big Lebowski* by Joel and Ethan Coen. In contrast to its original meaning, "dude" as it's used in these works denotes everlasting youth, unhurriedness, and all the pleasures of lassitude, indifference, and irresponsibility.

"Dude" wallpapers our culture today. It's affectionate, ageless, and everywhere. Siblings holler the word at one another from different floors of the house. Girls and women use it to address boys and men and, occasionally, other girls and women; and men use it with other men, and sometimes when they're talking to women, too. I've heard kids call their parents "dude," and parents use "dude" to address their younger, teenaged, and college-aged children. Everyone calls everyone "dude" and has for the past few years. Why does it matter? Because people across all generations are now using the word "dude," so it's a prime example of the flattening I mentioned, one in which technology obliges us adapt to and even take on the sensibilities of the mostly young men who drove the internet's creation. "Dude" is a presenting trait of a new informality that has infiltrated every aspect of our lives, chipping away at any and all relationships once based on hierarchies of age, position, achievement, or expertise.

Thanks to the internet and our mobile phones, we're all twenty-two years old, stubbled, socially challenged, wearing an unflattering T-shirt, and busy typing out our private obsessions. But if everyone's a "dude" today, who's the boss? Are authority, formality, and chronological age relics from a recent past? If they are, how has this affected the relationship between parents and children, writers and readers, doctors and patients, politicians and voters, musicians and music fans, and others? How have our phones transformed our relationship to the past, to the things we own, to life itself?

These questions around relationship fascinate me because in some respects I symbolize the flattening of authority and tradition myself.

I've spent my career in this new digital frontier. In most big companies, there is a head of digital and a head of media. The head of digital is often focused on buying the advertising across new platforms like Facebook, YouTube, and Twitter. The head of media is focused on spending on what we more commonly consider advertising—sponsorships of large events, outdoor billboards, and TV and radio advertisements.

The two carry out their duties in different fiefdoms—and with very different budgets. Historically they're in battle, or at least their relationship is fraught. I spent my whole life trying to get large organizations to understand the value of digital and move from what I saw as the small-budget kids' table over to the grown-ups' table, where the traditional media folks had large spending power.

Two years ago, when my now-boss, Dana Anderson, told me she wanted me to take charge of Mondelēz International's entire media future, I thought at first that we were both hallucinating. Never mind that I'm black and was not yet forty. For the fifth-largest food company in the world, and the thirty-third-largest media buyer in the marketplace, to hire a thirty-five-year-old digital guy to drive the future of *all* media buying was, if nothing else, a symbolically profound and even futuristic decision. The only advice Anderson gave me was, "Don't mess it up." Later, she explained, "I knew that as a company we needed to be informed, and that the windows we looked through had to change. Otherwise, we would never be able to move forward fast enough."

Still, during my first few weeks as I went around trying to figure out what to do and how to do it, the responses and the advice I got were mostly the same: *You should do what we've always done.* A few old-timers looked at me with bemusement. My age and enthusiasm probably reminded them of their younger selves. Surely the enthusiasm would be beaten out of me soon enough, just as it had been thrashed out of them. From others I got the sense that like the technology I loved and advocated, maybe I lacked perspective, a sense of the proofs and tides of history. Why wouldn't I, since compared to them I was just a kid?

But if history and perspective are on the table, here's an analogy: If I knocked on your office door in the early 1950s, at a time when there were roughly 40 million radios in the

US versus only 44,000 television sets, in an effort to convince you, a marketing department, to invest heavily in this brand-new medium called television, chances are good you would have said no. Radio, you would have told me, was working just fine. Today, history is repeating itself, and every one of us has the opportunity to get in on the ground floor. I don't only believe that mankind's future is wrapped around mobile phones, I practice that belief every day with the gut-sure conviction that if people and organizations don't keep pace with what's happening right in front of them, they are headed for irrelevance.

Whatever terms we use—"equalization," "flattening," "democratization"—the digital world, and the ubiquity and universality of mobile phones, has created new challenges in all our relationships, which, in this early stage of the internet, most of us are still trying to name, come to terms with, and in some cases redress. It's not always easy. Equality and access of the virtual kind aren't necessarily democratic, and at worst they can be unstraightforward, disorienting, and problematic. When I look across the digital environment, the big questions I keep asking are: How have our relationships changed across the social landscape, and in what ways? Are these changes positive, destructive, or somewhere in the middle? What does it mean be a leader—a parent, an artist, a boss—in a conversational environment that doesn't trust past forms of authority and leadership, that sees slowness and inequality as "old-school," that worships at the tabernacle of "real time" and "now-ness," and that often, due to immaturity, lacks perspective as to where digital technologies might be taking us?

Another thing: When you spend close to a year writing a book, it's with the confidence and conviction that the issues you're writing about will be relevant for a year, five years, ten years, maybe even longer. But when you write about digital technology and mobile phones, both of which are in their infancy, the only certainty is that everything is in flux. Every object, person, and trend comes across in retrospect as quaint, but technology has accelerated everything, including the time it takes us to deem a style, look, or belief charming and passé, and to romanticize the past. Having said that, in a digital era where the birth and death of a thing often occur only minutes apart, my job is to focus on what is relevant right now. The same fear of obsolescence that haunts one's attempt to write about technology also gives this book an urgency that comes from passion and—here's that word again—relevancy. My goal for this book, then, is to explore those ground-zero moments when traditional relationships were subverted, resculpted, and transformed—and why. It's also to provide a history lesson in how mobile phones, unlike any other technology, have changed our identity and existence.

I have one last reason for writing this book, one that links back to my own professional life. It's the disconnect that exists between institutions and organizations and companies . . . and the rest of us. Outside of work, as everyone knows, our mobile phones are with us all the time. Inside most organizations, aside from the obvious use of emailing and text-messaging, it's like entering a separate solar system, one unimpeded by progress. Why do these two planet-worlds collide but almost never intersect? By exploring some of the ways in which the internet and mobile phones are transforming traditional relationships, one of my goals is to do everything possible to help bridge that gap.

"Man shapes buildings, and then buildings shape men," Winston Churchill once said. The same is true for the internet and mobile phones. If man has shaped mobile technology, I'm proposing that, in turn, technology has been busy transforming our every relationship to the people or things we love or admire: our children; our parents; the people we elect into office, or ask to keep us healthy; the past; the things we own; our mortality; even life itself. In the pages ahead, helped along by the opinions, perspectives, and experiences of some of the most insightful people I know, we'll explore what being connected via mobile phones is both giving and taking away from us, often in the same breath. Along the way, we'll come up with answers and solutions to some of the thorniest questions posed by one of the greatest technological advancements of all time.

HOW TO TXT ME

I want to know what you think!

Text me at (646) 759-1837 with your answers to any of the questions called out throughout the book. I'll text back with my thoughts.

Just remember to include the hashtag of the question you're answering in each text!

• • •

Participating in the *Txt Me* experience may unlock exclusive deals and special offers. As your contribution is important to me, please keep in mind that standard carrier rates regarding SMS or data may apply, and you can opt out whenever you wish by texting "STOP".

1

language

S TARTING WITH HIS THIRD ALBUM, *Controversy*, the pop
star Prince began doing strange, willful things with the
English language. Before that time, his songs had stan-
dard, if slightly suggestive titles: "I Feel for You," "Uptown,"
"When You Were Mine." But that all changed in 1981, when
Prince began substituting letters and numbers for key words.
"I Would Die for You" morphed into "I Would Die for U," "How
Come You Don't Call Me Anymore?" became "How Come U
Don't Call Me Anymore?" "Rave Unto the Joy Fantastic" was
reborn as "Rave Un2 the Joy Fantastic," and "Tonight" was
reworked as "2nite." Prince's album liner notes and eventual
online communications followed suit.

There was more. A decade or so later, in the course of a
contractual disagreement he was having with his label, War-
ner Brothers, Prince announced that he was retiring his name
in favor of a symbol, a superimposition of the centuries-old
symbols for Mars and Venus, male and female. This dimin-
utive, curly-ladder black shape had something to do with
universal harmony. And sex. And male and female desire

and desirability. More to the point, Prince's glyph denoted a set of meanings that words would have taken too long to explain, which is why the media began referring to him as "The Artist Formerly Known as Prince." Prince eventually retired the glyph and went back to being Prince, though he kept his spelling funky, original, and, it later turned out, prescient. Unwittingly, the informal innovations he'd created in language would later come to influence the communication style of an entire culture.

Cut to a few years after Prince traded in his name for a symbol, when I was working at PepsiCo. One of my responsibilities there was to help determine why sales were flat for one of the company's leading brands, Gatorade, the yellow-green sports drink favored by student athletes. In an effort to find out what consumers were actually saying about Gatorade, our Chicago-based marketing team launched what we called the Gatorade Mission Control Center.

Mission Control was a combination war room and social media command center. Picture NASA or the CIA as it's portrayed in the TV series *Homeland*—with half a dozen oversized computer screens feeding our brand teams real-time data visualizations of national sports trends, online mentions, tweets, Facebook posts, and all-purpose buzz relevant to the brand and its rivals among the three demographics that matter the most to Gatorade: sideline moms, athletic directors, and lead athletes.

What we found over the next few weeks surprised us. Young athletes weren't drinking Gatorade in the Clear-Eyes-Full-Hearts-Can't-Lose spirit we thought they were. No: Eighty percent of the conversations we monitored were focused around how adolescents and college kids drank Gatorade to ease their hangovers. The sports drink was less *Friday Night Lights* than it was *Barfly*. Gatorade's television ads may have shown real athletes dunking basketballs into hoops and powering backhands across tennis nets, but Mission Control was telling us Gatorade's core audience was more interested in getting drunk on weekends, and also that sideline moms found Gatorade's high levels of sugar intolerable.

Obviously, the marketing team needed to rethink the brand, especially the way it was communicated. We needed to focus on the language we used. Whenever in-house marketers talked about Gatorade, we used words like "hydration" and "high-performance" because, hype aside, Gatorade is actually constructed on sophisticated scientific principles. But outside of an organization, who talks like that? From that point on, Gatorade would talk to consumers as informally and conversationally as they talked among themselves.

Over the next few months, we gave Gatorade fans increased access to the brand's athletes and scientists. Via a streaming video platform called Ustream, Gatorade lovers were invited to interact with football players during the Super Bowl and to ask as many questions as they liked to a sports nutritionist that Gatorade made available on Facebook. If in the past companies and consumers had once dined formally, with Gatorade seated at one end of the table and everyone else at the other, we were now eating tuna sandwiches together on the grass.

This new conversational strategy worked. Less than a year later, almost all the Gatorade dialogues the marketing team continued to track via Mission Control had shifted over to how the drink improved athletic performance. Hangover mentions were down, and sales were up. The old-fashioned idea of *Us* versus *Them*, of an organization talking down to the people who bought and used its products, felt like an ancient memory.

Prince and Gatorade both represent pivotal points where language, and the way we talk and write, evolved to where it is today. Aside from being something of a genius, Prince was also a soothsayer. More than three decades ago he invented and popularized a fast-paced communication shorthand used today by people of all ages with a text-messaging plan. It's sexy, elliptical, alive with innuendo. In the case of Gatorade, Pepsi's marketing team found that to retake control of the brand, it had to lose its formal, paternal tone in favor of a vocabulary, a persona, and a way of speaking similar to what we use with our friends.

Subtly and over time, in the same way a gear gets ground down, the internet and mobile phones have created a new relationship between communicators and audiences. It's more or less flat. It cheerfully dishonors old-fashioned boundaries between writers and readers, professionals and amateurs, paid opinion-makers and unpaid commentators. The distance separating those who create words, articles, essays, or books, and those who read them, has never been closer.

Most of us are taught how to spell and write as young children. Still, it wasn't until the internet came along that the ability to use writing to share one's thoughts with a mass audience, something historically limited to professionals, became available to everyone. There are roughly 156 million public blogs across the internet today, with 200,000 new ones added daily, and over a billion unique website domains. Of course there are also Facebook, Twitter, YouTube, Vine, and photo-based media like Instagram, Snapchat, and Pinterest; not to mention sites from Amazon to Yelp that encourage visitors to contribute their two cents in reviews or comments. What used to be said privately is today typed out, innocently or ragefully, for the world to read. Millions of voices and opinions have been freed, without realizing they had been locked up or silenced in the first place. Internet users making their way through the online jungle of misplaced apostrophes, misspellings, opinion, wit, and venom could easily convince themselves the internet is single-handedly responsible for degrading language and writing. But if the web has in some ways devalued language, in large part because there's just so much of it online, the mobile phone can be credited in turn with rescuing the importance of words and meaning. Armed with our smart phones, we have entered a new communication renaissance, in which the increasing speed of online conversation has necessitated new and novel uses of language.

ONLINE, THE NEW INFORMALITY that has overtaken the English language shows up everywhere, whether in corporate communications, blogs, social media comments, even political fundraising requests. Take, for example, one division of Tesco's communication with its online consumers. A publicly owned British multinational supermarket, Tesco is the second-largest retailer in the world, with stores in fourteen countries. Tesco Mobile provides mobile phones and service plans from locations within Tesco's supermarkets. Tesco Mobile's signal and clarity aren't great, but the products and plans are so cheap that the company will always have customers.

A decade ago, there would have been a formal division between Tesco, a monolith with a sterile communications department, and the people who shopped there. If you or I weren't happy about something, and wrote or emailed the company, we would have felt fortunate to receive an answer. But last year, Tesco Mobile's Twitter account responded to one consumer's tweeted complaint in this way: *That's just how we roll, haters gonna hate, potatoes are gonna' potate.*[2] That was it. That was all Tesco Mobile's customer service representative had to say. When the comment was retweeted numerous times and someone else commented, *omg hahahahahahahah I'm proud to say that I am on Tesco Mobile*, Tesco Mobile wrote back: *Wahoo, you're one cool cookie.* Later Tesco Mobile posted this: *Beware—81% of mobile shopping results in impulse purchases.*

Now we own 50 potato peelers. Sometime later came another one: *Seriously, 5.1 billion mobile owners in the world but only 4.2 billion own a toothbrush? Own up, who's sharing?*

Tesco isn't alone in this shift to informality. Google, of course, has a search button marked "I'm Feeling Lucky." When they drag a file to their cloud-storage provider Dropbox folders, users are told, "You've connected a new file to your Dropbox. Awesome! Happy Dropboxing! The Dropbox Team." These are just a few examples among many of how many companies and brands today have lost any pretense of authority, and have begun engaging consumers as if they were friends or junior colleagues. In only two decades, technology has accelerated the evolution of how we write and speak from structured to casual, from felt to ironic, from considered to staccato, from age-appropriate to ageless. It is no coincidence that many of today's college and university catalogues are designed instead to look like websites, with page after page bulging with colors, graphics, links to online videos, and fiats like "Dream!" and "Imagine!" Organizations and companies are still in the business of selling you things, and no one will deny that hierarchies still exist in the world, but you would never know it from how we have taken to addressing one another online and off.

Groupon, the daily deal company, was among the first companies to use language itself as a selling point. At one point Groupon had approximately sixty writers and sixteen editors on staff, with 40 percent of them having prior experience in journalism and two-thirds with a creative writing background.[3] Groupon attracted early interest and attention for its witty, sometimes psychedelic deal descriptions. One Groupon description for a deal on marinades read, "Spicy sauces are great for deterring children from licking frozen poles, substituting lost winter coats, and swiftly ending staring contests." Another read, "Six pages of dinner options ensure that no appetite exits with its former owner, and a Mexican hot chocolate offers the perfect transition back into frosty thoroughfares and the cocoa-less monotony of everyday life." Every Groupon offering was saturated with a sensibility best described as "internet," comprised of irony, outsiderliness, knowingness, powerlessness, and a *Seinfeld*-esque sensitivity to minutiae that twenty years ago would have been placed in a bin marked "Passing Thoughts of a Twenty-Something-Year-Old Male." It's a style that's still prevalent online today.

More obvious is that we now inhabit a world in which conversation has no beginning and no end. "Marriage is a long conversation," Robert Louis Stevenson once wrote, and so, it now seems, is our collective communication style. One example is the number of people who begin their sentences with "So," as if resuming a conversation that began days, weeks, months earlier. "So everyone is starting sentences with the word 'so' these days," a *Slate* article from last year began. According to Professor Galina Bolden of Rutgers University, "so" is generally used to signal that a new subject is primed for discussion.[4] Others would add that by leading off a sentence with "So," a speaker conveys interest, engagement, and enthusiasm. But from my perspective, the now-ubiquitous use of "So . . ." as a conversational starter has a clear implication: Speakers are always reopening or joining a dialogue already underway and yet to be concluded.

"So" is unauthoritative and nonconfrontational. Its soft-broom momentum comes across as ever so faintly craven. It doesn't exactly inspire confidence. "So" also correlates with a near-universal spike in "uptalking," a term generally, and usually negatively, associated with adolescent girls, who often don't speak their sentences with conclusive endings but instead inflect them as a slightly audible question. Similar to "So" as it leads off a sentence, uptalking conveys an overall lack of assuredness and a fear of contradiction. Via uptalking, a traditional command like *Put that book over there!* sounds to a listener more like *If you put that book over there, that would be optimal and we can go forward from there, would you be okay with this?* as if the speaker doubts his own reasoning or even sanity. Just as the slight tonal ascension at the end of *You did a really substandard job on this report, Bob* sounds a lot like *Bob, I could be wrong here, I'm certainly not mad at you, but could you and I possibly figure out a reasonable, amicable way to deal with this issue?*

Everyone uptalks these days—parents, bosses, heads of organizations, even the president. If memory serves, uptalking took root around the same time technology began to level old-fashioned notions of formality or authority. "So . . ." and uptalking both suggest that speakers could easily be challenged or even demolished by a simple internet search.

"If there was an inflection point when this new off-handedness in language began seeping in, I would have to say it was 2008," says Bryan Wiener, the CEO of 360i, a mobile advertising firm. "By 2010, every organization and every brand was transforming, or trying to transform, the way they communicated." Today, Wiener says, practically every business and brand in the world is trying to come up with a human, approachable "persona" to which consumers can relate.

David Droga, the creative chairman of his eponymous New York agency, Droga5, tells me that "the new informality," as he calls it, has affected not just brands but also academic institutions and politics, and has even redefined the concept of leadership.

IN SOME RESPECTS, today's more lowercase communication style is a return to a very recent past. In the mid-1980s, customer service was focused around engaging in dialogue with consumers, which is why and how the 800 number was invented. Then, in the late '90s, customer-resource-management, or

CRM, software came to market;[5] companies started using call centers, consumer analysis, and data mining rather than discourse. This growing use of automation reinforced the formality of most institutional communications—and frustrated customers. When Facebook and Twitter came along, organizations realized that the internet had created new tools and opportunities to talk to customers in ways customers preferred. But new rules had to be established.

Says Droga, "At the same time, if every brand and organization is your friend, then wouldn't it follow that nobody is your friend? The downside to informality is that everyone is trying to be personal, and with it, and super-casual and chatty. Frankly, I don't really want to be best friends with my corner deli, my bank, my hospital, and my children's schools."

> "Frankly, I don't really want to be best friends with my corner deli, my bank, my hospital, and my children's schools."
>
> *Droga5 creative chairman David Droga*

What Droga seems to be asking is, Who's in charge now? It's a good question, and I think the answer is that, at least at this point in time, no one really knows.

The informality of language is not just about our changing notions of authority, but about the combination of a leveling of power and our desire to get as much as we can said in as short a time as possible. Nowhere is this more clearly the case than in how we communicate with our phones.

Today, text-messaging, a language most of us used to associate only with teenagers, has replaced emailing, and buried the idea of calling someone on the phone. What fascinates me most about texting is the speed with which the two most recent ways we communicated before texting came along—emailing and phoning—have, in a very short time, taken on formal, borderline archaic meanings. Today, calling someone up on the phone feels symptomatic of a past era when we had lazy afternoons, time to spare, and a genuine eagerness to hear other people's voices. Today, who calls someone when they can email them and who emails them when they can text them? Who uses a phone as an actual phone unless there's an emergency?

Few people I know are immune to the Morse Code pointedness of text-messaging. Laura Desmond, the CEO of the global media agency Starcom MediaVest at Publicis Groupe, says, "In my personal life, texting is 85 to 90 percent of how I communicate with my closer personal friends and family circle and even my partner at home. Somehow it enables you to speak your feelings easier. It's a more informal, more personal format, and the emoticons are fun and add to the layering and the texture of the conversation. Email has become tone-deaf, which is one reason why my work colleagues have so many meetings, and why they text so much more than they used to."

> "Email has become tone-deaf, which is one reason why my work colleagues text so much more than they used to."
>
> *CEO of Starcom MediaVest at Publicis Groupe Laura Desmond*

The turning point, Desmond says, came in 2010, when smart phone use reached critical mass. Today, she says, 90 percent of her interactions in the business world are either text messages or face-to-face business meetings. As for the phone, "I don't do that a lot, unless it's a prior orchestrated teleconference call that includes two or more people. Unless it's for a group, I've noticed that phone conversations are declining in general." As a rule she doesn't leave voicemails, nor does she listen to the ones friends and colleagues leave on her phone. "People just don't have the time to listen to voicemails, or they plain don't want to. Everyone I know wants things in real time."

Of course, texting has its downsides, as well as a protocol. Renny Gleeson, the director of interactive strategies at the advertising agency Wieden+Kennedy, notes that as long as human beings have existed, there has been human drama, and texting creates its own version of that same drama. "Texting presents an entirely new set of ways to be dissed," Gleeson reminds me. "An unanswered text is a great way to indicate to somebody that he or she is not a priority in your life." If Gleeson gets back a reply to his text in five minutes or less, he knows he's on that person's front burner. "But if it takes a day or more for them to get back to me, it's clear I'm not a priority, and I operate accordingly. The cues are all there, and in my experience people figure them out quickly."

Within this new text universe, who is allowed to text you, to duck under the purple rope into your personal VIP channel? Your family and certain close friends, of course, but what about work colleagues? Is there a time of day after which a text message from a male or female colleague comes across as inappropriate? Does text-messaging keep office hours? David Droga believes that once he gives someone his cell phone number, he has given that person tacit permission to text him, "just as in the old days we used to give someone our home number, as opposed to our work number." Bryan Wiener agrees, though he also points out that text-messaging is an inadequate long-term conversational medium, and on those rare times he emails his eleven-year-old son, he first sends him a text message to remind him to check his inbox.

The two most recent television shows featuring Sherlock Holmes, BBC's *Sherlock* and the American remake, *Elementary*, take place in contemporary London and New York City respectively. In both series, Holmes and Watson take maximum advantage of cell phones, texting, photo-taking, and using GPS. In one episode of the former, the following exchange takes place: Holmes texts Watson, "YT? ND U

How long does it take you, on average, to listen to a voicemail? #1A

ASAP" and then to Watson's reply texts back: "IMLTHO: No. IMPORTANT. CUS!" Later Holmes explains to Watson that IMLTHO means, "In my less than humble opinion." Tiredly, Watson replies, "Your abbreviations are becoming borderline indecipherable. I don't know why, because you're obviously capable of being articulate." To which Holmes says, "Language is evolving, Watson—becoming a more efficient version of itself. I love text shorthand. It allows you to convey content and tone without losing velocity."

To echo this modern reimagining of Sherlock Holmes, communication today has everything—*everything*—to do with velocity. Brevity is nothing more than a symptom and a consequence of that velocity. Velocity is about dispensing a maximum amount of germane information in the fewest possible words or characters while interfering the least with whatever else we happen to be doing at the time. Why do slow computers or slow-loading websites infuriate us? If we thought about it (most of us don't have time), what offends us most is that our computers are moving more ponderously than our brains. We're just bending, cracking, angling, and scissoring language, both to match today's increasing speed and to counter the increasing complexity of the digital environments in which we spend more and more of our time.

It's a given that text-messaging has transformed the way we punctuate, but my perspective on the seemingly slapdash, ungrammatical spelling that many fear signals the end of a literate society may be different from most people's. First, let me summarize what everyone already knows, but may not always be aware of:

The apostrophe has vanished. Few people seem to care anymore about the difference between *it's* and *its*. Nor do they distinguish *their* and *there*. *You* is *u* and *are* is *r*. In the same way baby boomers insist on informality around younger people, capitalization is mostly dead, too. Most of us write in lowercase. We sign our emails with our initials, if we sign off at all. The exclamation mark, obviously, has made a theatrical comeback as a cornerstone of texting. Once a seldom-used mark used to show happiness or anticipation, exclamation marks, along with the "Sent from iPhone" or "Sent from Galaxy" messages that fill out the bottom of mobile-sent emails, keep our communications from sounding robotic, terse, bizarre, or hostile.

The period (.) has taken on new meaning, too. Writing for the *New Republic*, journalist Ben Crair notes that in emails and texts, the period now signals anger, disapproval, or passive censure. He draws an example: If a man was texting a woman, "I know we made a reservation for your bday tonight but wouldn't it be more romantic if we ate in instead?" and the woman texts back "we could do that," then most likely the woman agrees with the man that eating at home is a good idea. But if she texts back, "we could do that.", with a period at the end, the man will know she disapproves of this change of plans.[6]

Punctuation is no more formal in the corporate world. Most of Laura Desmond's friends and business associates communicate not only in words but also in emoticons and pictures. "It seems to me that words and letters are migrating towards pictures very rapidly," Desmond says. And though she doesn't say so outright, her understanding of this trend matches mine—that a haphazard mixture of pictures and words represents the quickest, most energy-preserving way of conveying the velocity of the twenty-first-century brain.

In a pioneering 1980s study on nonverbal communication, Professor Albert Mehrabian found that our feelings about what others say are based 7 percent on the words the person uses, 38 percent on their tone and voice, and 55 percent on their facial expressions.[7] The picture-based communication that has been integrated into text messaging restores some of this nonverbal communication. Stickers, gifs, and other images available on apps like LINE, Facebook Messenger, and WhatsApp help us place emphasis, highlight importance, and reveal tone.

But what strikes me the most about the changes in language and punctuation is not how trivial and careless words and spelling have become. Rather, it's how mobile phones and texting are helping users develop an intuitive relationship to language and meaning that would be impossible to teach in any school or university. In response to critics who say the internet is making people stupid and superficial, I would argue that the velocity of communication, and the need to distill meaning into fewer words and characters, whether via SMS, Twitter, or Facebook, has made us all more, not less, sensitive to the nuance, meaning, subtext, and intention of words. "Don't play what's there, play what's not there," jazz trumpeter Miles Davis once said. Twitter and text-messaging ask us to spell out and unlock the implications, presence, and absence of words with the souls of lyric poets who moonlight as cat-footed private eyes.

Take Facebook, which, by its nature, is a curated piece of personality theater, and whose photographs are often as eloquent and suggestive as short stories. "Home," as in "Facebook home page," is as good a description as any for that digital space: We upload art and pictures onto our digital walls, add magazines, books, movies, interests, and preferences to our digital coffee tables, keep a visual list of friends within reach like an open address book.

Every Facebook user's social experience will vary depending on their friends, but in general, little of what we or our friends put online bears much resemblance to our real lives, which is why Facebook, so unifying and beneficial in so many

Do you think people present a false self on Facebook? #1B

ways, can be so maddening in others. Via photos, posted links, or personal comments, users "say" one thing while communicating something else entirely that's connected to their social, economic, genetic, or superior spiritual status. An album of vacation photos taken on a trip to Brazil or a visit to the Turks and Caicos is a statement of taste and adventurousness, and a secondary declaration of economic status, among other things. The postings and articles we share with friends reveal our interests, our education levels, and our intelligence. Parents pimp out their children's beauty and accomplishments, but if called out would deny ever doing such a thing. On Facebook everyone is always selling something, usually themselves.

In just a few years, Facebook has schooled us all in the cellophane lingo of the implied and unsaid. Over time we've learned to read between spaces, to interpret the presence or absence of a "like," to exhume hidden meanings in photos and videos—in short, to decipher the site's contemporary cave drawings while hoping we have enough self-awareness to be more genuine about the way we present ourselves on our own home pages.

The older generations have developed this digital sixth sense, but children and adolescents are being raised in this environment. Via an online remark they find out about a party to which they're not invited. A photo of a girl hugging a boy signals to her rivals he's off-limits, no words needed. It's a veritable feast of passive aggression. Boys post pictures of themselves experimentally shirtless, as if seeking clues about their own desirability, and girls who post new profile pictures know full well they'll get back a thread of comments about how beautiful they look.

More to the point, teenagers read, and write, their own text messages with the care and attentiveness of semioticians. A few months ago I sat down with half a dozen juniors and seniors at a local high school to discuss text-messaging habits, protocols, and punctuation. I expected the session to last no more than ten minutes, but an hour later the students were still talking.

I wasn't surprised to learn that every one of their parents texted, and also used text-based punctuation. But I found out the difference between abbreviating *okay* to *K*, versus shortening it to *Kk*. *K* means that the person texting is angry at you, whereas the latter signals "Okay—that's cool." A smirking emoticon sent by a male to a female, or vice versa, is a sexual invitation. For both parents and teenagers, *Hey* has replaced *Hi*. No one says *Hi* anymore. It's sinister and alien in its peppiness, and if they do, it's *Hi!* On the other hand, *Heyy* signals a feeling of ambiguity toward the person being texted, whereas *Heyyy* means the game is on. The short shelf life of *Sweet!* has given way to the affectless, all-purpose *nice*, and *super* and *crazy* have made comebacks as synonyms for "very," as in "I'm super excited" or "This meal is crazy good." A smirking yellow emoticon, or a *what's going on . . .* texted after, say, midnight on a weekend, is an invitation to romance or more. If someone is angry at you, his or her incoming texts will be short and clipped and may even end with a period. I left the meeting feeling that children coming of age today are developing a new, visceral, almost synesthetic relationship to language borne, again, of velocity, with technology serving as an on-the-ground teacher.

What this shows is that the tools for writing are changing. What we will come to see as "good" writing in the future may be defined as an ability to communicate a message in the most succinct way possible. The question, perhaps, is whether we will consider social media's postings and micro-blogging as "writing." Certainly, a lot of content is being produced. But how do its producers know if it's any good? Often the only feedback writers get back is praise and backslapping through likes and retweets. I wonder: Will the number of shares or favorites become the new metric of excellence in writing? Has it already?

David Sable, the global chief executive of advertising firm Y&R, reminds me that the most critical commodity, as ever, is talent. "Today every schmuck can write or post something. But it's only the stuff that's really good or interesting that people pay attention to—and that comes from people who are great writers, or great photographers, or great singers. Just because an art or a craft has been democratized doesn't make it any good—in fact, it just makes apparent the amount of mediocrity in the world, and how easy it is to put it out there."

At a tech conference, Sable notes, everyone was going around advising the younger generation to study code "and all this other digital bullshit. I was saying, 'They should read *The Iliad* and *The Odyssey* and ask themselves, after 3,000 years, why are people still telling these stories?'"

As writer Nicholas Carr argues in his book *The Shallows*, the internet has had a big influence on how most of us read, digest, and remember information. If an article is too long, or visually dense, or if the language is too challenging, we can easily find another, more approachable article, or even hunt down a bullet-point summary. People I know who read seriously and often tell me that they like grappling with a complex book, but most say the internet has chipped away at the patience they once had to read material they enjoyed as recently as the mid-1990s.

> "Today every schmuck can write or post something. But it's only the stuff that's really good or interesting that people pay attention to. Just because an art or a craft has been democratized doesn't make it any good—in fact, it just makes apparent the amount of mediocrity in the world."
>
> *Y&R global chief executive David Sable*

Some people have likened the internet to a city, a teeming, foaming metropolis. If you've ever spent any length of time in an urban capital like New York City, it doesn't take you very long to notice how quickly and purposefully residents make their way along the sidewalks. Where is everyone going? If as an out-of-towner you stop, or even pause, the natives will simply elbow past you. After spending a couple of days there, chances are good you will begin walking as pointlessly rapidly as everyone else.

If the internet is a city, then our brains have subtly, quickly adopted the urban equivalent of fast walking in the way we read, write, and communicate. But does this new velocity endanger books, or reading? After a day of spent scanning and skipping over articles, headlines, emails, texts, tweets, and Facebook posts, can we still give ourselves permission to immerse ourselves in an actual book?

Many of us spend our workdays poring over screens, dealing with facts, figures, and other fragments of information. When evening comes and we have the time to read long-form articles for pleasure, we are tired of reading. It's a problem that my friend, and digital prophet at AOL, David "Shingy" Shing, refers to as TL;DR ("too long; didn't read").

At the same time, the continued success of novels tells me there's still an enormous market for an uninterrupted soak inside a good long book, for the simple reason that it's a relief to get away from learning things all the time. We need, and read, to escape the web. Books are a reprieve from a day spent grazing and quick-switching across 100 websites or more. As a culture, I'm happy to say, we are reading more books than we ever have before, switching fluidly and unself-consciously between printed and electronic books.[8]

Do you think the internet has affected your ability to read print books? #1C

The changes in our reading habits have consequences for how we write. In his 1946 essay "Politics and the English Language," George Orwell drew up a few rules for writers. Among them: "Never use a long word where a short one will do." "If it's possible to cut a word out, always cut it out." "Don't use jargon." And, finally, "Break any of these rules sooner than saying anything outright barbarous." If nothing else, the internet reminds us of the enduring importance of this advice.

The success of Vine, the micro-video platform, teaches us that today stories can be told briefly, suggestively, fleetingly, in seven seconds or less. Even a six-and-a-half-second Vine can tell a story. As we watch we are reminded how our own imaginations always fill in what's implied or unseen.

Then there are emoticons.

Across the world there are countless words with no English translation. One of them is the German *maskenfreiheit*, which means, roughly, "the freedom conferred by masks." Another is *verschlimmbesserung*, meaning a supposed improvement that in fact makes things worse than before. *Aware* is a Japanese word denoting the beauty and melancholy of a transient moment of time, and the Russian word *razbliuto* describes the feeling we have for someone or something we loved once, but no longer do. Outside their native countries, these words take a few moments to communicate, but inside, their meanings, however complex, are simple and direct.

In this way, they are similar to emoticons and hashtags, which, however simple they may appear, carry unexpected weight and nuance. Like Prince's glyph, emoticons are visual mini-narratives that convey what would otherwise take too long to say. We see the same economy in hashtags, which can be as eloquent as courtroom summaries. Both remind us how

How do you use emojis to communicate things texts can't? #1D big a role our imaginations play in shading and coloring the spaces around meaning.

I found out about the importance of visual narrative for myself during the work I carried out with Oreo cookies. With the underlying mission of making Oreos relevant, my company launched a 100-day campaign we called "The Daily Twist." Every day we posted an image of an Oreo cookie in a new guise, costume, or role. Our inspiration came from whatever was trending culturally that day, week, or month. We posted a Shark Week Oreo, a Mars Rover Oreo, and an Elvis Oreo. One Oreo celebrated the birth of Shin Shin the Panda's baby. Another featured the silhouette of a raised human hand to commemorate the unofficial anniversary of the high five. To mark the passage of gay marriage legislation in the United States, we posted to Facebook an Oreo with half a dozen multicolored layers—red, yellow, orange, green, blue, and purple. Not surprisingly, it was loved, hated, denounced, adored, shared, tweeted, and retweeted millions of times, with the pro-Oreo crowd vastly outnumbering the people who wrote in to tell us they would never buy the brand again. The Daily Twist taught me that what took Oreo 100 years of brand-building to create can today be done in 100 seconds. That's velocity, via brevity, and it's here to stay.

Communicating, I'm glad to say, is still the most important thing we do. Laura Desmond reminds me that during the Great Recession of 2008, every sector in the economy in advertising and media was down significantly. Two, though, sustained during this slump. One was healthcare, the other telecommunications.

"These statistics told me something really important about people," Desmond says. "People want their meds, and they want to be able to talk to each other. When the economy is tanking, humans will sacrifice eating steak and even hamburger, but they want to keep their health and their mobile lives going strong."

The last word belongs to Stefan Weitz of Microsoft search engine Bing. "The internet has democratized the ability people have to use language in any way they see fit—slang and informality is now the norm—it is no longer something we look down on." He adds, "Remember Ebonics? A lot of people were saying, 'This is the end of the English language!' Today, they've forgotten all about it."

> "The internet has democratized the ability people have to use language in any way they see fit— slang and informality is now the norm—it is no longer something we look down on."
>
> *Microsoft senior director of search (Bing) Stefan Weitz*

2

rebellion and anxiety: iParenting and kids

URING THE 2013 SUPER BOWL, Samsung broadcast what is widely considered a brilliant television commercial. Dubbed "The Next Big Thing Is Already Here," the ad featured a crowd of college kids standing in lines along wintry city sidewalks. The advertisement never mentioned the word "Apple," though it was obvious to viewers the people in line were awaiting the latest iPhone.

As the crowd pushed forward, the kids began contrasting the new Samsung Galaxy phone with the phone they were waiting to buy—everything from the Galaxy's design to its faster speeds to its wider screen to the fact that two people can swap music playlists by tapping their phones together. Then, realizing the deliverance they were anticipating was right in front of them, the kids began wondering aloud about what, exactly, they were doing outside in the cold. As the commercial ended, two good-natured, middle-aged parents appeared to reclaim the space in line their son had been saving for them.

The Samsung commercial was heralded across the industry as an inflection point for Samsung in its ongoing battle to wrest market share from Apple. To me it told a deeper, more relevant story about parents and children in today's technological culture. If you're a parent who owns a smart phone, and it's hard to imagine you're not, maybe you know what I'm talking about.

Maybe you've stood there yourself, bundled up in a long queue for the latest black-boxed piece of tech out of Cupertino, or ambled through Apple stores, those digital candy mountains. You've bought Shure, Bose, Beats, or Jaybird headphones that you hooked up to music players the same colors as your children's old pink and blue baby furniture. Via home-sharing, you've appropriated your sons' and daughters' Drake, Actress, Sia, Lady Gaga, and Solange playlists, in the same spirit that they pinched all your Beatles, Stones, and Wilco. No matter how old you are, tech companies seem recognize in you a coolness-addicted, text-message-crazy adolescent. Isn't the technology you own, use, read about, and stand in line for every six to eight months proof of this?

More than adolescents or college kids, it's parents who eagerly anticipate the latest phones, the latest OS, the sleekest hand-feel, the apps that seem to jab and skate along the nerve endings of *now* itself. Moms have become the largest game-playing demographic on earth.[9] For reasons endemic to their generation—an inability to set limits on themselves, a reluctance to be seen as older or as authority figures— many parents today see themselves as the bellwethers and beneficiaries of everything in technology that's small, hot, fast, fiery, and new. Perhaps they feel it's their reward for a life that until now has been marked by inconvenience, immobility, and an overall lack of access. The problem is they're diving into something that doesn't properly belong to them.

Nowhere does the razing of the traditional relationship show up more vividly than in the relationship among parents today and their children, who share the same technologies and the same tastes. In most areas, the flattening of hierarchy is a good thing, but in the case of families, I can't help but believe it has taken away as much as it has given.

Recently my longtime friend Jonathan drove down from Vermont with his wife to drop off their daughter, Lucy, in New York City. It was the beginning of her college freshman year. Jonathan and his wife picked up Lucy's lanyard, found her dorm room, unpacked milk crates and book cartons, made the bed, helped hang up clothes, and sat around speculating what their daughter's new roommate from Malaysia, who hadn't arrived yet, might be like, though the two girls had already made each other's acquaintance on Facebook, Twitter, and Instagram.

Later, when the three of them found themselves at a Chinese restaurant for a farewell meal, no one seemed hungry and no one said very much. They had emptied their pockets, surrendering their devices on the table, making it an obvious point not to look at them. In the New England town where they lived, all three of them were buried in their phones most of the time, but the density and quick pace of urban life seemed to fulfill a thirst usually gratified by new texts, emails, calls, updates, and news headlines. Real dopamine versus the screen kind, maybe.

Outside the dorm, Jonathan and his wife tightly hugged Lucy good-bye. And then the two of them were back in the car, heading home.

"You think she'll be okay?" Jonathan's wife kept asking.

"She'll be grrreat," Jonathan said, sounding just like Tony the Tiger.

But he wasn't as confident as he sounded. In the next hour, he texted his daughter three times: *How's it going so far?* followed by *Call when you figure out what your classes are!* and finally *Love ya lots!* When there was no response, he interpreted Lucy's silence as a sign he was overdoing things and should back off. Maybe she'd gone for a walk. Maybe she was at a freshman orientation. Maybe her phone had lost battery power. While his wife drove, Jonathan played Zombie High Dive, Touch Racing 2, and Crash Bandicoot Nitro Kart2 on his phone. "You're like a little boy," his wife said at one point, kindly, and neither of them took offense at this. At a McDonald's off the highway that he had geo-located via the Fast Food Finder app, Jonathan used Star Walk to map the black nighttime autumn sky. Back on the road, he Shazam-ed a song on the radio, before plugging his phone into the car's sound system so he could stream a playlist he'd put together of songs by John Legend, Nicki Minaj, Iggy Azalea, Lester Young, and Ella Fitzgerald, which he'd given the name "Fast Trainin' Just 'Cuz."

When they reached their highway turnoff, Jonathan texted Lucy again: *Did you remember your cell phone cord? Let me know, I could overnight it to you!* He scanned his emoticons—he had hundreds, including a syringe, flaring nostrils, a boar, a pistol, a pig face, a ladybug, and neat rows of yellow cat heads—and in the end texted Lucy a gangsterish-looking red stiletto. What could be more downtown! By 8 PM, when he still hadn't heard anything back, Jonathan's brain began agitating: Lucy had been kidnapped; she had forgotten her own name; she was at some rooftop party in Bushwick, Brooklyn, like the one he'd seen on *Girls*; she'd been mugged; she was in the hospital. He checked Lucy's Facebook page and Twitter account. No new status updates, no new friend requests. Her lack of communication was making him almost physically ill.

"I just got off the phone with Lucy," Jonathan's wife said before coming to bed. "She sounds tired but good. Long day. She says to say hi."

It turned out that Lucy had left her phone in one of the moving boxes, and when she found it, it had run out of juice. She was charging it now, but she was about to grab a slice of pizza and go to sleep; she'd text them in the morning. From then on, she and her parents texted two or three or four days a week, along with the occasional Facebook message, Skype, Facetime, email, and phone call. This lasted until November, when Jonathan and his wife drove back down to New York to pick Lucy up for the Thanksgiving break, at which point the three of them, while obviously glad to be reunited, found that they didn't have much to say to one another that they hadn't already said.

WHAT'S NOT TO LIKE ABOUT ANY OF THIS? If communication between parents and their children is generally conceded to be "good," it would follow that more communication and more conversation between parents and children is "very good." But rebelling, or at the very least breaking away from one's parents and developing an identity independent from one's family, is a necessary developmental stage that crosses all racial, cultural, social, and economic classes. How, in a digital age when more ways exist than ever before to check in, and when anything short of an immediate response is cause for parental alarm, do kids take risks and experience the happiness, disappointment, and disillusion that comes from adventurousness and trying on new identities and even

Are you in touch with your kids more now that there's text and social media? Do you communicate with them differently over these platforms than in real life? (What might you say on Facebook that you wouldn't say to their face?) #2A behaviors? I'm not talking here about what's come to be known as helicopter parenting; I'm talking about iParenting.

My clearest memories of my childhood, in fact, involve taking risks. I was born in New York City, on 14th Street and 5th Avenue, grew up in Harlem, and spent my first eighteen years buzzing around the city sidewalks. I cut classes, took the Q train out to Coney Island, swarmed city parks with my friends. At fourteen or fifteen, I took the subway late at night to unsafe Brooklyn neighborhoods, now and again crossing under the river to New Jersey via the PATH train to crash Mac User Groups alongside other errant computer romantics. The only parental boundaries my folks put in place were that I come home at a reasonable time and not to talk to strangers. Did I bump up against predators and bullies on the streets of Harlem and elsewhere? Of course. I also learned to spot, predict, and dodge them. When I think back on those days, a lot of the joy I associate with being young links back to those feelings of independence, the feeling that no one was watching me and that I was meant to figure out things on my own, mess up, right myself, and then figure things out some more. That's how we all grow up.

My freedom lasted until my junior and senior years of high school, when I asked my parents for a beeper. I thought it would be cool to carry one, not realizing it would serve as a combination leash and leg iron. The beeper lit up whenever somebody was calling me, which left the burden on me to ring back the caller—usually my parents—on the nearest pay phone.

I left the beeper and New York City behind when I went upstate to college. As an eighteen-year-old freshman, I stood in line with the other kids in my dorm to call my folks once or twice a month. During those conversations, my parents took my emotional temperature, made sure I liked the courses I was taking, and had friends and enough money, at which point we agreed to check back in with each other as needed. Contrast this to nowadays, where parent-child communication is an ongoing conversation, a run-on sentence of elliptical chirps inscribed in green and gray speech-bubbles that look like a Roy Lichtenstein painting. This stream of consciousness has no beginning, no end, and no geography to speak of. Your children may be in college, or living on another coast, but they might as well be upstairs in their bedrooms. So tell me: How good is all this for kids who are making their way out into the world for the first time, where the unspoken mission of growing up involves engaging in a series of quiet conversations with oneself?

It's not just how children are expected to develop and foster their independence in the digital age that raises interesting questions. How are parents expected to maintain their own authority when their worlds map so closely to those of their children? Traditionally, as was the case when I wore a beeper, it's the older generation that teaches the younger generation how to use technology. The elders were the ones who set down the rules and as such were the authorities. Implicitly, they wrote the owner's manual.

But in the digital age, that tradition has been subverted, if not inverted. The technology children use today is more or less the same technology parents use. Jonathan, who nearly lost his mind after not hearing from his newly enrolled college daughter for twenty-four hours, is forty-eight years old, owns a smart phone, and has a Facebook page and a Twitter feed. He has sixty-four apps on his phone and uses maybe two. He text-messages both his children, and uses emoticons, too. He even mimics his younger daughter by texting the word *OK* as *Kk*, despite the fact that abbreviating an abbreviation fills him with the sickly suspicion that by using these devices and shortcuts, he, like all the other parents he knows in their forties and fifties and sixties, is in the thick of a socially approved midlife crisis. These devices, gadgets, and gizmos have turned every adult he knows into tech-bedazzled, quick-fingered people who have lost some core sense of who they are. He's grown so accustomed to how efficient, convenient, and superior the digital and mobile world is to anything he grew up with that he doesn't stop to think that by Facebooking, tweeting, text-messaging, and emoji-ing he's smoking out every site and experience his children should be able to call their own.

Moreover, he and everybody else over the age of forty consider it their duty to create parameters around their children's screen access, even though they're not quite sure how well they are handling their own. Until they turned twelve, Jonathan's kids were only allowed to use the centrally located family computer. Jonathan bought them laptops when they were in middle school, but forbade them to use the Wi-Fi while they were doing their homework. He didn't want them using their computers in their bedrooms, though after a while he caved in—it was too much trouble to monitor. Meanwhile, downstairs out of sight, he alternated frantically among a MacBook Pro, an iPad, and his iPhone. He needed them for work. He needed them to keep up. What if something terrible, or great, happened, and he was the last to hear about it?

Now think back on the equipment and the music and the movies and the television shows you shared and had in common with your own parents. Was there much overlap? No. One of the defining elements of being young is the drive to explode out of your parents' space and into your own. In the 1970s and 1980s parents listened to the music of their era, while kids listened theirs. Old stuff versus new stuff. Old tech versus new tech. The record player versus the cassette player. The cassette versus the portable CD player.

Then came the internet, and portable MP3 players, and smart phones, which smoothed out any technological divides and even tastes. Today, visit just about any house where there are kids and you'll find a silver-bells showcase of hardware and software—smart phones, laptops, tablets, e-readers—that evoke an eternal, unisex, dorm-room collusiveness. Everyone in the family uses Skype or Facetime. Everyone goes onto YouTube. Everyone uses Spotify or Pandora. Everyone plays the newest games and chats with one another via texts, emails, Facebook accounts, Twitter, and, when the stakes are high enough or if something very serious has gone down, on the phone.

Today, rather than children asking their parents how to use the record player, parents ask their children why the internet connection is so slow, what the cloud is, and why their podcasts won't sync properly with their phones. Parents continue to be the acquirers of household tech—they're still the ones with the money—but they're probably no longer the experts on how to use it.

All this shared technology leads, inevitably, to shared cultural references. A video of a badly behaving teenaged pop star will show up on *The Huffington Post*. It creates enough commotion to inspire a *New York Times* meta-story that several people then post on Facebook. Or there's a long article about the climactic episode of a popular television show. Parents might forward this video or article to their kids—are they aware of this singer, this series? Their curiosity piqued, parents test the waters themselves. It's part of living in the now, of not slipping behind the times, of beating back the years with your fingers. Before long they're hooked on *Pretty Little Liars* or *Orange Is the New Black*, and while they may feel nothing at all for Katy Perry or Pharrell Williams, they know who they are and even turn up "Roar" and "Happy" when they hear them on the radio. If it's true that inside every fifty-year-old is a young man or woman wondering what happened, thanks to smart phones, today they need wonder much less often. And who wants to get older anyway?

So here's the question: If parents are busy helping themselves to a technology that doesn't really belong to them, what does setting limits and being an authority figure look like? In an era when adults and children share identical technologies and cultural references, and can select among a half-dozen ways to connect to one another, how do children, teenagers, and college students rebel? Relatedly, do smart phones, which most parents see as a solution to their free-floating anxieties about their kids' safety and well-being, in fact end up making parents more apprehensive?

Who better to contemplate these answers than people who are creators and captains of this emerging technology and are also parents? To them I posed questions not only about rebellion in the age of digital and mobile technology, but also whether or not technology was in fact importing more anxiety into the home. Their responses were varied and insightful.

The head of sales for music and entertainment at Viacom, Jeff Lucas, has two children currently in college, and a third away at boarding school. While agreeing that there will always be adolescents who drive parents crazy—who drink, lie, shoplift, plagiarize, break windows, crash cars, and so on—Jeff believes that digital and mobile use do provide a space within which children can rebel. "Rebellion [in the traditional sense] just isn't necessary anymore because these days, kids have an outlet for it," Lucas says. "Children growing up today can still get outraged by things—by politics, or the environment, or whatever else—but today there are all these ways kids can communicate and express their feelings in real time, so that things don't build up inside them. No one is pushing them down. It's like an instant release." Once his own children began engaging with social media, "they felt that much more connected to something bigger. Even if they're upstairs in their bedrooms, even if they're not engaging with whatever group they belong to, they still feel a sense of belonging. With rare exceptions, things no longer reach a boiling point."

A recent research study from *The Journal of Adolescence* shows that by facilitating "checking in" with one another during the day, digital media helps adolescents develop a sense of belonging. The internet tells teenagers, "You are not alone," usually when they are alone. This immersive experience, Lucas believes, is what allows for a connection to something bigger than themselves. You might even argue that immersion is crucial to the formation of identity. When you're thirteen or fourteen years old, who mirrors back who you are? Family members, classmates, friends and the people in your town or community, all of whom today make up our social media circles.

> "Children growing up today can still get outraged by things—by politics, or the environment, or whatever else—but today there are all these ways kids can communicate and express their feelings in real time, so that things don't build up inside them."
>
> *Viacom head of sales for music and entertainment Jeff Lucas*

Gail Heimann, the president and chief strategy officer of Weber Shandwick, reminds us that kids can still rebel in subtle digital ways. "The first rebellion comes when your child is somewhere in between the tweens and the teens," Heimann says, "which is when they unfriend you on Facebook. In a mobile and digital age, unfriending your mom is the most profound, singular rebellious act that can occur."

"Some kids even have a secondary Facebook page," Lucas points out, "which is not their real one, and that their parents probably don't know about." Then of course there's Twitter, which can be anonymous if a user wants it to be. Instagram connects via a Facebook page, but via Twitter, users can potentially set up entirely different social internet identities that allow for alternate behaviors.

Another outlet for digital rebellion, Heimann notes, are selfies, the self- or group portraits taken via a smart phone or handheld camera that parents are generally prohibited from seeing. Selfies have become the main mode of communication on Snapchat, the popular photo-messaging app founded by two Stanford University students in 2011, in which sent images disappear after a preset time limit and whose main demographic is ages thirteen to twenty-three. Snapchat cofounder Evan Spiegel told *Forbes* he came up with the concept after observing that adolescents generally feel compelled to create and curate idealized, unreal online identities due to the longevity of personal information on social media. "It takes all the fun out of communicating," Spiegel said.

TO UNDERSTAND ALL THIS, it's worth casting a glance at the larger social media backdrop. In a landscape where traditional hierarchies have mostly collapsed, it would be tempting to believe that the concept of an oligarchy has collapsed alongside them. It hasn't. In only a few years, Facebook has evolved into The Establishment—the Metropolitan Museum of social media—and not only because everyone's parents are on it, either. Facebook has become a thirteen-year-old child's rite of passage, except rather than entering a den-room filled with cool kids, new Facebook users are obliged to sit at both the children's table and the grown-ups' table. There, along with their peers' status updates, they also have to scroll through kale-and-potato recipes, animal videos, and comments about whether the *New York Times* op-ed that morning was on the money. Before long they figure out what we all know, namely, that Facebook users squeeze out their remarks as carefully as witnesses on the stand at a murder trial. The vibe is feel-good and confirmatory. Dark or conflicted sides of human nature are unwelcome. There is no "Dislike" or "I Object" button. Created by a college student for college students and originally a place users could hang out with friends away from the prying eyes of family, Facebook today is likely to come across to a thirteen-year-old like a weekly family dinner at which they must sit in their stiff Sunday best while their grandmother, aunts, and uncles all shout their opinions.

Rebellions are historically built on the starkest possible dichotomies between the present and the previous generations. This is where the latest platforms for digital rebellion, text-messaging apps, come in. Most are created by twenty-somethings for twenty-somethings. They reflect a time-honored adolescent complaint—that teenagers have to "be" a certain way, or adapt to an unspoken etiquette that feels inauthentic or overly rigid. And they represent one of the few possible ways teenagers can escape the loose boundaries of contemporary parents. "Apps," says Heimann, "might very well be today's generational divide."

At twenty-two, Brian Wong is an entrepreneur who, along with two cofounders, started and runs Kiip, a mobile rewards network that allows companies and brands to reach consumers via badges and other levels of accomplishment inside games. As of this writing, Kiip has a presence in over 1,000 apps, and partners with brands including American Apparel, Amazon, Verizon, and McDonalds.

Facebook aside, most adolescents, Wong says, belong to three or four different networks, including Twitter and Path. "On Twitter," he says, echoing what Jeff Lucas said, "you can say things, and send photos, that you would never, ever dream of posting on Facebook." As for the other post-Facebook landscape for teenagers, Wong lists off a few of today's most prominent text-messaging apps, including WhatsApp, MessageMe,

WeChat in China, LINE in Japan, and in Korea, KakaoTalk. Their primary appeal is privacy, friendship, and, of course, preventing FOMO, or The Fear of Missing Out.

The statistics bear this out. Across the UK, WhatsApp has more than 450 million users. Roughly 90 percent of all Brazilians, 75 percent of Russians, and half of all Britons use the free messaging app; WhatsApp is on 95 percent of all mobile phones in Spain.[10] In the face of the fifteenth gluten-free recipe that week posted by your mom, what child wouldn't want to go undercover, or seek out a close-knit virtual space where only the shadiest grown-up would ever go?

Teenagers are known for coining their own private languages, and many of these text-messaging apps are barely word-based. Instead, users can swap snapshots, emoticons, and minivideos. Snapchat's new "Story" functionality allows teens to craft their own narratives from images taken throughout their day and share them with a curated friend network.

Again, the lure of mobile text-messaging apps is that they are beyond the reach of the family plan. Parents can't swipe, eavesdrop on, or oversee them. Text-messaging apps are physically and psychologically divorced from desktop computers and platforms and, in fact, were designed exclusively for mobile phone use. To teenagers, these handheld, standalone social networks feel personal, authentic, private, and most of all, free from parental boundary issues.

The explosion of text-messaging apps is the direct result of a contemporary culture in which children realize early on that at every turn they have to stay one step ahead of their parents' digital foraging. This is one reason why Facebook and other online originators are busy scooping up younger, hipper platforms, as if to retrieve a bolting younger generation. Google recently merged with Waze, the popular GPS app. Twitter bought Vine, the purveyor of short-form videos, while

Facebook bought Instagram—which makes sense given that teenagers prefer Instagram over Facebook,[11] and Instagram's popularity highlights the fact that the days of text-based status updates are probably numbered. Again, older platforms like Facebook were designed and rolled out for a desktop generation. As companies and developers begin to take notice of global trends, today almost everything is mobile-first.

It came as no surprise last year to read that Facebook had made its largest acquisition ever when it paid $16 billion to buy WhatsApp. The acquisition helps Facebook strengthen its penetration in places like Mexico and India, compete against Asian behemoths such as Japan's LINE, China's WeChat, and South Korea's KakaoTalk, and also make inroads in developing markets like India and Indonesia, where most consumers access the internet for the first time via their mobile phones.

The acquisition also, like the earlier purchase of Instagram, helps Facebook recapture a younger demographic who have been increasingly moving to other platforms. A few days after the WhatsApp sale was made public, the *New York Times* speculated that more and more people are growing tired of clamorous social networks like Twitter, Instagram, and Facebook—out of an average of 300 friends, an average Facebook user speaks regularly to maybe two of them— and equally weary of relentless advertising and the idealized image-curation that social networks require. Not surprisingly, kids seek out the company of their actual friends. As the *Times* put it, "In buying WhatsApp . . . Facebook is betting that the future of social networking will depend not just on broadcasting to the masses but also the ability to quickly and efficiently communicate with your family and closest confidants—those

How many of your Facebook friends are also friends IRL? Do you wish you had more in-person time with your Facebook friends, or do you like keeping them in the digital world? #2B people you care enough about to have their numbers saved on your smart phone."[12]

IT'S NOT ONLY THE ISSUE OF REBELLION that comes up as one of the ramifications of the constant stream of communication between one generation and the next. It's also the reliance on our phones as replacements for the tacit dialogues and realizations that young people engage in during their early twenties. What is my relationship between "me" and "others"? What is my relationship to alcohol and drugs? What is my relationship to romance, to my own gender, to the opposite sex, to my race and other races? As the Buddhists say, the only way out is through, and this leads to the first soft cementing of identity. But instead of checking in with themselves, everyone's first instinct is to check in with their smart phone, which can't answer these questions.

Of course, for many families, at some stage of a child's development, the capacity for constant communication is incredibly helpful. For Carolyn Everson, a Facebook executive and a mother who oversees more than twenty teams around the globe, text-messaging her two young daughters has been an invaluable way to maintain the semblance of a traditional family life. "With my schedule and the amount of flying around that I do," Everson says, "the ability for my girls to send me a quick text, or post something—they use Instagram, since they're too young for Facebook—has been a fantastic way for me to stay in touch with them in a really light, easy way."

But there should be a limit. "Today your kids can text you every little question," Lucas says, "in contrast to the way it was when I was growing up, where we had to find stuff out on our own. Kids also have the expectation that you are at their beck and call. Now, my own dad was great, but

I can tell you for a fact he was never at my beck and call."

If you are in an ongoing dialogue with your children, as Lucy was with her parents except for the few hours during which she misplaced her phone, don't life's most significant entry points—leaving home for college, getting married—lose their momentousness? Are parents so seduced by technology's sheer awesomeness that they've forgotten what it means to be authority figures, and to allow their kids to experiment? Once, parents mailed their children articles they cut out of the newspaper or the latest *Parade*. Today these same articles exist inside blue-lit links, like digital marquees, and children are as likely to forward them to their parents as their parents are to them. "Let's all be friends," technology seems to be telling us, resulting in an anomalous new informality that has become the norm in many families.

> "We figure it's better for us to be a peer with our kids than some horrible scary gray-haired authoritative figure."
>
> *Weber Shandwick president and chief strategy officer Gail Heimann*

As far as parent-child communication is concerned, "I think there are a lot of forces at work here," Heimann says slowly, "and one of the biggest is the way my generation has raised the next generation of kids with more of a peer sense, and that's all mixed up with our fear of aging. In the end, we figure it's better for us to be a peer with our kids than some horrible scary gray-haired authoritative figure."

But what is gained is also lost, and what is potentially a quiet victim of technology are those moments every parent faces when they must acknowledge that doing nothing is of more benefit to their child than intervention. This letting go is less and less likely, considering that cell phones ignite fear and anxiety among parents more than they bring relief or happiness.

Think about it: In the days before the internet, kids played outdoors, biked and walked through their neighborhoods, shattered living room windows with baseballs, endowed their dolls with superpowers, and lived to tell their own children about it. Nowadays many parents fear that if their children don't respond within two minutes of receiving a text, they've been kidnapped. They feel justified in their paranoia, too. Every parent I know with school-age kids looks me in the eye and swears that life today is more violent than it's ever been, with more murders, shootings, natural disasters, explosions, barroom fights, high-speed highway car chases, and generally untrustworthy people on the sidewalks than ever before. The statistics, in fact, say exactly the opposite.[13] But thanks to digital and mobile, every news event, no matter how isolated or far away, feels as if it's taking place two houses away from us. Among its other attributes, the mobile phone, one of the greatest tools for free-ranging anxiety ever invented, has transformed parenting into an extended nervous breakdown, from a child's birth to adolescence. Ironically, the mobile phone also has the magic, power, and reach to redress and relieve parents—as long as they maintain constant communication with their offspring.

While agreeing that cell phones alleviate parental anxiety—almost everyone I spoke with remembers a night growing up when they came home late at night or in the early morning only to face a crying or angry mother who, having been in a communications blackout, was convinced the worst had happened—Jeff Lucas admits that when he contacts his own kids via text message or phone, he expects them to return his call promptly, "Which is interesting, since my own parents could never ever expect that of me."

Has the mobile phone made you crazier as a parent or a kid? How?
#2C

Heimann expects the same of her children. "When I text my children and they don't answer, it creates a nanosecond or two of panic. I think, 'Maybe she doesn't have her phone with her,' followed by, 'But hey, wait, that's not possible.' Overall, though, I would say having a smart phone at my side has been a helpful ally in combating fear."

I understand—but disagree. If the new normal among parents and children is a continuous conversation tapped out via text, then an unreturned "How are things?" will automatically induce genuine disquiet and fear, just as a child not answering our question would concern us if he or she was in the same room with us. The expectation of a split-second response on the part of parents, who after all pay for the family's unlimited text-messaging plan, is high. Texting has transformed children's "wellness" into a moment-by-moment bulletin chronicling the ups and downs of impulsive and undeveloped brains. To draw an analogy, one also enabled by technology: It's the difference between observing the stock market in real time versus waiting to see if the Dow Jones average was up or down for the week or month. The *now*-ness of technology destroys the perspective that would otherwise soothe or de-stress the mind. To be witness to the volatility of adolescence and college is alarming enough, and it only becomes worse via real-time text-messages.

A friend of mine goes so far as to make distinctions on the emotional tone of the texts he gets from his college-aged daughter to determine whether or not to answer them. Some seem to be asking him to hold her hand, to tell her everything will be okay. Depending on the situation, my friend will either reply or fall silent. Other texts from her are chatty and friendly, and these he answers immediately. In a crisis,

Do you think the *now-ness* of technology is inherently anxiety producing? #2D he would be at his daughter's side in an instant—what parent wouldn't?—but other times he knows that answering her text would do her a disservice. No good can come when college-age children constantly reach for a smart phone for an outer authority and bypass the development of an inner one.

Over the past few years numerous articles have appeared about why college-age kids today seem to be having a harder time than past generations "growing up." Some use the term "emerging adulthood" to refer to the extended adolescence that delays adulthood for as long as possible. The slow economy and longer life spans are two reasons why, but rampant technology use may be another cause.

According to *Slate*, "A 2012 study by the American College Counseling Association reported a 16 percent increase in mental health visits since 2000 and a significant increase in crisis response over the past five years."[14] I'm guessing that excessive connectivity doesn't help. Parents throughout history have worried about the health and safety of their children, but today's technological umbilicus has become a stranglehold that damages and unsettles both parents *and* children. Moreover, by refusing to let their children go, parents have much less of an idea who they are once their kids leave the house. Via technology, they're forever on call, never off duty, never able to face their own losses, their own aging, the new empty or silent spaces in their own homes, relationships, and identities. And isn't this lack of independence precisely what most parents fear mobile technology is doing to their children?

Do you have rules for when you answer certain people's texts, and when you don't? What are they? #2E

3

the new sex education

THE MUSEUM OF SEX is located along a strip of lower Fifth Avenue in New York in a neighborhood most people walk through in order to get someplace else—Times Square or Rockefeller Plaza or Washington Square Park or Greenwich Village. Two years ago, around Valentine's Day, as a February blizzard was making the sidewalks un-navigably slushy, I bought a ticket as the museum was opening up, and made my way up a flight of industrial stairs to the second-floor exhibition room.

According to CEO Daniel Gluck, the Museum of Sex, or MOSex, is a leading attraction for out-of-town tourists, and last year welcomed more than a quarter of a million visitors. The museum recently installed a downstairs bar and lounge, in addition to the high-end sex toys for sale in the lobby. Many of the exhibitions at MOSex are selected for their timeliness, Gluck says, adding that in addition to a permanent collection of 15,000 objects, the museum has hosted exhibits ranging from the sex life of animals to the evolution of Japanese pornography from *shunga* to anime.

I was there to see the main exhibit, entitled "The Universe of Desire: Type, Swipe, Search, Upload, Download, Post and Stream," based on research taken from the 2012 book *A Billion Wicked Thoughts: What the Internet Tells Us About Sexual Relationships*, by Ogi Ogas and Sai Gaddam. Using a meta-engine that compiles search terms from Google, Bing, Yahoo, and other platforms, the two authors had analyzed roughly one billion web searches, a million websites, a million erotic videos, a million erotic stories, millions of personal ads, and tens of thousands of digitized romance novels to come up with a portrait of the ways in which, as the sign at the entryway said almost ominously, "desire has gone viral."

The authors of *A Billion Wicked Thoughts* didn't distinguish between male and female or heterosexual and gay searchers. Regardless, in the course of their research they found that across the globe, humans seek out identical sexual motifs. Age dominates sexual searches. "Teenage" and "college" are common search descriptors and for every search for a "thin" or "slender" woman are three more for a "fat" one. Breasts, regardless of size, are the most popular body part in America, Russia, India, Germany, Japan, and Saudi Arabia. As most females are aware, men are preoccupied with penis size, much more so than women. No matter where we live in the world, human taboos—rape, incest, and bestiality—are the same, too. To no one's surprise, males are turned on by explicit imagery, whereas women, who can be physically aroused while remaining psychologically disinterested, are more likely to be stimulated by stories, relationships, and romance.

On my way out of the museum, I stopped for a moment to study a wall covered with every single text message ever exchanged between former New York congressman Anthony Weiner and Lisa Weiss, the Nevada blackjack dealer who went public in 2013 with their online affair.

From the latest iPhone to free-with-most-plans clamshells, cell phones have grown beyond being merely gadgets, a wall-sign read. *Light-years beyond dialing, they now serve as camera, Internet, personal organizer, and best friend. We rarely use these little objects to call each other anymore, but rather fill them up with 160-characters-or-less worth of texts, sexts, chats, and BBMs. They become virtual mirrors as we Tweet each other pictures of ourselves and share them on Facebook. Entire websites, like GuysWithiPhones.com, are dedicated to user-uploaded self-portraits taken by camera phone and amplified for public enjoyment. Downloadable applications, such as Grindr, utilize GPS location technology to help find potential sex partners, further blurring the line between public and private.*

The sign ended with this: *As we continue to send each other information over cellular networks, these devices serve both as portal and memory bank. From love notes to dirty pics, entire relationships can exist on these phones, often discarded along with our next upgrade. Moving from model to model, data plan to 4G, the record of our culture's personal life may soon lie trapped in landfills across the world.*

THAT THE INTERNET AND OUR SMART PHONES have transformed what we think about when we think about romance, intimacy, and sex comes as no surprise to anyone with a hand and a keyboard. They continue to reinvent the ways we seek out one another, flirt, meet up, find out if our partners have been unfaithful, and break up. But rather than solidifying the inequities between men and women, digital apps and even pornography have gone a long way toward flattening the balance between the sexes.

The web would appear to be a platform tailor-made for connection and relationship, two areas of life in which females

Do you keep sexts or dirty pictures on your phone? Why? #3A

tend to excel. Over the past five years, women have used social media in higher numbers, more dependably and for more purposes—staying connected to family members, posting photos, asking for and getting information and advice—than men. Women are the dominant users of Facebook, Tumblr, Pinterest, Instagram, and Twitter, with 33 percent of online female adults using Pinterest versus 8 percent of men. Women also use their mobile phones and tablets to access social media sites more than men do. Generally speaking, men use social media for transactional and business reasons, which is why more men than women visit LinkedIn.[15]

The internet is a glass-bottom boat that reveals, for good and bad, our social and cultural prejudices, stereotypes, fears, preoccupations, and resentments. Social media in particular can be a convenient tool for reaffirming one's existing beliefs about others. For example, men who believe women gravitate toward trivial topics or want to be told repeatedly how attractive they are and spend their free hours taking pictures of themselves, can riff through social media sites and easily come away with their convictions confirmed.

Also thanks to social media, what used to be private is now public—including our faces and bodies. Everyone knows that Facebook, Instagram, and Snapchat increase the pressure to always be conscious of how we come across to others, whether we're alone, at a party, watching a ballgame, or picking apples from a tree. Far less emphasized, however, is the power these platforms give us to curate our own existences. Today, thanks in part to the rise social media, we have far more control over how we "present" to the rest of the world. It's up to us to decide whether we're willing to own our own appearances, flaws and all, or leave undocumented the parts of ourselves we don't like.

This has enormous ramifications for our romantic and sexual lives, as shown by a look at how the internet, especially via mobile phones, is transforming traditional love affairs. Today, the traditional steps to courtship have their own digital corollaries. We meet someone we like, online or off, through a mutual friend. Later that day, we may friend that person on Facebook. We trade cell phone numbers, and maybe arrange a face-to-face meeting. If we like, or end up loving, that person, we might inform Facebook we are now *In a Relationship*. Vacation photos, inside jokes, and other references begin showing up on our timelines, alerting our friends publicly that we now have an ongoing private life with someone else—intimacy as exhibition. If and when the relationship ends, one of us will alert Facebook to change our status back from *In a Relationship* to *Single*.

Facebook knows a lot about us, including what we are about to post or comment on before we think better of it or lose our nerve or get self-conscious. In 2014 the site's data scientists released a study based on a sample of anonymized, aggregated timeline posts over a period of three-and-a-half years. Facebook showed that in some cases it is possible to forecast when two people are about to make their romance official. In the roughly one hundred days before two people get serious, Facebook evidently observes a slow, predictable increase in the number of timeline communications between the prospective couple. "We observe a peak of 1.67 posts per day 12 days before the relationship begins . . . [and] when the relationship starts ("day 0"), [those] posts begin to decrease," Facebook data scientist Carlos Diuk wrote, adding that timeline posts between the couple reach their lowest point of 1.53 posts per day "eighty-five days into the relationship." He added, "However, don't be discouraged by the decrease in online interactions, as the content of the interactions gets sweeter and more positive."[16] The decrease in postings, Diuk speculates, comes as a result of the couple deciding to spend more time together in the real world.

I write about text messaging in the language chapter (and elsewhere in this book), but nowhere are the Rorschach-like meanings of texts, and the etiquette around texting, more elusive or confusing than when two people are in the flirtation stage, or even in a committed relationship. How does a person convey meaning, or intent, or even lack of intent? Even emojis can only do so much. What, for example, does it mean to not text a romantic interest back within a minute? What about five minutes, an hour, twenty-four hours? Does it convey dislike, apathy, nothing at all? Is it a good idea for a committed couple to know where the other person is every minute of the day? Shouldn't some things remain a mystery? Few people want to be perceived as eternally available, either emotionally or physically, and in romance, chasing and being chased, not to mention being unreachable, can be compelling. With our phones always turned on, what becomes of unavailability and its mystique, and how does that influence our romantic imaginations and capacity for desire?

"Ghosting"—a term that refers to breaking off a relationship by intentionally ignoring another person's texts or calls—has even made it into the lexicon. Quoting an *Elle* magazine survey, the *New York Times* reported that 16.7 percent of men and 24.2 percent of women had been ghosts—or ghosted—at some point in their lives. As one respondent noted, "People don't hold themselves accountable anymore because they can hide behind their phones."[17]

The internet may reflect who we've always been as humans, but the digital world and mobile phones also create wholly new behaviors and expectations. For anyone straight, gay, looking, in love, sexually involved, or celibate, technology serves as a wordless chaperone, carrying out a series of roles that are less straightforward than one might believe. Online data today is used to pre-vet the people who interest us: Their backgrounds. Their educations. Their job histories.

Their friends. The places they live and they work. Mentions of that person in every imaginable situation. The internet, and mobile phones, have turned every romantic and sexual relationship into a threesome or a foursome—while also creating a universe where the fantasy of infinite possibility is often more seductive than the person who's right in front of you.

Since 2004, when he was named editor of the *New York Times*'s "Modern Love" column, Daniel Jones has witnessed up close how technology has transformed two-person relationships into double dates. Over the past decade, Jones estimates he has read 50,000 submissions from here and abroad, of which he estimates 75 percent were written by women. He published some of his observations in a book, *Love Illuminated: Exploring Life's Most Mystifying Subject (With the Help of 50,000 Strangers)*.

When Jones began editing "Modern Love," digital and smart phone use immediately began figuring in the submissions he received. "Facebook was, and still is, a perennial theme in relationships, especially among middle-aged users. One essay topic I see over and over again has to do with reconnecting with someone with whom you went to high school or college. Clearly there's an inborn trust there, in that you feel you know these people already, that they're somehow 'safe.' I can't help but get the feeling that the idea of going back out into the singles market at a certain age is just too overwhelming for most people."

In 2008 "Modern Love" commissioned a nationwide college essay contest, followed three years later by a second one. In 2008, the most common essay topic among college undergraduates was their struggle to make sense of hooking up, e.g., sex with no strings attached. ("I don't think the hooking-up culture has helped women any," Jones notes. "In fact, I feel it's been incredibly damaging, making women feel as though they have to act like men.") By 2011, our relationship with digital technology began to dominate the submissions. "I started getting more and more essays that focused on online love affairs. In just three years' time, college kids had gone from trying to make sense of hooking up—navigating sexual relationships that excluded emotion—and now were trying to figure out how to navigate emotional online relationships that excluded sex."

What does nonsexual online intimacy mean exactly? Like Facebook's masked ball, in which what we reveal is only a carefully edited version of ourselves, an online romance provides only the illusion that we "know" another person. "Even if you really truly believe you're pouring your heart out into your Gchat boxes and laptop cams," Jones says, "online flirtations or romances are all about self-protection and invulnerability."

> "Online flirtations or romances are all about self-protection and invulnerability."
>
> *New York Times's "Modern Love" editor Daniel Jones*

A common essay subject is one Jones calls "Soulmate-in-a-Box," which he defines as "a person we rarely meet in person, and in some cases never actually speak to on the phone, but to whom we grow closer than anyone else. It's an object lesson in how relationships that start online can't hope to compete with reality."

It works this way: Two people cross paths online. At first, it's harmless, guilt-free fun, especially if they're separated by great physical distance. We are always seeking ways of finding love that don't prompt vulnerability, or insecurity, Jones points out, because who wants to feel insecure and vulnerable? "Hiding behind a digital identity frees us up from feeling those things."

Typically, after a period of intense cyber-intimacy and confession, the couple meets up in person. On rare occasions such an online relationship might lead to something in real life, but more often the connection that was built up online disintegrates. "The body doesn't match up with the sensibility they've come to know online," Jones says. "It's just too hard to square the person to whom you've been baring your heart with the actual human being seated across the table from you."

Not surprisingly, Jones explains, "Online, we get to know whatever the other person chooses to serve up, which is typically a two-dimensional collage of images and text and audio. We create unreal, idealized versions of ourselves." There's another, more poignant explanation Jones offers that anyone who saw Spike Jonze's 2013 film, *Her*, will understand: "The urge to seek pleasure and excitement and even perfection through a device rather than through another person can be an extremely hard habit to break."

Jones describes a woman who carried on a months-long online relationship with a man who lived 900 miles away. Their connection became so intense, so "real," that the couple mutually decided to take things further by meeting face-to-face. The woman rented a car and drove eleven hours to where the man lived. "It went fine at first," Jones says, "but it quickly became clear to them both that their online chemistry had no parallel in real life." Their conversations swiftly devolved into long silences. Soon the man began sneaking glances at his phone. "The woman was left sitting there as the guy searched online for the emotional fix he'd grown accustomed to finding there."

Our devices are good not only at fostering an inauthentic sense of chemistry, but also at flagging our disloyalty. These days when people stray they're more often than not busted by their own phones and texting history, to the point where potential cheaters would be smart to buy a second "secure"

Do you believe online chemistry can carry over into real life? #3B phone. Many individuals in their teens and early twenties snoop on their partners' phones all the time, a phenomenon that reflects the idea that the emotional or tonal read of a text can serve as evidence of emotional or even sexual treason.

Inside a relationship, receiving a text from another person has its own set of subtle implications. A friend of mine still recalls the day he got a text message late at night from a mutual female friend of his and his partner's. Why was she texting him? Why wasn't she texting *them*? Did he even know her well enough for her to text him, and at what point, exactly, had he given her the emotional permission to do that? Should he tell his partner? Was he being disloyal in spirit to his relationship by not telling his partner, or by texting the woman back? What if the entire thing was in his head? (It was.) Texting has opened the door, in fascinating ways, to a whole new world of relationship anxiety, not to mention paranoia.

Only a decade ago, if you were to ask most people to free-associate about the words "online dating," most would respond with some negativity. Online dating was for sad sacks with something wrong with them. In 2013, however, the Pew Research Internet Project revealed that one in ten Americans, as well as 38 percent of people who identified themselves as "single and looking," had used online dating or a mobile dating app, and that most respondents knew someone who had successfully found a partner that way. In 2013, only 21 percent of internet users agreed with the statement "People who use online dating sites are desperate," an eight-point decline from the 29 percent of people who believed the same in 2005.[18]

Have you ever looked at your significant other's texts or emails without their knowledge? Do you think it's okay to do so if you suspect they are cheating? Do you consider sexts cheating? #3C

Online dating today is a crowded, competitive industry. Among the biggest, best-known companies are OKCupid, Match.com, and eHarmony. Over the past few years, mobile-only dating apps have made it possible for users to find love on the move, no matter where they happen to be. Among today's most popular are Zoosk and Tinder, the latter allowing users to swipe through a revolving cast of men and women who live nearby as they're sitting in a coffee shop or buying a wrench at the hardware store.

How did online dating shed its underground associations, and so quickly, too? "If we forget online versus offline, and think about dating, period, the issue for most people is that their social group is fixed, and they work extremely long hours," says Shayan Zadeh who, along with Alex Mehr, founded Zoosk, which is available in twenty-five languages in more than seventy countries. "The times we serendipitously run into a new person have decreased, because of the amount of time we are either working, or hanging out in a closed world." In other words, online dating became more acceptable because it's practical. Zadeh also credits positive word-of-mouth to reinventing the reputation of online dating. "Many of us have friends who tell us they met so-and-so on this or that platform, and are extremely happy—which can't help but make us wonder, 'Why wouldn't it work just as well for me?'"

Zadeh attributes Zoosk's specific success to its technology. Most dating apps give users a huge group of people who match their checklist, "but every psychology study I've ever read tells us that when it comes to dating and romance, we basically have no clue who we are interested in. Most of the time our perceptions are wrong, and ultimately we end up with people who are interested in us." To address this issue, Zoosk takes note of how its users interact with potential romantic partners. If they receive half a dozen messages, which ones do they answer? Zoosk feeds this individual behavioral data into an engine, and the next person the app recommends has that much higher a likelihood of matching what the user wants. "In some ways," Zadeh says, "the technology does the work of your subconscious." Netflix, Pandora, and Amazon do something similar, he notes. Zoosk is just the first company to apply individual algorithms to romance.

Grindr is the geo-social networking app for gay men that identifies potential romantic partners within a nearby geographical radius. CEO Joel Simkhai launched Grindr in 2009, and when asked why, told me, "As a gay man you are always wondering who else is gay around you. Even though the internet is a good way for men to meet up, it's inefficient and clunky and not exactly what you'd call location-aware." When Steve Jobs announced the release of the second-generation iPhone, Joel was convinced it was the technology his idea had been waiting for. Grindr exploded virally almost as soon as it was launched; today it has over 7 million users, 3 million monthly users, and 1.5 million daily users. Not entirely facetiously, Simkhai says that Grindr gives gay men around the world a superpower of sorts—the ability almost to see through walls—"which I consider to be both brave and empowering."

In 2014, news reports came out that Grindr's usage had tripled during the Sochi Olympics, which gladdened anyone displeased by the Russian government's treatment of its gay and lesbian community. These statistics didn't surprise Simkhai, considering the strong role Grindr plays in travel culture. "If a user is in any new town, or location, [his] Grindr usage goes up. It's also a great way to find out what's going on, where the good bars are, and what might be happening that night in an unfamiliar city."

In the evolution of online dating, mobile apps like Grindr have normalized the idea of connecting with others based almost exclusively on their physical appearance. Simkhai doesn't believe this is a gay-versus-straight distinction but instead, about being male. "Our primary identity is as men, which both governs our identity and the way we look at potential mates, period. For various evolutionary reasons, women approach mates differently. Key for any app will be the recognition of that difference—how to make things comfortable, safe, and in control, which matters a lot to women. So to me, the bigger question is, Which dating service or app really allows women to feel comfortable? Because at the end of the day, if women are there, the men will show up."

Today, women are using new technology to create dating apps tailored to their own desires and build communities around their own experiences. Launched with fanfare and publicity in 2013, Lulu, which has been called "Yelp for Men," is a crowd-sourced female rating system that allows female users to rate men in categories that range from "ex-boyfriend" to "crush" and to use hashtags as shorthand descriptions of these same men. Users can select from hashtags Lulu provides, including but not limited to #Sexual-Panther, #WillWatchRomComs, #LoserFriends, and #NoGoals, or create new hashtags of their own. Lulu's algorithms then calculate a score from 1 to 10 that shows up in the app, superimposed over the man's Facebook profile picture.

> "The question is, Which dating service or app really allows women to feel comfortable? Because at the end of the day, if women are there, the men will show up."
>
> *Grindr CEO Joel Simkhai*

Some critics, many women among them, find Lulu disturbing, vengeful, and even antifeminist. In 2013 in Brazil, where Lulu is the number-one downloaded app, one man filed suit against the platform, resulting in the app adjusting its terms of use so that Brazilian males had to actively affirm that they wanted to be rated or reviewed before showing up on the site.[19] I'm not the first person to point out that this adjustment is antithetical to the spirit of the app—and that Lulu is a case in point that often men can dish it out but can't take it.

In fact, in contrast to over-the-top male "revenge porn" websites, Lulu has never been shown to be destructive. A year after its launch, *New York* magazine noted that among Lulu's 2.5 million reviews—500,000 of which were requested by the male subjects themselves—the median score was 7.5 out of a possible 10, and that, "Among reviewers who self-identify as ex-girlfriends and hookups, 70 percent of reviews are 7.0 or higher. When the reviews come from friends, 80 percent are higher than 7.0."[20] As the *New York Times* remarked, "Apparently, many believe it's better to have been badly reviewed than never to have been reviewed. Some guys have even taken to Twitter to brag about their score or campaign for better reviews."[21]

Still, far and away the most dominant player in the world of mobile dating apps—made up most recently of players like Hinge, which includes matches drawn from users' Facebook friend group, and Happn, which uses GPS technology and tracking to show whether two parties have recently crossed paths—is Tinder, whose estimated 50 million users make roughly 1.5 billion swipes daily. "If you chart the growth of Tinder against every other dating app in history, and place that on a global level, the lines of Tinder's competitors are almost invisible," notes Tinder founder and CEO Sean Rad. Moreover, the level of engagement among Tinder users is staggering. According to information the company provided the *New York Times* in 2014, "On average people log into the app 11 times a day. Women spend as much as 8.5 minutes swiping left and right during a single session; men spend 7.2 minutes. All of this can add up to 90 minutes each day."[22]

Since its launch in 2012, Tinder has infiltrated pop culture, with "swipe right" and "swipe left" becoming well-known, and knowing, references. It's also been a magnet for controversy. But I disagree with Tinder's critics. By shifting the power dynamics of dating, searching, and seeking out love in a way that helps equalize the playing field between men and women, Tinder is a game changer in ways that might not be immediately apparent.

Consider this: Until Tinder came along, what women wanted out of a dating app bore little relationship to the $2 billion online dating sector, which was uniquely tailored to the hunter and the ogler, not the hunted and the ogled. Once inside a dating site, the culture, as *Fast Company* notes, "is for female users not to initiate contact, but to field hundreds of incoming, often sexually charged, messages"[23]—which is precisely what most women *didn't* want. Exploring the world of online dating for women in the *New Yorker* in 2013, writer Ann Friedman noted that based on her conversations with female-founded dating sites and apps, "women want authenticity, privacy, a more controlled environment, and a quick path to a safe, easy offline meeting."[24] Fittingly, the name of her article was "Overwhelmed and Creeped Out."

So what's different about Tinder? First, some context. As Dr. Jessica Carbino, PhD, a researcher at Tinder, explains to me, the human brain has always made instantaneous appraisals, a practice known as "thin-slicing." The term, drawn from psychology and popularized in Malcolm Gladwell's bestseller *Blink*, refers to the human ability to make rapid, unconscious inferences about someone (or something) that are often more accurate than judgments based on far more information. We thin-slice everything from a person's socioeconomic status to their personality. In short, every time you and I walk down the street making eye contact with others, we are, in effect, swiping left or right.

Tinder also taps into and builds on another natural human behavior: sociality. In the years after graduating college, Rad points out, many young men and women find themselves in a friendship wasteland, where they no longer have access to individuals from the wide variety of social and economic groups provided by higher education. They are suddenly constrained to their existing friend groups and work colleagues. Tinder expands and enriches its users' worlds in unexpected ways.

"Meeting new people is a key part of everyone's lives," says Rad. "Meeting people is difficult. Love is difficult. At Tinder, we asked, 'How can I make it incredibly easy to form quality relationships, all of which will have the impact and potential to change your life and give you a bigger perspective on the world?' That really is Tinder's mission." One way the company found to improve the process, Rad adds, is "by removing the question and the friction of who wants to meet you. There's a lot of potential rejection involved in meeting people. Tinder came in and said, 'Let's solve that.'" He adds, "The biggest innovation of Tinder is actually not the swipe. It's what we call the 'double opt-in.' It's the fact that two people [have to] have expressed interest in each other anonymously. We see this principle applying not just to romance but also to friendship and even business. No one wants to be the first to put him- or herself out there. They're afraid they're going to get rejected—which is a problem that Tinder solves."

> "The biggest innovation of Tinder is actually not the swipe. It's what we call the 'double opt-in.' It's the fact that two people have to have expressed interest in each other anonymously. No one wants to be the first to put him- or herself out there—a problem that Tinder solves."
>
> *Tinder founder and CEO*
> *Sean Rad*

Since its founding in 2012, Tinder has created 10 billion new connections that otherwise probably would never have existed. And that number is growing at a rate of around 26 million a day. The app facilitates over one million in-person dates every week. But Tinder is being used for more than just dates. When Rad and his team study Tinder data, they find everything from business professionals meeting up, to trainers looking for clients, to casting directors looking for actors, to restaurants seeking chefs. Some Tinder users who are traveling out of town match up with locals who provide restaurant recommendations. And plenty use it to make new friends. As Rad puts it: "If Facebook's mission is to define the graph of who you're friends with, and give you the tools to connect with them, Tinder's mission is to expand the graph."

Still, Tinder's greatest contribution has been to even the dating playing field, by helping shift the traditional balance of power. Almost all first-generation internet-based dating services and apps, by allowing their female users to be deluged with messages from men in whom they had no interest, put women at a disadvantage. Tinder was one of the first to address and resolve this issue. A male Tinder user cannot leave a message to a woman he is interested in unless the woman has also given the go-ahead, giving female users a greater degree of agency, autonomy, and choice. This shift in dynamics regarding typical online engagement is expedited by the "double opt in" feature of Tinder. Women on the platform have to actively engage with other users to be able to talk to anyone, which effectively neutralizes the playing field of initiation.

Clearly, dating apps have infiltrated the mainstream, and they may have done so as much as they have for reasons driven by digital culture itself: dating apps not only facilitate romantic and sexual relationships, they also reflect the habits of time-starved people whose heads, hearts, and fingers are buried in their phones. The popularity of dating apps has exploded in response to our preoccupation with our phones and to what Dr. Belisa Vranich, a New York City-based clinical psychologist and author, describes as the contemporary trend of "hypomania." "We've grown conditioned to think that people who talk fast and never slow down are fast thinkers," Vranich tells me. "Our culture is all about being driven to the point where we actually glorify stress." She notes we've reached a point where if we have a free moment, rather than stopping and pausing we whip out our phones. "Unless we're putting out information or getting other people to resonate with us—like bats—humans are finding it harder and harder to capture any sense of their own being. I have a funny feeling sometimes that people put information out to discover how they should feel, that they're no longer even sure themselves."

Of course, this has implications for romance. Many of us are so accustomed to efficiency and time-saving that we've adapted a *Click Now/Add to Cart/Delete* philosophy to our romantic and sexual lives. Wading into a party or room only a decade ago, we might have made eye contact with another person, or picked out a personal detail, whether it was the color of someone's socks or the quality of someone's smile. Today, most of us are so absorbed in our screens we wouldn't see a potential partner if they were standing right in front of us (so perhaps we should be grateful that phones apps now allow us to find out what romantic possibilities are around us!). Among the most popular features of Craigslist is a section known as "Missed Connections," which is devoted to moments where users spied an attractive or intriguing person who got away from them. It wouldn't be a surprise if the reason they got away were that we only we only removed our mobile blinders in time to glimpse them and murmur, "Wait—."

It's worth reminding ourselves that we are living through a time of profound social change. *The Christian Science Monitor* reports that in 2014 the number of unmarried US adults was higher than the number of those who were wed. In 1950, 4 million Americans lived alone; in 2014, it was 31 million. Twenty percent of American adults have never married. In 2010, four out of ten Americans told Pew researchers that marriage was becoming obsolete. Traditionally, a big factor for women in getting married was financial stability. But with roughly 70 percent of all women working outside the home, is financial stability as important a driver as it once was? The increase in singles could be an extension of today's "rental" economy (why commit to, say, a house, a car, or, in this case, another person, when you can lease it instead?). Or it could be the result of living in an entirely new world shaped by digital connectivity. Think about it: we inhabit an era where it is possible to scour the world to find a potential soul mate.

Some people worry that by inspiring romantic and sexual FOMO, or the Fear of Missing Out, dating apps are, in fact, inimical to committed relationships. But Tinder and other apps cannot be held responsible for engineering abundance of choice. Abundance already existed, just imagined and unseen. Humans have always felt anxiety about missing out on people and experiences. Tinder and other dating apps only fill in what—or who—we already imagined was out there, and in fact may even redress this anxiety by serving up actual faces and names.

What dating apps do offer that's new is the exploration, and discovery, of potential relationships (whether romantic or otherwise) in ways, and at a pace and scale, that humans have never experienced before. And with women increasingly empowered to shape technology based on their needs and desires, we are perhaps seeing the onset of a new world more empowering to both sexes than any of us could have ever imagined.

IF SOCIAL MEDIA AND DATING APPS hadn't already transformed or, rather, uncomfortably clarified the male relationship to women, there's always pornography.

It's difficult to overemphasize the extent to which the internet has enabled porn to infiltrate and transform our culture. Ten, twenty, thirty years ago, porn was a niche thrill, thrilling in large part *because* it was niche. But in a UK study commissioned for the Channel 4 documentary *Porn on the Brain* in conjunction with *The Telegraph*, 97 percent of boys and 80 percent of girls who responded to a survey in England of study subjects between ages sixteen and twenty said they had looked at porn. In the US, the same survey reported that one in three women regularly watch porn, while 70 percent of men aged eighteen to twenty-four visit porn sites at least once a month, and I suspect the other 30 percent may not be telling the truth. Pornhub.com, which according to Alexa is the world's biggest porn site and among the 100 most popular websites worldwide based on page views and unique site users, has around ten million visitors a day. At the same time, as a culture we treat porn unseriously, using the term to denote any delectable, covetable, close-up object. Thus we have food porn, real estate porn, and, on Pinterest alone, shoe porn, cookie porn, book porn, craft porn, barcodes porn, even kayak porn.

Most of the articles I've read about pornography and the internet focus on the negative ways it affects men. In 2013 the actor Joseph Gordon-Levitt directed and starred in *Don Jon*, a film about a twenty-something man whose real-life relationships can't compete with the sex he watches online every day. Earlier that same year, *Salon* published an article by a pseudonymous journalist, Isaac Abel, called, "Did Porn Warp Me Forever?" In it Abel describes how his porn habit desensitized him to the extent that he quickly fell down what he calls a "kink spiral," that kept him searching out videos that gave him the same "toxic mix of shame and lust." In bed with actual women, he had trouble getting and maintaining an erection, and his brain would be dreaming the entire time of images borrowed from porn clips. Of his own millennial generation, Abel writes, "A decade before we were having intercourse, our neural pathways associated ejaculation with an addictive, progressive perversity that demanded a superlative overstimulation—skipping from climactic scene to climactic scene."[25]

More accurately than anything I've seen, the male characters in HBO's *Girls*, whose actions are often met by the young women sharing their beds with upset or bemused bewilderment, embody the default sexual expectations of men who have come of age with porn available anytime on their phones. In a 2012 article in *GQ*, journalist Siobhan Rosen writes, "Almost every female friend of mine has had an experience with pornified sex super-early in a relationship."[26] Rosen likes sex. She's not a sexual neo-con, and neither is she antiporn. But, she writes, it hardly seems right to call some of the sexual encounters she's had "sex." They are "more like masturbation with a fellow 3D person."[27]

Porn has even infiltrated the ways we use words to describe sex, and male and female sexual organs—at least the ones that don't sound like they come from a middle school anatomy class (like, for example, "sexual organs"). Jane Pratt agrees. "I was on a television show once, and I used the word 'intercourse,' and my staff teased me about it afterwards, but what else was I supposed to say?"

Pratt is the founding editor of *Sassy* and *Jane* magazines, the current editor of the online magazine *xoJane*, and the host of her own TV show, Jane Radio, on Sirius XM. I wanted to get her perspective on how internet porn may be affecting not men—they've been written about enough—but women, now and in the future.

Pratt agrees that porn has infiltrated everything, adding as an aside that it's tricky for her to explain to *xoJane* writers how to write about sex so that it doesn't sound like porn. "Sex aside, my female readers also write in to say they feel an added pressure to have porn-like bodies—to fit one very specific body ideal. Another powerful porn influence is that many young women have come to expect that men are hooking up with them only for their bodies. Not only is every female expected to be hairless now in all the right places, they even have to think about the style of their *pubic* hair. Is it a landing strip? Is it completely bald? Is it bedazzled, or whatever that expression is?"

But the *do I measure up?* phenomenon can cut both ways. Porn serves up innumerable images and videos of men and their bodies—their penises, their youth, their vitality, their willingness to take risks—placing men under their own type of pressure. In an industry where only the best-endowed men are chosen to be stars, how does what men see in porn affect the male psyche?

Porn is, in a sense, a training manual, and today, thanks to mobile phones, it's a portable one, too, able to be accessed anywhere from a college library to the passenger seat of a car. Young people may see porn as an infographic, growing up to believe that there are specific ways they ought to act in bed, specific positions and techniques they should master, and specific experiences they should expect—and if they themselves don't, their partners, also well schooled by porn, likely will.

"It's not just porn, either," Pratt notes. "It's also the countless YouTube sex tips videos, too, and the celebrity sex tapes that are leaked online. You'll notice in all of these tapes that it's never about the woman enjoying sex. It's about Kim Kardashian and Paris Hilton posing for the camera and trying to

Have you ever looked at porn on your mobile phone? #3D

look and sound as much as possible like the women they see in porn. There *is* so-called female-friendly porn out there, but I doubt that appeals to women, because women were raised watching this other kind of porn, so objectification itself has become a kind of turn-on."

Inevitably my thoughts turned to Cindy Gallup. Gallup is a former advertising executive and the founder of the website MakeLoveNotPorn, who in 2009 gave a TED Talk about sex that quickly became among the event's most popular offerings. Gallup has been quoted as saying that today's unfettered freedom of access to online hardcore pornography has met up with a global reluctance to talk candidly about sexuality— and that as a result, for millions of middle school and high school boys and girls, porn is the closest thing they have to a sex education class.

In an interview I conducted with Gallup, she expanded on her thoughts, and also gave me a rundown on some of the more violent terms and expressions for sexual acts trending online, many of which, she notes, were undoubtedly dreamed up by men who've never been forced to perform them. What bothers Gallup most is how most male fantasies reflect behaviors most men would seldom be able to get away with in real life, with a real female. But as porn becomes even more mainstream, it turns fantasy into baseline reality. "Is this really what we want eight- to eleven-year-old boys absorbing as the paradigm of male-female relations?" Gallup asks.

Digital services arise to fill the void created by the absence or failure of something. In this case, that something is sex education in schools, which, at least across the US, is practically nonexistent; only twenty-two American states require sexual education in school at all. Online pornography fills in the gaps. (It's not only pornography that has come to the

Do you think porn is a form of sexual education for teenagers? #3E rescue here, of course. Though it may be thick with misinformation, in the absence of trustworthy sex education programs the internet has taken on the role of an authority that both teens and grown-ups can ask for advice or information without anyone else being the wiser.)

But what has porn done to those born after 1990, and what is at stake? What are the consequences of a generation of girls and boys growing up thinking that the porn they see online is the way people have sex? The power relationship between the sexes as depicted in porn is very different from the one we see today in the real world, where dating apps have given women more agency in relationships than ever before, where porn has obliged men to consider their own sexual capabilities in ways they never had to before, and where women are just as important as men in the bedroom.

As Paco Underhill wrote in his 2010 book *What Women Want*, 70 percent or more of American women work outside the home. It's a world where women dominate higher education and outnumber men on North American college campuses by at least sixty to forty, a gender gap that's only expected to increase. A world where record numbers of women are attending business school or preparing for careers in engineering, physics, and computer science. Today's young women are growing up at a time when, in most major cities in America, women under the age of thirty have overtaken men in earning power; a time when, as of 2010, gainfully employed females between the ages of twenty-one and thirty earned 117 percent of the wages of equivalent working males.

They are also inhabiting an influential parallel universe where they begin their lives as Lolitas. Before long they'll become Lusty Cheerleaders, Kinky Teens, or Insatiable Nymphomaniacs. In college, they'll evolve into Girls Gone Wild and Sluts Who Want It Bad. As life and time goes on, they will take on the personas of Hot Slutty Librarians, Lusty Pregnant

Moms, Horny Bored Housewives, and Sex-Starved MILFs. After that will follow their Cougar and Horny Grandma years.

Of course, young men are subject to a similar trajectory. In porn, they begin their sexual life as My Son's Best Friend, the Pizza Delivery Boy, Young Stud, and Horny College Boy. They age into the Guy Next Door, the Boss, Daddy Knows Best, and Dirty Old Man. Porn objectifies and categorizes almost every possible interaction, human behavior, and body type. The simple act of having to search and find interactions not only means that such categories become necessary, but that interests and fetishes are laid out without nuance or apology.

Given the amount of time and energy we spend, as a culture, searching for those specific sexual interests, why, in the early twenty-first century, are we still so incapable of talking openly about our sex lives? Sex is in commercials, in books, in magazines, politics, in movies and television shows. Ninety-five percent of all Americans have sex before marriage, and the US has the highest rate of teen pregnancy in the developed world, but as a culture, the last things we seem to want to talk about are boys and girls and sex.

Parents used to be able to ignore the *Penthouse* under their sons' beds; online porn is harder to ignore. It is, after all, the biggest secret we all have in common. And so the pervasiveness of online porn may create an unintended beneficial consequence: pushing the subject of sex into the open. Because as long as we change the subject, and allow porn to remain a ubiquitous subterranean secret, it will continue to cause as much harm as it does good.

Porn does have its pluses, after all. As Daniel Gluck points out, "You can find at least one other person, if not an entire community, that likes exactly what you like sexually somewhere in the world—whereas before 1995, you would probably remain closeted and frustrated." The internet in general, and porn especially, has probably rescued or invigorated as many relationships as it's unraveled. For Generation X'ers in tired or passionless marriages, porn can provide excitement and relief as much as it can erode real-life sexual relations.

Correlation is not causation, but a recent statistic I saw has even made me wonder whether online porn, the access to online health and sexual education, or both, might in fact be curbing sex. A 2015 survey of 2,000 boys and girls aged fifteen to nineteen and 1,770 young adults twenty to twenty-four published by the Centers for Disease Control and Prevention Health Statistics shows that only 41 percent of teenagers claim to have had sexual intercourse—a significant drop from 1988's figure of 51 percent. In 1988, 51 percent of teen girls had had at least one sexual encounter; in 2013, the figure had dropped to 44 percent. Among girls ages fifteen to nineteen, births have also declined, from eighty-four per 1,000 teens in 1991 to twenty-six in 2013.[28] During their first sexual encounter, 79 percent of female teenagers and 84 percent of male teenagers also reported using some method of contraception. These statistics could be credited to smarter education being available online, but it could also be argued that easy access to taboo imagery online has altered the way we act on our desires.

Maybe some things, some of the time, are better left to the imagination or to fantasy. Or maybe, thanks to the accessibility of online porn, sex has lost some of its forbidden nature, leaving this generation with the capacity not just to reframe their own relationship to sex but to create altogether new models of relationships, much in the same way apps like Tinder are reshaping how we meet and interact. The most likely scenario is that, again, the internet has created an issue it has simultaneously solved—and, by providing unprecedented amounts of information, in pictures, videos, and words, has given us an unprecedented amount of freedom to make up our own minds about sex, and everything that goes with it.

4

gum, mobile phones, and the future of buying

ACROSS THE WORLD, chewing gum sales were down and no one knew why. After decades of steady growth, one-fifth or more of the globe's gum chewers had stopped buying gum, and the remaining four-fifths were buying less gum in general. In four years, the decline in US gum sales has been 11 percent.[29] The biggest slump took place within the category's two biggest, most dependable demographics: adolescent males and young men between the ages of eighteen and thirty-four.

Somewhat counterintuitively, the overall snacking category—including coffee, chocolate, peanuts, yogurt, fruit, tortilla chips, popcorn, pretzels, muffins, croissants, soups, energy bars, and nearly all the other foods we put in our mouths in between breakfast, lunch, and dinner—was unchanged. Potato chips and nuts were selling. So were bottled water, cookies, energy bars, almonds, cashews, pretzels, sunflower seeds, and everything else that falls under the category of "snack," making gum's decline in popularity and sales all the more puzzling.

Some of this disparity is explicable through context. Salty, greasy snacks like tortilla chips and cheese puffs are positioned in the middle aisles of supermarkets and convenience stores. Coffee has its own standalone supermarket real estate, along with an old-fashioned grinder. Dried and canned soups generally form a hard-edged mural across one side of an aisle. Muffins, bagels, doughnuts, and bread are sold in the in-house bakeries many supermarkets have installed in the hopes of stirring people's appetites, which in turn induces them to buy things they had no intention of buying when they left home.

Gum, however, is displayed and sold in and around cash registers in an overcrowded peninsula of store real estate that marketers refer to "The Hot Zone." Along with magazines, lip balms, batteries, chocolate, and other pocket-sized items clustered around the point of sale, gum practically defines the expression "impulse purchase."

Unlike many other snacks, chewing gum tends to be a last-second gesture of improvisation. It seldom appears on shopping lists. It almost never directly drives us into stores. Regardless, it's always sold steadily and well. The problem was that for whatever reason, consumers across the world were buying much less of it, even across Brazil, one of the most dependably gum-crazy markets on earth.

Snacking is a multibillion dollar industry, which makes sense when you realize that nobody in the world doesn't snack. The first cup of coffee or tea we drink in the morning counts as a snack, and so does the glass of cranberry juice we drink in the early afternoon, the muffin or croissant we pick up at a bakery, and the bag of cashews we pick at during our commute home. A banana is a snack, and so is a bunch of grapes, and a slice of pepperoni pizza, and a tub of Greek yogurt, and a mozzarella cheese stick, and a family-size bag of potato chips.

We snack in between meals and we snack instead of meals. We snack in our cars, on buses and commuter trains, at our desks, as we surf the internet and watch television. We snack as we read books and magazines and lounge around in bed in the morning and late at night. And as we get busier—or rather, as we feel busier—more time-starved, impatient, and impulsive, the global snack food market grows. In 2014 it became a $374 billion industry.[30]

Snacking may involve a boundless variety of foods and beverages, but at its core it addresses several specific needs. My company, Mondelēz International, carried out extensive consumer research, ascertaining that the "snacking occasion," or the stimulus to snack, can be assigned to one of three standalone but occasionally intersecting Need States: *Boost*, *Fuel*, and *Treat*.[31]

Boost is self-explanatory. It's about shocking the brain to attention and alertness, usually with the assist of sugar or caffeine. Coffee, tea, energy drinks, and sodas fit naturally under the Boost category. The Fuel category comprises fruits, vegetables, yogurt, cheese, soups, bread, and cereals. These things end up feeding, recharging, and reenergizing our brains and bodies. Then there's Treat (e.g., cookies, chocolate, candy, crackers, potato chips, and so forth), whose underlying mission is to reward us or elevate our moods. Snack manufacturers subdivide these three categories into even more granular Need States, including "Morning Sustainers," "Rest-of-Day Fillers," "Mid-Morning Bridges," "Mouth Sensations," "Indulgent Rewards," and "PM Nutritionals."

Within the context of these Need States, where does gum fit in? While not really a big player in the Fuel or Boost category as the average stick of gum is no more than five calories, it can be considered a Treat. Your typical stick of chewing gum has approximately 1.98 grams of sugar in it,[32] a modicum of the daily percentage one is supposed to consume. Though not even half a teaspoon, this slight increase in sugar qualifies it as a treat. When one is craving something sweet, gum is a low calorie alternative to, let's say, a cookie. The wide spectrum of flavors ranging from fresh to fruity allows gum chewers to snack mindfully, enhancing gum's ability to be a healthier treat alternative. Despite all the positive attributes surrounding gum, in the past few years there has been a dip in gum sales.[33] For some reason, people have been cutting back on how much gum they are purchasing and consuming.

As a significant player in the world of gum tasked with helping reverse the slide in gum sales, there were a few concrete steps my company—which manufactures Trident, Stride, and other gum brands—could take. We could continue our marketing efforts to sell gum in developing markets like China and Russia, where more and more consumers are entering the middle class and eating and drinking on the go. At home, we could double up on our attempts to train kiosk employees inside airport convenience stores like Hudson News to ask consumers, as they're being rung up, "Would you like gum or water with that?"

But none of this really addressed the larger question of why consumers worldwide were cutting back on gum. However, as we looked further, we found research that observed and interviewed consumers of all ages on their current shopping habits. When we read the results, they made three decades of studying how you and I as consumers make, or rather, don't make, decisions about what we buy irrelevant. They also made it clear that companies and retailers no longer exert the power they once did over us as shoppers, and would have to come up with altogether new ways to sell to us in the future.[34]

The problem, of course, was our mobile phones. As recently as five years ago, you and I put up with waiting in line—or literally being put in our place by retailers—as one of those tedious, unavoidable acts of being human. Standing in a drug-store or supermarket a few feet away from a teenaged cashier, our eyes would find their way over to the gums, candy bars, and breath mints arrayed in boxes in and around the cash register. We would mentally preselect a gum brand, and when it came time to pay, grab it and pay. But if our studies were true, and there was no reason to doubt them, that era was over, and it had been collapsed by a single four-inch device. In the early twenty-first century, boredom and impatience meant that it was time to pull out our phones—that is, if we'd ever put them away—and go onto Facebook or Tumblr or Instagram, read the news or tweet.

Other impulse categories were suffering as well. Maga-zines rely as much on last-minute improvisation as gum does. Fifteen percent of all magazine sales take place at checkout, and single-copy sales of magazines had fallen even more pre-cipitously from a year earlier than gum.[35] Periodicals, as well as almost everything else stores put in our way, were the latest victims of what some in the industry were calling "mobile blinders." Thanks to a single device, the power once held by companies and retailers had been delivered back into the hands the people who buy things and who keep those orga-nizations in business. What did this mean, and was there any way retailers and companies could create a new, collaborative relationship with us?

Do you look at your smart phone while waiting in line at stores? What do you do on your phone while you're waiting? #4A

RETAIL HASN'T CHANGED IN YEARS, and most stores are similar in both appearance and atmosphere. If asked, most retailers would agree that their sole mission is to get consumers inside and "convert" them into buyers (stores talk about their "conversion rates"). Nothing exists or takes place in a store by accident. Too much revenue is at stake, and in supermarkets, the profit margins are too thin. Store-planning is, if not an exact science, then a highly considered discipline.

Consumer seduction begins with design. Most stores are laid out in one of four ways, to maximize the pedestrian traffic flow, the best-known being the Grid layout, the Free Flow layout, and the Loop. The Grid, where you and I walk up and down a sequence of aisles, with products on both sides of us, is the most common design in small markets. Target and other big-box department stores use the Loop layout, with a well-defined main aisle circling through the store like a high school track; while airport convenience stores and Disney stores, among others, use the Free Flow design, where there are no discernible aisles or even straight lines.

By now, many of us know about some of the unseen ways stores manipulate us, but they are worth remembering. Consider a supermarket. Right inside the entryway is an area known as the "decompression zone." Like a mudroom, or a dressing room off the main stage, it is generally plain and poorly lit. It's there to slow us down, reorient us, help our eyes adjust from the outdoor light to the bright, jam-packed new world we are about to enter. Just inside the second set of doors, an actual human being may even welcome us to the store. The presence of a greeter is said to reduce shoplifting, as you and I are likely to steal less from people we "know,"

What other things do stores or companies do to manipulate what we buy? #4B but a greeter's secondary purpose is, once again, to slow us down and convince us to linger and wander.

The first thing we see is the fruit and vegetable section. It gives off an aura of good health and freshness that makes everything else in the store seem healthier than it is, as do the smells wafting over from the in-store bakery. Staples like milk, eggs, butter, and orange juice are strategically positioned in the rear of the store, the goal being to tempt us with other products as we make our way there. Most drugstores use this same strategy by placing the pharmacy in back. The more "dwell time," which refers to the number of minutes we physically spend in a store, the higher the chances are we'll buy something.[36]

Inside the grid of aisles, top-selling items are positioned at eye level, with cheaper, less popular ones on the lower shelves. Right-side aisles are prime real estate, considering that most of us are right-handed and we list naturally in that direction. End-caps, which showcase razor blades or perfumes or granola or soft drinks on both ends of aisles, have the greatest visibility in any store. The sampling that often occurs there—in which, say, a kindly gray-haired woman asks if we would like to try a new jam or cheese—is also a billion-dollar industry, not only because it persuades us to try something we might not usually reach for, but also because when we receive something for free, we feel the urge to reciprocate by purchasing the product. Then there is the science of adjacencies: what foods should go alongside what other foods. Should peanut butter be positioned in the bread section, or should it be sold alongside the jams and jellies? Should sandwich bread be sold at and around the deli counter, or along with the rest of the bread?

Still, no section of any store is more carefully controlled or manicured than the Hot Zone. Impulse buying begins with exposure, with stores placing products as close as possible to our eyes, and as close as possible to the moment that we ring up our purchases. Any number of studies have gone into analyzing the optimal placement of products, to figure out the difference in impact when a lip balm is sold in a box on the counter versus on the shelf just under the counter. Store planners also devote a lot of time and thought to "line management," to the point of calculating how many loops of crowd control rope should surround us while we stand there bored and captive in line.

According to recent research, before smart phones came to market, 100 percent of all consumers were exposed to the Hot Zone. Slightly less than that number scanned the items there, or made eye contact with a pack of gum or a bar of chocolate, and an even smaller majority bought something. With the advent of smart phones, companies and retailers are up against some startling new statistics and behaviors. According to the research that regularly crosses my desk, 43 percent of us use a mobile device in-store for shopping purposes; 21 percent of us hunt down coupons on our mobile devices inside stores; and 52 percent of us use our devices in-store for advice on buying decisions.[37]

This means, too, that the relationship between retailers and consumers, which has long favored stores, is now in flux. Retailers have the home-court advantage, but we, the visiting team, are now calling the shots. We can comparison shop. We can research products online, check out what friends or strangers have to say about them, and read about a product's nutritional value or lack of it. We can scan articles or watch videos about a company's politics, diversity, history, leadership, and labor policies. We can do all of this in the middle of an aisle, too.

This shift in power was sudden. It had begun a few years earlier with the mobile-phone-based phenomenon known as "showrooming," where retailers found out the hard way

that we could now take photos or short videos of the products that interested us in stores, then go home and buy them
more cheaply online. Still, based on a 2014 study of more
than 30,000 global consumers, showrooming has fallen
from 50 percent of online purchases in 2012 to 30 percent in
2013.[38] For that you can credit retailers who, acknowledging
what was happening, did everything they could to merge
the offline world with the online one. Some, including Best
Buy, accomplished this by guaranteeing to match any prices
found online as well as offering free in-store pickup, thereby
saving us shipping costs.

Showrooming has been accompanied by another internet-
driven change in purchasing practices. One intriguing trend
of the past few years finds that shoppers research products
online and go into stores having already made up their minds,
a process known as "reverse showrooming," or "webrooming."
Reverse showrooming now happens more often than showrooming itself, and a 2014 Harris poll found that across the
US, 69 percent of respondents reverse showroomed, mostly
for electronics, shoes, cosmetics, and sports gear, in contrast to
46 percent who prefer to showroom the old-fashioned way.[39]

Retailers have shown they are willing to acknowledge
the problem of mobile phones in their midst, and counter-
attack. So what could they do about the widespread myopia
that was taking a huge bite out of not just Hot Zone sales, but
sales in general?

Joe Tripodi, the chief marketing officer of Coca-Cola,
reminds me that despite the science that goes into store design
and planning, the impulse category isn't terribly complicated.
Companies and advertisers first create awareness about a
brand, then consumers develop a history with it—meaning

Have you ever bought something online after seeing it in a store,
before leaving the store itself? #4c

that Trident gum or Ritz crackers have an emotional and functional meaning to us, and we identify with and trust these brands. The rest comes down to a stretch of boredom or free time, the products in question being placed before us, and a spontaneous purchase. Joe regards smart phone use from an angle relevant to any kind and size of company or retailer, one that has to do with the hours or days before we even enter a store.

"As many as 70 percent of shoppers do some kind of digital preparation or list-making before they leave the house," Tripodi says. This preshopping behavior ranges from researching prices, to finding digital coupons, to watching how-to videos, to going on social media networks to decide where to shop in the first place. "Our research shows that this is actually leading to smaller basket sizes. Which is why," Tripodi adds, "right now, Coke is looking hard at 'list-building.' The question becomes, when consumers are first making out their shopping lists at home, how will companies get in there and enter that space?"

> "As many as 70 percent of shoppers do some kind of digital preparation before they leave the house. The question becomes: How will companies get in there and enter that space?"
>
> *Coca-Cola chief marketing officer Joe Tripodi*

It's a good question. More than one-fifth of us go online to find information about food and beverages, one-third go online to hunt down the best deals on pet products, and 40 percent do prior research on baby products.[40] Which means that conventional in-store marketing—oversized cardboard displays, or splashy window promotions—may no longer complement today's mobile-phone-using consumers. More crucial for food companies are recipe websites and apps, from Epicurious to Pinterest. If you've shopped a supermarket recently, you've no doubt noticed that a lot of people are wandering the aisles gazing down at one or another site that lists off the ingredients for the meal they're planning on making that night. Maybe you've done it yourself.

Companies and retailers have had to begin using strategies to reach us where we are, namely on our phones. If Epicurious or Pinterest were accompanying us through the supermarket aisles, then companies themselves had to go onto Epicurious or Pinterest, by sponsoring pages or even via direct advertising.

In fact, by embracing the mobile phone revolution, magazines, another staple of the impulse category, have found innovative ways to fight back against declines in print sales. Lou Cona, the president and chief revenue officer of the Condé Nast Media Group, reminds me that although the impulse category remains a big part of their industry, magazines have migrated from an in-store experience toward a multiplatform model involving home delivery, tablet access, phone access, or a combination that allows continual engagement with readers. It's worth noting that Condé Nast was one of the original parties who urged Apple to create a digital newsstand. Thanks to this instantaneous digital delivery, today magazine purchases are more impulsive, and their subscriptions more profitable, than ever before. As such, Condé Nast is currently working with Delta Airlines to allow flight passengers to download magazines from a server while they're in flight.

Another way companies can meet us on our phones is via gamification, which has shown up across all industries in the past few years, and for good reason, too. We all have a deep human desire to compete, and win, and have something to show for it, whether we earn points, badges, levels, or other marks and notches of accomplishment and status. Research from leading technology research company Gartner suggests that over 70 percent of Fortune Global 2000 companies use gamification to sell or enhance their products.[41]

Game strategies have been adopted by everyone from eBay to flash-shopping sites like Gilt, Ideeli, and Rue La La to hotel chains ("Are you a Marriott Gold Rewards member?) to the airline industry. ("Sapphire Gold Premium Platinum first-class passengers may now board the aircraft.") Even the Buy-Ten-Get-One-Free card you get stamped every time you pay a visit to your local coffee shop is a form of gamification.

Alone among big-box retailers on Black Friday last year, Walmart showed an increase in impulse sales by using geo-location services. As soon as consumers with Walmart's app on their phone were within a mile of a Walmart, the store sent them a message or a coupon offering ads, special offers, or daily deals. Walmart credits its Location Services program with helping preserve the company's bottom line on the busiest shopping day of the year. Geo-location's downside, of course, is the creepiness factor some of us feel knowing a company as powerful as Walmart can now monitor our whereabouts.

"There is definitely value in geo-location fencing services like Foursquare," says Tripodi, adding that these services, which alert companies and stores to consumers' precise whereabouts, can potentially target Coke drinkers who have liked the brand on Facebook by sending them coupons or special offers for old and new products at specific times of the day.

Facebook, Twitter, and other social media sites play decisive roles in this new ecosystem. "A couple of years ago, we did an alliance with American Express where users could sync their Amex cards to Twitter," says the company's chief operating officer Adam Bain, "at which point, any merchant accepting American Express could ask credit card holders to reply to them using a certain hashtag in return for $25 off their next purchase." Syncing a credit card to social media

Would you link your credit card to a social media account? #4D makes impulse purchasing easy. Says Bain, "I'm not going to see you and say, 'Hey, thanks for hanging out, here's $1.85.' But soon I could tweet you a coffee. It's easy and frictionless." There is no scanning of your phone. No barcode-swiping. The lightweight impulse transaction doesn't even feel like you're spending money. Right now, he says, Twitter is experimenting with how Twitter users with Amazon accounts might someday have a friction-free buying experience. "What if [you tweet that] you buy something on Amazon, and I reply to that tweet with '#AmazonCart,' and Amazon proceeds to place that purchase in my Amazon shopping cart. The next time I'm on Amazon, it's in my cart, waiting for me."

Another way Bain believes that Twitter can influence impulse purchases: by revealing plans or preferences that can help companies target us on our mobile phones at the point of sale. "If somebody tweets that they are going to the gym, a sports drink could tweet back that it hopes the workout is a success and that the person enjoys the product. Or if a New York Giants fan announces that he's heading to an upcoming game at AT&T Stadium, AT&T can target that user in a way that capitalizes on its game and field sponsorship. It could do this via certain keywords. And the moment a user tweets out one of those keywords, it's sent to that user. Again, if our users go onto Twitter to find out what's hot, what's new, what's happening in the world, or what's going on in *their* world, they may not be in a mode where they have made up their minds already—which makes the impulse part of that equation interesting, and worth watching."

Along with other advertisers, companies are using Twitter "product cards," a new advertising offering available both on the web and on mobile phones. Whenever users share a product with their followers, the card displays that product along with a short description. Let's say that you're tweeting about, say, a discount on Trident gum on sale at participating Target stores. Via a Twitter product card, a photograph of

Trident shows up along with its discounted price, a few lines about the gum, and a link to the Target website.

Another way to reach us on our mobile phones is via Facebook. There's a spike in active users in New York during the region's prime commuting hours of 8 AM to 11 AM. If companies spend a chunk of their advertising budgets marketing gum to us on Facebook via our phones during those hours, they're more likely to catch us when we're on the train, or in line for our morning coffee, and open to the impulse purchase.

Then there are GPS apps. Waze is a popular, free, downloadable, crowd-sourced geo-location app for commuters. Waze describes itself as "a community of 40 million people who hate traffic and are working together to outsmart it." Last year, my company partnered with Waze and Target to incorporate "pins" onto the Waze screen—tiny logos denoting the presence of nearby Target stores. Imagine you and I are in our cars on the highway, sipping lukewarm coffee, our phone mounted on the dashboard and our Waze app open to track our journey as we swap traffic tips with other Waze-users. A Target logo suddenly pops up, alerting us to the presence of a nearby store. When a Waze user presses the pin, a "Buy Trident Today" message appears, along with directions to the nearest Target. Waze then navigates us to the Target, where we pick up a pack of Trident Strawberry Twist.[42]

What if you and I don't have Waze on our phones, or it's not activated? Some companies have struck partnerships with Google, so that whenever you or I access Google on our mobile phones—and most of us do—companies can advertise to us alongside our search results. In essence, there's no getting away from companies until they convince us to start buying gum again.

Among the phenomena created by the Information Age is that events and products have a radically foreshortened shelf life. If I may put on my marketer's hat for a moment: The new abbreviated lifespan for a CD, a movie, a television show, or the popularity of a musical artist has transformed our thinking around how consumers receive and process information. In an era where a lot of things become obsolete after only a few minutes or days, my mission as a marketer is to echo the state of our brains by creating a series of short-term interruptions. Selling things today is less about whether or not something will last, and more about how and if it is current or relevant.

The future of reaching and influencing and engaging consumers, then, is via "micro-content"—a continuous scroll of brand reminders both in-store and out, across television, mobile devices, social media networks, and downloadable apps. Instead of creating a single narrative around a brand, companies today fire out smaller bits of content in the hope that the sum of those parts will add up to something consumers remember. For better or worse, this seemingly fidgety, scattershot approach complements the fishnet mesh of our twenty-first-century brains.

"Basically there's a need for more and more content that's more available more quickly," Tripodi confirms. "It forces companies to react and respond more quickly, which also means we are that much less focused on perfection. If someone tweets something about your brand on a Friday, you can't wait until Monday to respond via social media. It's simply not the world in which we're operating anymore."

In 2014, for example, Honey Maid, the makers of graham crackers, ran a thirty-second television ad showing a diverse cross section of American

> "If someone tweets something about your brand on a Friday, you can't wait until Monday to respond via social media. It's simply not the world in which we're operating anymore."
>
> *Coca-Cola chief marketing officer Joe Tripodi*

families, including a single father, an interracial family, a military family and, notably, a family made up of two dads and a child. The tagline was, "No matter how things change, what makes us wholesome never will. Honey Maid. Everyday wholesome snacks for every wholesome family. This is wholesome."

End of story? No. As the *New Yorker* wrote, "Honey Maid knew its ad would provoke controversy, and it did."[43]

It's safe to say most people don't spend a lot of time thinking about Honey Maid, but what the company did next in response to its first ad was brilliant. Honey Maid released a follow-up spot on social media. "Some people don't agree with our message," the lettering read, showing a blizzard of tweets containing emails and words like "disgusting" and "horrible." Viewers then found out that Honey Maid had asked two artists to transform the negative commentary it had received "into something else." The two artists rolled up the negative comments into weirdly beautiful white funnels, arranging them into four letters that spelled out the word "LOVE." Before the spot ended, viewers read, "But the best part was all the positive messages we received. Over ten times as many." In its first twenty-four hours, the follow-up Honey Maid commercial had 1.5. million views.[44] Nearly as important as the message the brand was conveying was that it was responding to consumers, lovers and haters alike, in (almost) real time.

One of the brands I work with, Stride, whose target audience is young males, has long advertised its appeal via action sports. That said, according to social analytics company Klout, the two most popular topics on Twitter today are music and musicians.[45] Which is why we might soon consider connecting a brand like Trident to music. What if, via Twitter, you and I could sync our mobile phones to an artist featured on Stride's packaging that would let us download a new unreleased cut by that artist or unlock an opportunity to receive two VIP tickets to an upcoming concert or music festival? At this writing, companies are hard at work on all these prototypes.

Still, this begs a bigger issue: If mobile has brought a new mind-set to shopping, how can physical stores live and breathe the new mobile mind-set? Free Wi-Fi and physical pickup of products ordered online is a good start. Walmart has launched a new strategy that it calls "endless aisle," whereby if you can't find what you want in one of its stores, Walmart asks its clerks to refer you to the Walmart website. Companies are increasingly working to better connect their customers' on- and offline experiences. But all of these strategies address the symptoms, not the epidemic itself.

Retail hasn't been reinvented for years. But if it's to recapture our attention, it will have to be. Its future involves two issues that online retailers, and one offline retailer, Apple stores, have already mastered: reducing the number of things for sale, and encouraging us to use our phones as personal shoppers. In short, retail going forward has to involve exporting what is best about the mobile experience into the physical offline world.

Aside from the overall atmosphere of electrified Zen, what is the appeal of Apple stores? They are simple. They are curated. Basically one thing is for sale—in assorted colors, sizes, and data storage options—with clean wooden spaces in between the displays and tangled cords concealed from view. There is no Hot Zone, no line, no waiting, and no check-out counter to speak of. Give a blue-smocked employee your credit or debit card, and he or she will swipe it on the spot. You sign your name with your fingertip, arrange to get your receipt emailed to you, and are free to go. Or you can just use Apple Pay and walk directly out of the store.

More to the point, Apple delivers an entire ecosystem around learning. Apple stores are devoted to showing you how to get the optimal use out of the company's hardware and software, knowing that educated consumers will come back for more, and also buy more. Apple offers classes and workshops in using iPhoto and Garageband. It teaches us how to edit movies and what the cloud is. We can even sign up for one-on-one tutorials. There is a casual, freewheeling atmosphere. The stores feel dressed-down and collaborative. They seem to acknowledge we are all in this world of new tech together, and the more we know about it, the better off we'll all be.

By now we all know that when faced with an infinite amount of selections, say, sixty television sets or forty different brands of cookies or five pages of restaurant entrées, our gut instinct is resentment and confusion—a phenomenon that psychologist Barry Schwartz wrote about in his book *The Paradox of Choice*. We shut down.

For stores that aren't Apple stores, the biggest problem is that there are too many things on display, too many colors, sizes, aisles, sections. By attempting to give us a single solution to all our needs—by becoming grocers, pharmacies, clothing stores, kitchen suppliers, music stores, hardware emporiums, electronics suppliers, and sports-equipment purveyors—big-box stores turned into a cluttered garage sale that in the end actively discourages us from wanting to buy anything at all.

But by aligning themselves with our phones and online habits, physical stores can transform the retail experience and take back some of the power now held by phone-gripping consumers. Amazon, for example, is a website that, like it or not, remembers our name and knows our tastes and interests. It may have a stupendous number of things to choose from, but it curates the products it puts before us based on our past

Are you comfortable with more personalized marketing, even if it means companies know more about you? #4E buying preferences. In the future, is anything but a stubborn refusal to acknowledge what's happening in the mobile world preventing physical stores doing the same?

If technology offers us anything, it is the most granular data ever, data leaps and bounds over any traditional research. Today websites can measure, track, and get real-time feedback on just about anything and everything. If Facebook, Google, or Amazon ran brick-and-mortar stores, stores would look very different from how they look today.

The transformation of stores will happen when the physical world of retail and the customized online experience unite, not in an either/or way, but fluidly and unself-consciously. It will happen when companies and retailers acknowledge that the offline world isn't just a temporary suspension of our online behaviors and desires, but a companion to the online world. The average Walmart stocks 120,000 items.[46] Walmart doesn't have the time or the resources to sift through a shopper's individual likes and dislikes. If shoppers respond best to a curated selection of goods, and stores cannot reduce their total number of offerings (as products are paying for their space on the shelves), it makes sense to limit instead the number of offerings *on display*—and the best way to do this is via our mobile phones.

Imagine for a moment that Google owned and ran your local supermarket. After you entered the store, the first thing you would do is dock your phones onto a waiting basket. Everything taking place in the store that day would pop up. Your phone would alert you that a barista is in aisle 17, handing out free samples of a new Guatemalan coffee, and showing off the differences between a Chemex drip and the Melior plunge. A sushi chef is in aisle 7, making California rolls, and a vintner is in the wine section, offering samples of a new Australian Shiraz. Were you aware that consumers who bought that Shiraz also bought a particular brand of crackers, and a particular cheese to accompany it? Would you like to see a video? What about a recipe?

Aware of all the recipes and photos you have studied on Pinterest, or that you've recently visited a party board, or seem to like one particular Pinterest-inspired mood, your phone will make additional recommendations tailored and shaded to your likes and dislikes. Scanning your calendar and extracting a family reunion, your phone can send you two or three appetizer recipes, or ideas for a dish you're supposed to bring to a potluck dinner at your child's middle school orientation that very night.

Our smart phones ask from us one thing: They want to understand what *we* like, whether it's a Facebook page, an Instagram photo, or a Pinterest board. They pick up signals about us and what we do and what we're interested in, all day every day, to the degree where someday they will begin to anticipate our needs and habits better than we do ourselves.

Do online shopping sites have a Hot Zone? No, because most websites themselves *are* Hot Zones. Extending this model into a brick-and-mortar supermarket, is there any hard-and-fast rule that says that impulse buying has to take place at the checkout counter? Why does candy have to live in the candy aisle? Why not put chocolates next to a display of condoms? Why not store Ping-Pong balls in the beer section, the better to propose the idea of beer pong?

Money has been spent for decades on science, planning, and focus groups, to ensure that no accidents happen in stores. You and I were the beneficiaries or, some might argue, the prey. Today, thanks to mobile phones, that relationship between stores and customers has been derailed. Today, you and I have the capacity to *not see*. In response, stores need to provide as compelling an experience as our phones do, by collaborating with us *and* our phones. The only thing holding them back is an old-fashioned mind-set, or a quixotic belief that mobile phones are a short-lived fad no different from hula hoops or Tamagotchi pets. They aren't. And the future of retail is a customized experience that combines the thrill of discovery with the freestyle mixing and combining of our online and offline selves.

5

rockin' in the free world: music in the digital era

B Y MOST DEFINITIONS aside from the word "musician," Bruce Springsteen and today's artists have almost nothing in common. Springsteen rose to stardom in the early 1970s, during a time when consumers bought albums and listened to hit songs on the radio, and musicians needed managers, agents, record labels, and marketing teams in their corner to hope for popularity or commercial success. Today, in an era when the relationship between the music industry and musicians, the one between musicians and fans, and even the one between musicians and their own music has been utterly transformed, a Bruce Springsteen no longer happens. These changing power dynamics, which are still evolving, are creating new models around marketing, selling, buying, playing—and even how we listen to—music in an Information Age.

Let's go back to predigital times. Born in 1949, Bruce Springsteen grew up in and around Freehold, New Jersey.

Called before the Vietnam draft board in 1968, he flunked the physical exam, which freed him up to form his first local band, the Castiles. They began playing at New Jersey venues ranging from sweet sixteen parties to drive-ins to mobile home parks. In addition to his vocals and guitar playing, it was Springsteen's songwriting skills that first attracted the attention of music managers Mike Appel and Jim Cretecos and, later, talent scout John Hammond, who signed Springsteen to Columbia Records in 1972. Marketed by the label as the "new Dylan," his first two albums, *Greetings from Asbury Park* and *The Wild, the Innocent, and the E Street Shuffle*, were both released in 1973. Though critically acclaimed, neither sold well.

Three years later, *Born to Run* dropped. Four songs off the album, "Born to Run," "Jungleland," "Thunder Road," and "Tenth Avenue Freeze-out," received national radio airplay. Springsteen's arrival was sealed later that year when he appeared on the covers of both *Time* and *Newsweek* in the same week. In 1999 he was inducted into the Rock and Roll Hall of Fame. Today he's sold more than 120 million albums globally and won twenty Grammy Awards. At sixty-five, his live shows are still almost four-hour-long spectacles.

Here's a story of another musician who made his way, thirty years later:

Born in 1983, Ben Haggerty came of age in Seattle, Washington. *"I grew up on Capitol Hill with two parents and two cars/ They had a beautiful marriage, we even had a swing set in our yard,"* Haggerty rapped later in a song called "Ego." Like Springsteen, he was a born performer; after seeing the play *Cats* as a boy, he dressed like one every day for a year. A beat-boxer and a fan of underground hip-hop, he was fourteen when he wrote his first song. Haggerty spent his summers working at the Seattle Zoo and also as a security guard at a youth correctional facility. He had problems with alcohol and drugs.

In 2000, while studying at Evergreen State College in Olympia, Washington, Haggerty recorded and distributed his first EP under the name "Professor Macklemore," and went around petitioning Seattle record stores to carry it. Five years later, he released his first full-length record album, *Language of My World*. But substance-abuse issues caught up with him, and it wasn't until he joined up with a local dee-jay and producer named Ryan Lewis that his career started to take off.

In 2010, they became known as Macklemore & Ryan Lewis and created their own label, Macklemore LLC. One self-produced single and mixtape after another followed as the two performed in any venue and music festival that would have them. Luck came when the Miller beer company used the duo's song "Can't Hold Us" in a television commercial in the United Kingdom, and the licensing money helped to underwrite the making of a new album, *The Heist*, and a music video for a new song, "Thrift Shop."

With no record label support, Macklemore & Ryan Lewis did practically everything themselves. They laid down tracks using Pro Tools software. They designed and pressed their own T-shirts. They filmed their own YouTube videos. They made a one-off deal with the iTunes music store to carry their music, and hired a distribution company, ADA, to market "Thrift Shop" to alternative radio stations nationwide on a pro bono basis.

Looking back, Macklemore said he knew that, by going it alone, he would never get widespread radio airplay, or have a big advertising budget, or see his name on banner ads. "Yet in our minds, maintaining our independence and thus creative control was far more important in the end."[47] Macklemore credits his and Ryan Lewis's success to their fans, or to what Macklemore calls "the strength of person-to-person connectivity through music."[48]

The Heist debuted at #1 on the iTunes music store. In its first week it sold over 80,000 copies, and to date has sold more than a million. The single "Thrift Shop" has sold 5 million copies in the US and another 5 million in Australia, and the "Thrift Shop" YouTube video has been seen approximately 500 million times. When the song reached the #1 position on the US Billboard Hot 100 chart in 2012, it was the first time in two decades that a song had done that without major record label backing. In 2014, Macklemore & Ryan Lewis won Grammys for best song and album, beating out the critical and audience favorite Kendrick Lamar.

It's worth stressing here that aside from nonbinding deals with iTunes and ADA, no major industry label was ever involved in Macklemore & Ryan Lewis's career. In fact, in the early days all the labels turned them down. As they caught on with the public, record companies came around again, but by then it was the rappers' turn to say no. Why hire a mediator, a middleman, when in a digital age it seems you can do everything yourself?

Macklemore & Ryan Lewis are a phenomenon in a digital era where most musicians home-record their songs on industry-quality software. They design, create, distribute, and sell their music and merchandise online, and maintain an unremitting social media and video presence. It's an era when the playlist has taken the place of the record album, music is private rather than collective, consumers stream albums and songs onto mobile devices, the earbud and headphone industry has come back to life, and the concept of paying for music is seen by many younger consumers as incomprehensible. But if the internet, and the consumer, helped destroy the music industry as it once existed, the

Do you know the names of popular artists' albums, or do you just know individual songs? #5A mobile phone is primed to restore power to both companies *and* musicians.

IN A SPEECH I OFTEN GIVE no matter where I am in the world, I stand beneath a stage-size PowerPoint screen and argue that before and even after the internet exploded, many organizations were guilty of a sometimes-fatal case of short-sightedness. To illustrate, I tell the audience we'll play a game called "Digital Survivor."

"On our right," I say, as a photo appears of former US defense secretary Leon Panetta, "is the most sophisticated intelligence agency on earth . . . while on our left—" and now a photo of Julian Assange looms into view "—is a Brit, a handful of hackers, and Wikileaks." Other slides flip past, including the bookstore chain Borders on the left . . . and Amazon on the right. Blockbuster . . . and Netflix. Encyclopedia Britannica . . . and Wikipedia. And so on. "Failure to adapt," I continue, as Darwin's profile appears onscreen, "means failure to survive."

Everyone agrees that the internet is responsible for the large-scale destruction of the music industry. Having said that, the "failure to adapt" charge can also be pointed at the big labels. Until 1992, the industry was making money as they never had before, selling flimsy, easy-to-manufacture CDs for $17.99. Compact discs were chilly, unpoetic music delivery systems, but, persuaded that they offered a more technically perfect sound than records and cassettes, most of us willingly went about replacing our music collections at great cost.

When Napster came along in 1999, the free-music genie escaped the bottle forever. The big music labels made an unwise attempt to sue illegal downloaders, but soon backed away. In 2003, Apple rolled out its iTunes Store as a loss leader

Do you think listening to music isolates us or brings us together? #5B to encourage sales of its iPods. With CD revenues plummeting from their 2001 peak, the labels, finally realizing what was happening, began pouring their resources into digital downloads.

As MP3 downloads became the dominant medium for accessing music, and musicians were able to create and distribute music at low cost and huge reach, the internet further flattened the economic fortunes of the labels who ran and controlled access to the industry. The album as a concept fell away. Replacing it was the playlist, a co-creation of sorts between musicians and fans. You and I could now assemble a personal soundtrack to enhance a workout, a long drive, or a summer afternoon. Mirroring the flattening of age and cultural tastes occurring among parents and children, many playlists were cross-generational, too: a playlist including Eminem, Lorde, Talking Heads, Lil Wayne, Louis Armstrong, Rascal Flatts, and Shakira might culminate, beautifully and senselessly, with the Beatles' "Hey Jude."

As listeners, we were no longer willing to allow companies, or musicians, to have power over us, economically or emotionally. We would no longer permit record labels to choose which big acts to market and sell to us. We would discover the music we liked on our own. We would no longer respect the album as a delivery system, but instead would order à la carte.

Today, two decades after the internet and the MP3 came along, there are many more ways to get music online than ever before. The day after French electronic duo Daft Punk won Grammy awards for both Album and Record of the Year in 2014, their Grammy-winning album, *Random Access Memories*, was widely available online. It sold for $11.99 on iTunes. Amazon was selling the physical CD for $11.99, the digital download for $8.99, and vinyl for $28.99. Users could listen to *Random Access Memories* on Pandora, Spotify, Rhapsody, Grooveshark, Rara, Rdio, Songza, Beats, and any other music streaming service. *Random Access Memories*, as well as Daft Punk's three previous albums, could also be found in their entirety on YouTube—YouTube's free music videos have made it by far the most popular listening platform among young listeners, according to Nielsen[49]—from which listeners could copy and download them to their iTunes library using a YouTube-to-MP3 converter. If for some reason none of these options worked, a friend who owned a digital copy of *Random Access Memories* could email it via an online sharing service like Dropbox or Hightail.

Since 1993, the music industry has seen its overall value sliced in half. At the same time, the industry today is healthier than ever. More people are listening to more music, and from a variety of different sources, than at any time in history. The music world today encompasses iTunes, Spotify, Amazon, ringtones, streaming services, YouTube, Bandcamp, CD Baby, ReverbNation, and influential online music blogs like Pitchfork and Stereogum. Everyone's Mixtape offers users compilations with names like "Heartbreak," "Make Out," "Summer Barbecue," and "Sunday Morning." Live-concert revenue is at an all-time high, with the top worldwide tours of 2013—Jay Z and Justin Timberlake, Justin Bieber, Fleetwood Mac, Pink, Beyoncé, and others—taking in $2.43 billion, a 24 percent increase over 2012 ticket sales revenue.[50] Even vinyl sales are making a comeback.

The void created by shuttered record stores, and the sidelined role of record labels, has created an altogether new environment for artists. It has changed how musicians distribute their music online. It has changed how you and I discover new music. It has changed how artists market new music. It

What's your favorite streaming music service? #5C

has changed how musicians even think about their music. Let's look at these changes one by one.

First comes distribution. Among the new online models for getting music out there, and heard, is ReverbNation, a hugely popular online business that, among other things, offers independent musicians website hosting and promotion, fan-relationship management, digital distribution, sentiment tracking, and concert booking. "The job of the A&R guy in the digital age is a lot more difficult than it ever was," says Simon Perry, a successful music producer and the head of ReverbNation's A&R, short for Artists and Repertoire. In the old days, new music came to Perry's attention through friends, lawyers, agents, managers, and scouts. "With so much noise out there, with everyone out there busy marketing themselves, the job of an A&R guy in the digital world is to understand the difference between 'good' and 'great.'"

ReverbNation was launched in 2006 in response to the growing musical trend of DIY, or do-it-yourself, in which musicians like Macklemore take over many of the roles and duties that record labels offer their roster of artists. With over 14 million songs, and new ones uploaded every day from around the world, ReverbNation is a one-stop shop to millions of musicians, labels, and industry professionals, and even allows musicians to donate a cut of their revenues to one of thirteen charities. As Perry puts it, "For musicians, it used to be MySpace. Today, it's ReverbNation."

Perry empathizes with the major labels, whose demise he says is overstated and exaggerated. Big music corporations are no different from any other large publicly traded companies, he reminds me, accountable to shareholders and short-term quarterly earnings reports. "In the early nineties, the labels were trying to save their industry by selling plastic—and back then, selling plastic was how the industry made money." Today, the debate has shifted over to what role record labels will play in the present and future digital economy. "I don't think anyone knows yet what the equation looks like for monetizing music in the future. Even Pandora and Spotify haven't figured it out yet. But there's no question at all that the labels are still going to be a huge player in that space."

Instead of going meekly into obsolescence, record labels have been busy consolidating, while cutting smaller, less artist-friendly deals with musicians. Two decades ago, labels made money largely from album sales. The industry standard today is the "360-degree" contract, which gives labels a percentage of everything from musicians' merchandise to concert ticket sales. Which is one, though certainly not the only, reason why many musicians have migrated online to showcase their music and build and develop their fan bases. Technology didn't just disempower labels; it's also what has made the do-it-yourself phenomenon possible. Garageband, Logic, and Pro Tools software allow anyone with a laptop to make studio-quality recordings. Among the artists who have successfully produced "homemade" albums and songs over the past few years are Bon Iver, The Black Keys, Nine Inch Nails, Guided by Voices, Grizzly Bear, Vampire Weekend, and even Bruce Springsteen.

> "I don't think anyone knows yet what the equation looks like for monetizing music in the future."
>
> *Head of A&R for ReverbNation Simon Perry*

Another big online business and musical hub that is supplanting the traditional role of the big record label is CD Baby. "Artists send us five CDs, or they can upload their music, and we will rip and scan the CDs, and digitize them into dozens of file formats. We'll then distribute them to hundreds of retail outlets all over the world, including streaming services like Rhapsody, Beats, and Spotify," says former CD Baby president Brian Felson. Among the artists CD Baby connected with early on are Regina Spektor, Ingrid Michaelson, and even Macklemore & Ryan Lewis. "We also had a little song by a girl named Rebecca Black called 'Friday,'" Felson says, "and there is no earthly way that I or any other A&R exec could have predicted the massive success of that."

Other experimental "middleman" models have appeared online. In 2007, Radiohead made headlines by encouraging fans to pay whatever they wanted for their new album, *In Rainbows*, on their website. In just a few weeks, *In Rainbows* was downloaded 1.2 million times. One internet research firm, comScore, estimated that 38 percent of these fans paid around $6 per album, netting Radiohead around $2.4 million. When it finally came out in stores, *In Rainbows* reached #1 on both the UK Albums Chart and the US Billboard 200. To date, *In Rainbows* has sold 3 million–plus copies in both its digital and physical versions. The band's decision (or strategy) to distribute "free" music actually ended up stimulating paid sales.

"I feel that we, as musicians, need to fight," Radiohead's Thom Yorke said in a recent interview posted online. The most exciting aspect of releasing *In Rainbows* via the band's website, he says, was the newly simplified connection between Radiohead and its fans. "These fuckers get in the way, like Spotify suddenly trying to become the gatekeepers to that whole process. We don't need you to do that. No artists need you to do that. We can build it ourselves, so fuck off," says Yorke.

The digital music landscape begs the question whether, in an era where record labels no longer serve as gatekeepers, or key-holders, there even needs to be a middleman at all. The answer, with rare exceptions, seems to be yes, although the absolute power, and authority, of a middleman in the contemporary music industry no longer exists. You could argue that a site like Amazon serves as a middleman, but Amazon is also an open-exchange portal that allows you and me to make our own buying decisions. If anything, technology has redefined what it *means* to be a middleman. Thanks to the internet, labels can now hedge their bets by reviewing not just musicians' music, but their social media following, fan base, and overall online presence. It works the other way around, too. Musicians who have made a name for themselves online can potentially gain greater negotiating power by bringing proof of their popularity to the business table.

But what about the new relationship that the internet has created between fans and musicians? With music available anytime for download via YouTube, or courtesy of numerous streaming music platforms, listeners today feel entitled to the music they like when they want it. Music fans are generally inspired to play a song that matches or elevates whatever mood they're in. But the ease and convenience of MP3s, and the ability we now have to create a series of tune-paintings based on every dip and pinnacle of our inner lives, has transformed our relationship to the musicians who create the soundtracks of our lives. Put bluntly, we have forgotten about them.

In the digital era, music has become the customized score to hundreds of millions of interior amateur movies, each one called, simply, "Me." Today, the songs we choose to listen to are at the mercy of our emotional lives, as well as our impatience and changeability. Thanks to earbuds and headphones, we can now assemble a series of melodic spells to match whatever we're feeling, wherever we're feeling it—Erik Satie for a rainy morning walk; Nas before a night out; Kenny Chesney for those pickup-truck moments; and the Sugarhill Gang just because. If we're not sure what mood we're in, a compilation with a name like "Rainy Day," "Just Chillin'," or "Night on

Do you create customized playlists for different moods and activities? #5D the Town" does all the emotional heavy lifting for us. But where is the musician in this equation?

A look at the top twenty best-selling albums in the iTunes classical music store during the writing of this chapter shows the extent to which mood—*Mozart for Brain Power, Classical Music for Meditation and Yoga*—has come to dominate choice. Gregorian chant is marketed not as ninth-century sacred music but as an ancient mood stabilizer. Vivaldi has been recast as a Valentine's Day aural aphrodisiac. Starbucks, one of the few retailers that still sells CDs, even creates its own mood-based compilations. In addition to carrying new music from Sara Bareilles, Justin Timberlake, The Civil Wars, and Beyoncé, Starbucks' curated compilations include *Songs of the Siren* ("An international array of superlative women singers and songwriters steps forward with music that's rich in melody, soul, artistry, and insight") and *Big Waves* ("The heyday of the surf sound passed, but the music endures, still evoking the power, grace, and beauty of the waves").

If you have any doubts that mood has replaced genre, all you have to do is scan any number of new music apps and services. Last year Spotify released a service, Mood Agent, that gives listeners recommendations based on whether they're feeling "tender" or "sensual" or "happy." The Musicovery Player, an app, comes with its own touchpad, allowing listeners to slide their fingertip across and between categories including "calm," "energetic," and "positive." If listeners are feeling somewhere in the middle of calm and energetic, the position of their finger instantly generates a playlist to match their somewhat-calm, somewhat-energetic mood. Stereomood's tagline is "Turns my Mood into Music," and it offers a range of sensibilities including "Let's Party," "Magic," "Sleepy," "New York, New York," and "Melancholy." In early

Do you still pay attention to the genre of the music you listen to? #5E

2014, when Beats launched its streaming music platform, its interface was designed specifically for mobile use. Beats asks: "What if you could always have the perfect music for each moment—effortlessly?" Among the features of Beats music service is "The Sentence," a kind of Mad Libs for the moody. Fill in "Where I Am" (the options include On the Couch, In a Rush, In the Shower), and "I Feel Like" (Going Back in Time, Sleeping In, Breaking Stuff), "With" (My Pets, Robots, No Pants On), and "To" (Reggae & Dancehall, Musica Tropica, Indie), and you'll be rewarded with a bespoke playlist that more or less approximates that moment in your life.

Finally, the downloadable Pulse app acts as your own personal mood-deejay and psychotherapist. Place a finger over the camera lens of your smart phone, and the app will pick up and select music based on your heartbeat. The Pulse team includes a Chief Medical Officer and a pair of data-driven classical musicians. Company cofounder Dr. David Plans says he hopes someday to merge physiological data with social data, what he calls "connecting people through biometrics." He adds, "We can tell that something terrible happened yesterday, according to your level of stress. What was it? We're trying to work out the ethics of looking at your Facebook profile to determine whether you just broke up with someone."[51]

The demise of any physical representation—an album, a CD sleeve—detaches us further from the idea that a musician somewhere out there spent time, money, and effort writing and recording that music. One of the downsides of music on the internet is that it makes not just self-presentation and promotion, but also creation, look easy. The internet muddies the difference between Do-It-Yourself and Do-It-Yourself-and-You'll-Become-a-Star.

Do you think computer-generated playlists can capture your feelings and moods? #5F

The wisdom and tastes of the crowd—what other people like, or don't like, and are buying, and is reflected on best-seller lists—become that much more important when we have nothing in our hands to hold: no album, no cassette, not even a sheath of flat plastic. Listening to music on the internet, and on our mobile phones in general, further severs us from actual musicians in a way that, say, old Sony Walkmans didn't, because when the Sony Walkman came out, who wanted to carry fifty cassettes in his or her coat pocket?

DISCOVERY IS THE FIRST STEP TOWARD MONETIZATION, and new music discovery begins with curation. In the old days, you could huddle with one of the clerks at a record store. Let's say you were in the classical music section, hunting for the best recording of Chopin's *Preludes*. A clerk would tell you about a few options: the Martha Argerich version (fiery, fast), Maurizio Pollini's interpretation (just as good, though chillier), or if it was warmth and feeling you were after, how about Arthur Rubenstein? And you'd leave happy that you had made a match.

Yesterday's record clerk is of course today's algorithm. Just as Amazon recommends books we might like based on our and others' ordering histories, the artists whose music is selected to complement how we're feeling is based on other people's tastes and moods (an ironic contrast to the private, solipsistic approach to listening to music most of us have adopted). Nowhere are algorithms more in play than in music streaming, which the industry hopes will be its savior. Beats music service, which Apple bought in May 2014 for $3.2 billion, emphasizes the actual humans it has on staff to differentiate its music recommendations from its competitors'. By buying Beats, Apple acknowledged both a lack of

How do you discover new music? #5G

in-house innovation and the disappointing performance of its own iTunes radio station. But above all, the company was acknowledging that in a climate of free music, streaming music services, algorithm-based or otherwise, are the future. Napster and other free file-sharing sites showed the world the collegial power of what it meant to share music with millions of friends and strangers. Music streaming services, although initially controversial, allow that experience without sacrificing the livelihood of artists.

Today's most popular streaming music service, Pandora, has 76 million users in the United States, Australia, and New Zealand. Its main rival, Spotify, has 24 million active users, and though private about its finances, the *Hollywood Reporter* speculates that "nine million people pay $9.99 a month for an ad-free experience, high-quality audio, and the ability to download many of the 20-million-plus songs in Spotify's library."[52] Pandora is a young company, but already has a presence in fifty-five countries and to date has paid out over $1 billion to artists—some 70 percent of its earnings.

It's hard to predict the success of streaming services, since they are not profitable as yet, but in the absence of traditional "discovery" systems, like stores, and absent the recommendations of friends, or what we hear playing in airports, stores, and movie theaters, streaming music services are the closest thing we have to a contemporary discovery system. Says ReverbNation's Perry, "They provide what radio stations used to do. Radio stations had programmers who decided what music we were going to hear. Maybe you overheard it at your local record store—but that system of curation was really the one that worked best for any consumer."

My own preferred method of music discovery is Shazam, the smart phone app that can identify music you hear around you, giving you the name of the song, the artist, and the album. According to Shazam, their app has been downloaded onto more than 500 million devices in 200 countries, and adds another 13 million users per month.[53] Intriguingly, in 2013, the industry recognized Shazam as an almost unerring barometer for predicting Grammy winners, based on the "total activity" around these artists. Peter Szabo, head of music, was quoted as saying, "When people use the Shazam app to learn more about a song, it tells you more than just radio airplay information can—it shows you intent. Plus, because Shazam makes it easy for people to buy that track at the moment of the point of discovery, it also makes it a proven driver of sales and chart positions."[54]

FOR CONTEMPORARY MUSICIANS AND ARTISTS, distribution is only a small part of how music is being disrupted by mobile.

In the waning days of 2013, in the middle of the night, Beyoncé released her anticipated fifth album, the all-uppercase *BEYONCÉ*, exclusively for download via the internet. There was no warning, no marketing campaign, no advance downloads, no online teasers, no radio airplay. By releasing the album on the very same public channel used by her fan base—the digital download market—Beyoncé helped seal the burial of an old command-and-control music hierarchy. Twenty-four hours later, she had sold 430,000 copies in the US alone.

Obviously, an artist like Beyonce has the reputation, talent, brand equity, and intense following to succeed at whatever she wants. Other unsigned young artists have a more complex time of it. Zoe Keating is a self-described "non-mainstream" Canadian-born cellist and composer, currently unsigned to any record label. In a 2013 interview in the *U.K. Guardian*, Keating dissected how much she earns from the digital music economy.

During the first six months of the year, Keating earned $808 from 201,412 Spotify streams of tracks from two of her albums (as her distributor, CD Baby took a small percentage), which, practically speaking, earned Keating around 0.4 cents per stream. From Rhapsody, Keating took in another $54.40 from 7,908 plays, which comes to 0.69 cents per stream, and $13.38 from 387 plays of her music on Microsoft's Xbox Music service, at 3.5 cents per stream. Payments from Apple's iTunes Match and Amazon's Cloud Drive came to 0.2 and 0.05 cents per stream, respectively. From SoundExchange, a US company that collates royalties from Pandora, iHeartRadio, and Sirius XM, she earned $1,617, plus an additional $930.26 from You-Tube, making for a grand total of $3,454.28. Most of Keating's music earnings came from music sales on iTunes, Amazon, and from her own Bandcamp website: $47,000 from iTunes, $25,000 from Bandcamp, and $11,200 from Amazon.[55]

Keating isn't complaining. She's just estimating how much a musician who does what she does can expect to earn from today's digital platforms. Another musician who has had experience with the labels, but who has embraced the DIY platform—not to mention the concept of free music—is Amanda Palmer. In a 2003 TED Talk that has so far been seen by around 3 million people, Palmer, a former member of the cult cabaret group Dresden Dolls, reminisced about her early side-gigs, including working as a living statue in Harvard Square in Cambridge, Massachusetts. In the mornings, she spray-painted herself white and stood in the square handing out flowers to passing pedestrians. In her TED Talk, Amanda described her job as near-perfect preparation for teaching her how to connect directly with people. Since then, she has made an art out of asking her fans to help her.

Signed by a major label, the Dresden Dolls' first album sold 25,000 copies. While making it clear how big a push her label gave Dresden Dolls when they were starting out, Palmer says the relationship began deteriorating. In the wake of the Dresden Dolls' "failure" by industry standards, she began actively encouraging free downloading and ultimately severed ties with her label in favor of a crowd-funding project on Kickstarter. Her goal was to raise $100,000, but in the biggest Kickstarter project funded to date, she ended up with $1.2 million. When others inquired "How did you make people pay for music?" Amanda's response was, "I didn't. I asked them."

"There's really no name for what's happening right now in the music industry," says Palmer, who believes that, unique among other kinds of exposure, social media genuinely empowers contemporary musicians. Before Twitter, Amanda engaged with her fans only "when I had my ass parked in a chair with an internet connection." Now, suddenly, she could connect with her fans in real time. "Twitter was the biggest gift on the planet. Coming from a performance art and theater background, I've never been about mystique and wanting to be left alone. I wanted as few walls as possible, and to be able to communicate openly. I didn't want anyone telling me what to do, or how to act—I just wanted to be able to find the coolest people and hang out with them all the time."

> "Twitter was the biggest gift on the planet. I wanted as few walls as possible, and to be able to communicate openly. I just wanted to be able to find the coolest people and hang out with them all the time."
>
> *Dresden Dolls singer*
> *Amanda Palmer*

Twitter allows Palmer to broadcast whatever shows or appearances she has coming up next, and to ask her fans to spread the word to other Amanda Palmer fans. "It wasn't just about angst-y tweeted artistic narcissism, it was about connecting one person to another, and feeling like a helpful orchestrator of humanity rather than just another egotistical musician."

Brian Logan-Dales, the lead singer of the Summer Set, an indie pop-rock band who won the 2013 iHeartRadio Rising Star contest, tells me that far more than television appearances, social media underpinned the success of his band. After winning the iHeartRadio contest, The Summer Set appeared in the Macy's Day Parade, and played at the iHeartRadio Music Festival in Las Vegas alongside Justin Timberlake, Elton John, Sir Paul McCartney, and others. "I can't compare our TV appearances to our presence on Twitter and Facebook," Brian says. "Social media has been such a platform for our careers I don't think we could possibly even consider ourselves without it."

Music has always been a conversation between the people who create it and the people who listen to it, but today it's an almost literal dialogue, involving Twitter, Facebook, homemade playlists, and fan events and contests. At the same time, maintaining an ongoing relationship with hundreds, thousands, or millions of fans suggests that whoever makes the most noise online wins, and since when have artists been all that adept at self-promotion?

"We shouldn't expect artists to be marketing experts, as well as creative geniuses," Simon Perry says. "In some areas, younger musicians actually need someone to help them with distribution, or to provide services such as collecting foreign royalties or advertising revenue from places like YouTube. After all, you could change the oil in your car, but why would you want to do that? Asking musicians to do everything by themselves is like saying that someone who designs F16 fighter aircrafts also needs to be really good at flying them." Perry adds that the democratization of the delivery of content doesn't democratize the talent that's required to create it. "If a piece of music is terrible, it doesn't matter that you have shared it with 10 million people." On the other hand, he says, an artist can be a poor self-promoter, and have accomplished something great, and it won't ever see the light of day.

That the internet is obliging musicians to become self-marketers bothers him. "One problem with contemporary music schools is that they are graduating classes of modern artists who are incredibly good at promoting themselves, thereby enhancing a system that says, 'If we market something aggressively enough, then it's good enough.'" To him, Perry says, "a high social media presence is proof of one thing and one thing only—and that's how hard a band works at selling themselves."

Steve Stoute, the founder and CEO of the brand development and marketing firm Translation, and a former music industry executive who helped launch the careers of Nas, Will Smith, and Mariah Carey, sees "marketing" from another perspective. Gone, he says, are the days when music fans would sit around waiting for their favorite musician's new album. Today, artists are constantly "in artist mode," as well as incentivized to create and record great singles, as opposed to great albums. Social media obliges artists to be present, and resourceful, even when they're in between projects. And in the age of the iPod "shuffle," the concept album is a rare phenomenon. Says Stoute, "I don't think an album like Pink Floyd's *Dark Side of the Moon* could even *exist* anymore."

Another big challenge artists today face is maintaining mystique in a world where privacy no longer exists. "Overfamiliarity can become a big problem with some artists," Perry says. "To my mind Lady Gaga has been a genius at creating something whereby she engages constantly with fans, yet also maintains complete control and mystique." Fans may believe they want an up-close-and-personal relationship with the musicians they love, Perry says, "when what they really want is mystery, the equivalent of a forty-foot-high silver screen in a dark room. A clever artist will deliver them that experience via mobile, recognizing that it's all about escapism and dreams."

FROM A CREATIVE STANDPOINT, the internet has also affected how artists approach and create music. For those who see online videos as little more than a recycling of MTV, they're not. MTV was and is television-only. At its peak in the 1980s, MTV drove record sales, but its videos weren't shareable. And sharing is key to today's music ecosystem. Josh Cocktail, the vocalist for the trio Radical Something, tells me that thanks to technology, many artists are much more strategic in their approach to music videos. What kinds of videos could grow their fan bases? "As opposed to thinking about what they are writing, they are also thinking about the images that go with it," says Cocktail. "They want to make a video that is so shareable that even your mother's brother's sister's dog will want to see it and say 'Oh my God!'"

Technology blurs the lines between a shared video and a shared song. When listeners post, or share, or tweet, a music video, they are transmitting a visual representation of a song—a song that has been reimagined into film. The scale of this form of distribution of has, for the first time, made the music video as iconic as the music itself. What's more, when you and I access that video on our mobile phones, its impact is immediate, intimate, and personal in ways MTV never could be.

One concern that arises is whether social media makes artists too conscious of their audience, and as a result more likely to pander to them. But most artists reach a point in their careers when they realize they are creating art not just for themselves but for listeners. Having direct access to their fans or followers via social media has simply accelerated this arc.

Today the Beatles are considered great artists, but when they were just starting out their songs and lyrics were baldly commercial and even calculated. "You" appeared repeatedly in their song titles in the hopes that each teenage girl in the audience would believe the song was directed at her personally.

Artists today are also much more aware of the importance of branding—and in an online environment where everyone wants to stand out, branding is more crucial than ever. Jesse Kirschbaum, the founder and CEO of the NUE talent agency, told me more and more artists and managers have begun sending him mood boards, signaling what "vibe" they want to create with their band, how they want to sound, look, and feel. And in an era where tribalism is dead and mood trumps genre, it's in an artist's best interests to narrow his or her sound, the better to accommodate the specificity of moods of today's listeners. Whether it's intentional or not, bands like Fleet Foxes, Vampire Weekend, Sigur Rós, and Purity Ring have done just that.

As Translation founder and CEO Steve Stoute reminded me, the digital world also offers artists opportunities for collaboration that could have never existed before. "Being in different cities no longer matters. Not knowing each other personally doesn't matter. Thanks to the democratization of music, people who would have ordinarily liked different forms of the art are now being exposed almost voyeuristically to other forms—rock, rap, EDM, dance—and it's causing collaboration. The only thing that matters for collaborators is mutual respect."

> "Thanks to the democratization of music, people who would have ordinarily liked different forms of the art are now being exposed almost voyeuristically to other forms—and it's causing collaboration."
>
> *Translation founder and CEO*
> *Steve Stoute*

The internet has even affected the ways some musicians write songs. Traditionally, in popular songs, the title is front and center—"Message in a Bottle," "New York State of Mind," "Won't Get Fooled Again." The title of the song establishes the melody and recurs in the chorus and during the fade-out—all part of an effort to make the song stick in listeners' minds. Today, there are other ways for artists to make a song "sticky." In the digital music era, less important than a song's title is a catchy chorus, or scrap of lyric, with the potential to become if not a meme then a cultural "thing."

The ideal, perhaps, is what happened with Carly Rae Jepsen's "Call Me Maybe." The song's lyrics, which included the line, "Hey, I just met you and this is crazy . . ." were subsequently affixed to any number of online couplets, ranging from "I'm a dingo and I just ate your baby" to "But here's some scriptures, get baptized maybe?" More recently, Drake's 2013 song "Started from the Bottom—Now We Here" became a wildly popular meme, as did his "YOLO," short, of course, for "You Only Live Once," from his song, "The Motto." Tech N9ne's 2008 song, "Like Yeah" was a big hit, but more important than actual units sold was that the rapper's "like yeah" exploded virally. High school and college kids added "like yeah" as a suffix to whatever they were doing: nodding their heads "like yeah," ordering a cheeseburger "like yeah," meeting in the park after school "like yeah." Using "like yeah" was an ironic acknowledgement that you knew what was going on in the culture. The same went for Snoop Dogg's "Drop It Like It's Hot" and DJ Snake and Lil Jon's "Turn Down for What." It's hard to say what the latter title means, but it's vague and snappy enough for listeners to appropriate it for any situation—turning down for homework, dinner, a shower.

Maybe the best example of a musician collaborating with technology is Pharrell Williams. The release of the single "Happy" was accompanied by the launch of a website, 24hoursofhappy.com, that included cameos from Steve Carrell, Jimmy Kimmel, Magic Johnson, and Pharrell himself, dancing to "Happy" along the streets and sidewalks of Los Angeles. It has inspired countless copycat versions from all across the world, only increasing the song's popularity and sales.

ACCORDING TO THE RECORDING INDUSTRY ASSOCIATION OF AMERICA, the music industry in 2013 was flat, or rather holding steady, with sales at around $7 billion. This is a huge drop from the industry's pre-Napster, pre-iTunes peak in 1999 of $14.6 billion.[56] But most experts agree the industry has bottomed out. More optimistically, streaming service revenues have risen from 3 percent in 2007 to 39 percent in 2014,[57] one of the fastest growths of any digital music format, with digital downloads making up around 40 percent of US music revenue.[58]

Never before has music been less in the control of the industry that for decades controlled its distribution, image-making, and promotion. Never before have musicians had greater power to bypass traditional channels of control, and never before have their economic fortunes been more splintered, spasmodic, and uncertain. Napster may have put the music industry on an inexorable course of destruction, but as I wrote earlier, mobile phones are primed to rescue and restore the industry. The promise they hold out for both labels *and* artists is staggering.

Why does anyone hack or disrupt industries? Because those industries are broken. In the music industry, the breakage and mop-up has already occurred. In the future we will look back on the phenomenon of consumers not wanting to pay for music as a blip and aberration in music history. A generation of consumers across the globe will have grown up in families with shared Netflix, Amazon, and iTunes music store accounts. A decade from now, no one will remember what Pirate Bay was, or what a "bit torrent" is. And the reason is mobile phones.

Smart phones have created a simple, seamless, one-click purchasing structure that bills a single credit card account. Until the end of the month, listeners don't even realize how much money they've spent on music. Because we use our phones as both purchasing devices and music players, paying for music becomes the simplest, most friction-free way of downloading songs, which is why I believe phones will continue to inspire an increase in paid music.

Consider that, before smart phones, our desktops and laptops were co-conspirators and willing facilitators in illegal downloading. Our computers ensured we could tuck ill-gotten songs inside our iTunes libraries, or our Limewire or Frostwire folders. No one uses a mobile phone to pirate music. It's inconvenient. It takes time and effort. In an eco-system where we demand ease and seamlessness, it's much less painful to stream music instead.

Mobile phones also make music more portable than ever. The portability of music began with the Sony Walkman, stalled out, began again with the release of the iPod, and has now migrated to our phones, allowing us to have our favorite music, and our favorite music videos, with us every moment of the day. And unlike in Napster's day, thanks to mobile phones, discovery of new music no longer requires us to be chained to a keyboard. Shazam could never exist on a laptop or desktop. Why would it need to?

What's more, as music has become embedded in our phones, and as mobile phone use explodes across the rest of

When was the last time you listened to music on your computer?
#5H

the world, the global implications for the music industry are astonishing. Across Africa and in many countries outside it, mobile phones will not only be most residents' first phones but their very first access to the internet—and with it, a world of international music. Tencent, the Chinese media conglomerate, already has a huge music streaming service that has helped legitimize American music in that country. As a billion new consumers around the world bypass landlines, desktops, laptops, and tablets for smart phones, I can guarantee you that the music they listen to won't come from an illegal downloading site, but instead via an inexpensive streaming service, an online retailer like iTunes or Amazon, an app like Shazam, or any of several other models yet to be invented.

New mediums for music are proliferating. In the old days, the industry had a single revenue stream: CDs and cassettes. Our phones have not only created a new way to share music, they have created any number of ways for musicians to make money. There is in-the-moment purchasing: What if we are at a concert and we want the soundboard recording? We can buy it on the spot. We have Shazam, Pandora, Spotify, Beatport, and Apple Music, all of which help music grow in ways that benefit artists. In addition to Bandcamp, ReverbNation, and CD Baby, Gracenote, Next Big Sound, Musicmetric, and even Twitter are among the companies who are today scouring the internet for new acts, local heat, and undiscovered artists. What's more, the music industry has yet to take advantage of the gamification techniques popular in other industries. (e.g., "Buy this now, and you'll be eligible to receive this new album or music tracks.") Going forward, I'm convinced the industry will discover the advantages of push notifications, and other means of real-time engagement with listeners.

Thanks to mobile tech, the future of music will also place greater emphasis on sound and audio engineering. Neil Young is among the musicians who have taken a public stand against

the inadequate audio quality of MP3s and of streaming services in general. Young and others estimate that in their
heyday CDs gave listeners only 15 percent of the data from
a master track, and that MP3s and AACs (Advanced Audio
Coding) give listeners only around 5 percent.[59] "We are in
the twenty-first century and we have the worst sound that
we've ever had," Young has said. "If you're an artist and you
created something and you knew the master was 100 percent
great, but the consumer got 5 percent, would you be feeling
good?"[60] With venture capital backing and the full support of
major record labels, last year Young launched Pono, a music
delivery system that offers resolutions up to thirty times that
of MP3s. Launched on Kickstarter with an initial goal of
raising $800,000, it hit that mark in twenty-four hours, ulti-
mately raising more than $6.2 million, on the way to becom-
ing the third-biggest Kickstarter campaign in history. Late
last year, Deezer, a French streaming music service, joined
forces with the wireless speaker company Sonos to announce
that it would offer its paying customers songs with the same
high-quality FLAC (Free Lossless Audio Codec) sound that
Pono offers.

Any change in the music industry, and there have been
many over the decades, has always generated intense short-
lived panic. When jazz and popular music caught on, people
worried they would unseat classical music and lead to civi-
lization's wreckage. When recorded music became popular,
it was the sheet music industry's turn to tear its hair out.
When radio stations started broadcasting music, the industry feared that consumers would stop buying records if they
could hear music for free, and when the LP came along, the
industry worried that consumers would stay home rather
than attend live concerts. When cassettes hit the market,
there was just as much worry that consumers would home-
tape music and never go out and buy another record album.

But as Pharrell noted in an interview last year, "We never go backward. That's the plight of the human species, but also our privilege. As always, a new equation will emerge, and that will be led by the artists and likely powered by them as well."[61] Not to mention by mobile phones.

6

health and fitness: an iPhone a day keeps the doctor away

W HEN SHELLY PALMER FIRST BEGAN WEARING A FIT-
NESS SENSOR, he weighed 252 pounds. His blood
sugar was in the high-normal range. He had sleep
apnea. As the host of Fox TV's *Shelly Palmer Digital Living*, he
was working anywhere from fourteen to seventeen hours
a day. His physician told Palmer he would likely end up as
Palmer's own father had, fighting adult onset diabetes. He
advised Palmer to lose anywhere from thirty to fifty pounds.

As an advertising, marketing, and technology consul-
tant who had long urged his corporate clients to embrace
the Quantified Self movement—the trend of using technology
to measure and analyze everything we do, with the ultimate
goal of improved health, sounder sleep, and a generally better us—Palmer decided to place his health in the hands of
data. He bought his first wearable, a Jawbone UP, and downloaded MyFitnessPal, a food database, calorie counter, and
diet tracker. Palmer told me that it occurred to him that since

3,500 calories is equivalent to a pound, for every 3,500 calories he didn't eat he would plausibly shed that same amount of weight. He ate smaller portions of healthier foods. He walked 10,000 steps daily, and at night slept at least seven hours. In rain or snow, he motivated his walking regimen by blasting rhythmic march music at a tempo of 120 beats per minute on Spotify.

Today Palmer weighs 201 pounds. His cholesterol is down to 119. His blood sugar is ninety-one. His doctor told him that the last time his blood work was this good he was *in utero*, and that Palmer had just added fifteen years to his life.

To many observers, and Shelly Palmer is one of them, the contemporary epidemic of self-tracking and self-measurement comes across as faddish and solipsistic, the ultimate example of James Bond-esque, gadget-y foolishness run amok. And fitness trackers *are* modish, to the degree that right now they are in their infancy. But regardless of what they ultimately resemble, wearables are here to stay. They are also much more than they appear. They are the first step of a solution to the much bigger problem of taking back our health from the medical establishment, and potentially improving our overall health as a species.

Few doctors or patients will argue that American healthcare isn't compromised, bottlenecked, inefficient, and expensive. Compared to other countries, the high cost of most of our procedures and medications is scandalous. The US spends around 18 percent of its gross domestic product on healthcare, or twice as much as most other developed countries, and most studies show we don't receive measurably better medical treatment. According to a *New York Times* editorial, average Americans experience "higher rates of disease and injury, and die sooner, than people in other high-income countries," regardless of how old we are or our economic status; and compared to sixteen other affluent democracies, the

US had the highest rates of disease in nine categories, from heart disease to chronic lung disease to diabetes.[62]

In an era when, according to the Centers for Disease Control and Prevention, more than two-thirds of all Americans are overweight or obese, one core issue is how we deal with our health in general. Dr. Daniel Kraft, a Stanford- and Harvard-trained physician and entrepreneur, sums up how we monitor our own physical and mental fitness as "reactive and intermittent." Roughly 82 percent of us see our doctor for a yearly checkup.[63] The rest of the year we try to eat right and exercise, with varying degrees of success, while living with the expectation that catastrophe could happen at any moment. If and when it does, we give over our bodies to physicians, nurses, hospitals, emergency room personnel, and insurance companies. Even those of us who take good care of ourselves are bizarrely detached from our own health and well-being. We're not the experts, after all; our doctors are. They know what tests and medications we need. If any problems come up, they will work them out behind the scenes with our insurance company. And our doctors don't encourage us to do otherwise. In his new book *Doctored: The Disillusionment of an American Physician*, Sandeep Jauhar writes, "There has always been a divide between patients and doctors, given the disparity in power inherent in their relationship, but this chasm is widening because of time constraints, malpractice fears, decreased income, and other stresses that have sapped the motivation of doctors to connect with their patients."[64]

As patients we have only ourselves to blame for permitting and encouraging a relationship with physicians where they know more about our own health than we ourselves do. But thanks to technology, and mobile phones especially, we are fast-tracking into an era where you and I will soon

Is your health record digitized and available to you online? #6A know nearly as much about our health as our doctors do. And in spite of their resemblance to kids' toys, the first step is wearables. The second step involves the digitization of our health records, up to and including our genetic vulnerabilities and strengths, to create a brand-new paradigm of patient-led personalized healthcare. With the help of technology, we are disintermediating physicians without disempowering them. Along the way, the relationship we are creating, one where patients and doctors have equal access to the same fitness and health data, has the potential to transform our entire healthcare system.

NO ONE WOULD EVER GUESS that the Quantified Self movement is only a few years old based on the 100,000 or so health and fitness apps available for download today in the iTunes store, many designed to be used in concert with a wrist monitor. Today's best-known wrist-monitor wearables include the Fitbit, the Nike + Fuelband, the Jawbone UP, Withings, Fitbug, Omrom, and the Basis Health monitor, which was acquired by Intel in 2014. Activity trackers are big business, too, generating around $290 million in US retail sales in 2013, with the market expected to double by the end of 2014.[65] A survey by the Robert Wood Johnson Foundation cited industry experts who predicted that mobile health apps will increase by 25 percent annually for the foreseeable future,[66] while another study estimates that the larger Quantified Self movement, which includes smart phones, wristbands, glasses, and various other devices, will reach $5 billion by 2016.[67]

The biggest players in the technology sector have taken note. In 2014, Facebook bought Moves, an activity tracker, while Apple unveiled plans to bundle a new self-tracking

• • •

Do you think technology will one day make general check-ups obsolete? #6B app, Health, as part of its iOS8 operating system. Last year Amazon rolled out a standalone storefront dedicated entirely to wearable tech including smart watches, fitness trackers, and wearable cameras.

Thanks to wearables and apps, we can track our insulin levels, stress levels, cholesterol levels, and caloric intake. We can monitor our blood pressure and body temperature, check our body mass index, and record our heart rhythms and brain waves in real time. We can buy a bracelet that detects its exposure to sunlight, alerting us when it's time to put on sunscreen. Capable of sensing movements at all times, wearables can even determine if we woke up during the night and if so, what time we fell back asleep. In conjunction with apps like Runkeeper, Map My Ride, Push Ups Pro, and the afore-mentioned MyFitnessPal, we can do as Shelly Palmer did, combining our wearables data with our daily food consumption with our exercise regimes, all via our phones.

"You can't improve what you can't measure," says Jesse Stollak, the director of Global Digital Brand and Innovation at Nike Digital Sport. Nike, of course, is the maker of the Nike + Fuelband, which tracks the intensity and progress of users' workouts. The band connects, as all wearables do, to a Nike app, which also gives users daily goals. "Measuring," Stollak adds, "leads to motivation. And motivation leads to more measurement."

Most of us know the extent to which big data has revolutionized businesses and entire industries. But it's our very own individual "small data," the kind that wearables deliver, that may be key to taking control of our personal health. Wearables are a starter kit to our bodies and minds, with apps serving as coaches, enthusiasts, and companions. The wearables industry also intuitively understands the power of peer pressure and gamification. For example, in 2010, Nike rolled out Nike Grid, an urban gaming platform for runners that at one point turned London into a virtual game-board. Runners from the UK could make their way to various London checkpoints, earning points along the way. By connecting athletics in real time with digital and social media channels, Nike Grid created a community that ultimately arranged around 30,000 runs as well as its own celebratory wrap party.

The idea of competing against our past best performance, as well as against digital rivals, has found its way into sports as well. Babolat Play Pure Drive racquets, used by Rafael Nadal, Roger Federer, and other pros, are equipped with grip sensors that chronicle every aspect of your tennis game, from the velocity and typology of your shots to the success of your first versus your second serves. The microsensors in Babolat racquets are now also inside basketballs, with golf clubs, baseball bats, and footballs next in line.

Which inevitably invites the question: Who cares? Just because we can measure things doesn't mean we should, or that the data suctioned to the surface is useful or even interesting. Self-quantification can also slide off into deep-end extremes. In a 2014 *U.K. Guardian* article, a female journalist, Arwa Mahdawi, recalled that as an adolescent she went through a period of obsessive self-measurement. She cut back on eating, and number-crunched the calories she permitted herself. She weighed herself constantly, and exercised obsessively. "It was called anorexia," Mahdawi wrote, adding that she "would diligently feed all these numbers into a sort of anorexia algorithm, regularly adjusting different variables in order to maximize weight-loss efficiencies."[68] Mahdawi's weight dropped to 84 pounds, and her hair fell out in clumps. Nor is she alone in speculating about the potential for "a sort of tech-orexia that rewrites compulsive behavior as healthy."[69]

"There's always a potential for someone to become too obsessed with something," John "Ivo" Stivoric, VP of Research and Development at wearable company Jawbone, says, "but in general, how the collective intelligence and skills of the world are applied and distributed nowadays far outweigh any potential negatives."

Today, wearables, and the Quantified Self movement in general, are marketed to educated, tech-smart users, people willing to pay upward of $200 for a stone-gray wristband with an internal accelerometer. But this means the consumers who could potentially benefit the most from health trackers, including the low-income and elderly demographics, are excluded. Wearables will achieve mass adoption when prices decrease, and when wrist monitors become undetectable, fashionable, or both.

A year from now, wearables are likely to be disguised in earrings or bracelets, or buried in shirts and sneakers. Companies like Under Armour are already working to embed sensors in our clothing and footwear, and during last year's US Open tennis tournament, selected ball boys dashed out onto the courts wearing machine-washable Ralph Lauren–designed black nylon compression smart shirts with biometric tracking capabilities. Conductive threads were woven into the fabric, and a clip-on module was able to relay heart rate and breathing data to any Bluetooth-enabled mobile phone or tablet.

Apple has already made the wrist monitor fashionable— or at least is trying to. In the last couple of years, executives from Yves Saint Laurent, Burberry, and luxury watchmaker Tag Heuer joined Apple, which is why the sheer beauty of the company's new, sensor-laden watch came as no surprise. But the Apple Watch is also a comprehensive health and fitness device that tracks users' heart rate, daily activity, and calories burnt. It runs GPS (via your phone), plays your music, and is Wi-Fi-enabled. If you're so inclined, you can even share your heartbeat with other Apple Watch users.

At first glance, people might believe that the Apple Watch, which is poised to redefine mobile health, represents the demise of wearables, but if anything, it only motivated the growth and sophistication of companies like Jawbone and Fitbit. On the same day as Apple's announcement, Jawbone announced it was planning to open up its iOS and Android apps to support other companies' hardware—including Apple's. *Fast Company* noted that Jawbone's decision will make it easier for wearables companies and hardware to get fitness information in and out of their own systems, "and will presumably allow them to connect with the data that Apple's own device collects"[70]—all this without having to compete directly with the Apple Watch. In my opinion, a bigger obstacle to the widespread adaption of the Apple Watch is what the gadget does almost incidentally: tell time. Unless you're someone willing to pay several thousand dollars for a branded Swiss timepiece, mobile phones have made wristwatches anachronistic, especially among younger people. Why wear a sliver of chain mail around your wrist when you can glance down at your phone?

The wearables industry does face a notable challenge: high attrition rate among wearers. The *MIT Technology Review* reports that one in ten Americans today owns a tracking device made by Nike, Fitbit, or Jawbone, but "more than half of these devices are no longer in use." The study adds, "Of the 100,000-plus mobile health applications available for smart phones, very few have been downloaded even 500 times. . . . More than two-thirds of people who downloaded one have stopped using it."[71] In part these figures can be attributed to wearables' very own brand promise, namely, personalized results delivered *in isolation*. Wearables lack context or meaning. Right now at least, users can't compare and contrast their data to that of others roughly their age, weight, or physical condition. In short, biometric devices ask us to interpret data that we can't understand or put into any perspective.

To continue to grow, the Quantified Self industry will need to generate a host of new middleman businesses that are devoted to reading and making sense of our wearables data. Your resting heart rate is high—what now? Rather than calling a doctor, or driving to the emergency room, you can call, text, or email a company or platform that will analyze your results in real time and recommend a course of action, whether it's making an appointment with a specialist, drinking a glass of water, eliminating dairy products, or seeking immediate help.

Wearables, as I wrote earlier, are bellwethers with a far more profound role to play in the future medical food chain than may be apparent right now. Part of this potential lies in the "data exhaust" they and other health and fitness technology produce.

Data exhaust, or data byproducts, refers to information revealed almost by accident in the course of a technology that's otherwise engaged in carrying out its primary mission. Imagine, for example, that a garage door company that serves millions of homes around the world makes units that come equipped with surveillance cameras to alert homeowners they forgot to close their garage doors or if there's an intruder nearby. Incidentally, the company discovers that its cameras pick up other things, too. How many cars bought last year were red, or yellow, or black? How long does it take for the paint on an average new car to degrade? What might this incidental information be worth to car manufacturers or automobile insurers?

We don't know yet what role data exhaust will play within the Self Quantification industry, only that it will play one, and in fact, already has. For example, on the basis of data coming from users' wearables, Nike can now track real-time activity

Do you own a wearable? Do you use it? #6C

patterns in cities across the country at different times of the day. At 8 AM in New York, Nike wearable users are showing the first flurries of activity, whereas Los Angeles is at a standstill from 8:30 to 10 AM as the city's Nike wearers are imprisoned in cars on area freeways. Says Stollak, "This data tells us incredible stories that could someday correlate with our health, or our happiness, or our productivity."

Imagine you are an adult child of an elderly parent who lives on the other side of the country. The two of you are in regular touch via email and the phone, but you are also connected via a sensor attached to your mom or dad's refrigerator door, or coffee machine, that in turn connects to your smart phone. Experience tells you that your parent gets up every day by 8:30 AM and turns on the coffee machine no later than 9 AM. What if one morning the sensor shows that the coffee machine is untouched? The data from that sensor or, more to the point, the lack of data, could spell out the difference between life and death.

SO FAR MOST OF TODAY'S HEALTH AND FITNESS INNOVATIONS— not just biometric wearables but downloadable apps, medical devices, and more—exist in isolation. One or two of them may "converse" via Bluetooth, but the others are incredible devices in search of connectivity. How can we ensure that our data from various sources can be accumulated, centralized, and made available both to us and to healthcare providers?

Mana Health is one of the best of the new platforms designed to make life easier for patients, physicians, and caregivers. Similar to Blue Button, the protocol used by federal agencies including the Department of Defense, Health and Human Services, and Veterans Affairs that allows government employees and veterans to download their health histories, Mana is a patient portal that allows doctors and patients to see and interact in real time with every piece of their personal health data via a laptop, tablet, or mobile phone. Patients log on to Mana to find a customizable dashboard of tiles devoted to everything from Fasting Glucose Level, Breaths Per Minute, Height, Oral Glucose Tolerance Test, Calcidiol Mass Volume, and others. Mana explains each medical term or measurement and also allows users to add notes or reminders to themselves. If you go to a hospital and your blood pressure medication is adjusted, that change will show up in real time on the Mana website. Not only are patients privy to their own health information through Mana, multiple doctors are as well.

"One of our goals is to turn very complicated things into easy-to-understand graphs and visuals," says company cofounder and executive chairman Raj Amin. Mana also encourages patients to incorporate hyper-specific app data onto their personal portals. Amin predicts a day in the future when insurance providers offer consumers lower premiums in return for access to data that shows that they work out at the gym three times a week or attend yoga classes. "By seeing your activity levels, they're able to reduce their risks on you and qualify [you] for a lower insurance premium."

Proteus Digital Health is pioneering a new way to oversee the elderly's health and well-being. By creating FDA-approved "smart pills"—medication equipped with sensors—Proteus gives clinicians, patients, families, and caretakers real-time information about a patient's medication-taking, rest, and activity, helping all parties to safely maintain daily care while, ideally, reducing healthcare costs.

"By ingesting a tiny sensor and agreeing to wear a Band-Aid-sized patch on an arm, patients allow Proteus to capture their medicine intake, as well as their activity and sleeping

Would you be willing to ingest tiny sensors to track your activity, sleeping patterns, and medicine intake? #6D patterns," says Andrew Thompson, the CEO of Proteus Digital Health. He offers another example closer to home: "Let's say you're the parent of a bipolar teenager who is taking a typical antipsychotic drug. But you can never be certain if he has taken his medicine or not. Proteus allows you to track whether or not he's taking his medication, as well as his sleep patterns, data that is then fused with his body angle, heart rate, respiration, and temperature. Additionally, Proteus takes into account a sociability index—is he talking, texting, emailing?—which can give insights on his mania or depression."

Mana's Raj Amin foresees a time when physicians are granted access to patients' social media feeds to help them better understand patients' motivations. Knowing what motivates a patient is probably one of the most important things that primary care physicians can learn. "It might be losing that extra ten pounds so that they can walk their daughter down the aisle. Anything that helps doctors understand their patients' motivations will have a dramatic effect on the ultimate outcomes, and the cost, of healthcare in this country." There might even come a time when doctors have access to all patient data—not only the number of steps we take daily, or our Twitter feed, but things like whether we oversee the care of an elderly parent and the various factors stressing us out in our jobs. Already, physicians can make use of another new app, Ginger.io, which collects data from patients' cell phones, and the hundreds of micro-behaviors it has accumulated, to monitor the behavior of people with bipolar disorder, depression, and chronic pain issues. Is the person sleeping? Is he interacting with others? Has he made plans for the weekend? When something seems "off," Ginger.io sends an alert to the person and, with permission, to family members.

Would you want your doctor to have access to your Facebook account or data from your mobile phone apps? #6E

One common, long-standing concern with medicine is that it's too measurement-driven, and technological advances that create additional streams of data will likely just reinforce this model. Which is why going forward, Daniel Kraft believes, physicians need to maintain a balance between data and intuition. As I wrote earlier, data may disintermediate doctors, but it does not disempower them. After all, our fitness and health devices lack any ability to diagnose. They cannot pinpoint diabetes, or feel or photograph for throat cancer. They can tell you that your fever is spiking, but they cannot distinguish among pneumonia, malaria, and a passing flu. Physicians will always have the final say. Diagnostic intuition is just as important as data.

"As a doctor, I know the most important element is the doctor-patient relationship," Kraft says. "My hope is that these technological tools can actually support these interactions, so that patients can spend more time during their fifteen-minute visit on more important things than filling out a form or trying to remember their diet over the past few weeks."

What if we also added another piece of data to this mix: whether we carry genes for certain diseases or conditions? In 2013, the thirty-seven-year-old actress Angelina Jolie wrote a *New York Times* op-ed announcing that in the wake of genetic counseling, during which she found she tested positive for a rare genetic mutation known as BRCA1, she decided to undergo a preventative double mastectomy. The *Times* later explained that women with Jolie's specific mutation "have, on average, a 65 percent risk of eventually developing breast

> "My hope is that these technological tools can actually support doctor-patient interactions, so that patients can spend more time during their fifteen-minute visit on more important things than filling out a form or trying to remember their diet."
>
> *Dr. Daniel Kraft*

cancer, as opposed to a risk of about 12 percent for most women," as well as a heightened risk of developing ovarian cancer.[72] Jolie herself wrote that her doctors estimated that she had an 87 percent chance of someday developing breast cancer.[73]

Some medical observers found Jolie's decision extreme, but the attention she drew to her decision brought attention to the ability we all have today to pretest our genes for potential abnormalities, thereby giving us even more power over our future health.

Jim Plante, the CEO of Pathway Genomics, tells me that only 1 percent of the US population has ever undergone genetic testing, the overwhelming reason so far being to determine carrier status for recessive hereditary diseases like cystic fibrosis and sickle-cell anemia. But over the last few years, there's been greater awareness of the clinical benefits of genetic testing for diseases including autism, cardiovascular disease, and ovarian, thyroid, renal, and lung cancers. Pathway Genomics, he says, was founded in 2008, at a time when roughly twenty FDA-approved medicines wore labels alerting both prescribing physicians and patients that genetic testing might also be considered before taking the medication. That number has grown to more than 140 medications today.

A research study published in 2013 by United Healthcare showed that, rather than consigning genetic testing to a bin marked Science Fiction, a majority of patients surveyed believed that their physicians should use genetic testing as part of their prevention or treatment, and that a majority of doctors believe that many of their patients could benefit from genetic testing, too. How does Plante account for this enthusiasm? Not surprisingly, he credits the wearables industry.

• • •

Do you believe genetic testing should be a routine part of medical care? #6F

"Genetic testing is part of the overall trend of people realizing they want more access to their own personal, health-related information," says Plante. "Knowing how many calories you're burning and how well you're sleeping at night opens the door to more information. People are starting to want to be the CEO of their own health, and to do that they need access to lots of different kinds of information."

> "People are starting to want to be the CEO of their own health."
>
> *Pathway Genomics CEO*
> *Jim Plante*

Historically, only medical doctors could order up a genetics test and dispense the results to patients. But recently, the Center for Medicare & Medicaid Services, which regulates the genomic industry, passed a rule mandating laboratories to make the results of any diagnostic test available directly to patients. Which is another way of saying that genetic testing in general and the Pathway app in particular has the power to eliminate weeks if not months of trial-and-error prescription-taking. Another benefit of the Pathway app is that it's location-aware. In the supermarket, for example, it could notify users that, say, a Mediterranean diet is optimal for their particular genetic profile, and offer food recommendations.

"Patients have the right to their information, which I believe is entirely beneficial. It also fits in very well with the mobile app approach, which allows the patient to carry around their clinical health and genetic data. Basically," Plante concludes, "more information for the patient is better."

Plante expects the genetics industry to advance quickly. The Genetic Information Nondiscrimination Act (GINA) was signed into law in 2008. It states that genetic information can't be used in any way to discriminate against people if they are attempting to sign up for health insurance. It also prevents employers or companies from discriminating in any way in the hiring or management or treatment of employees based on their genetic data, protecting employee privacy and thereby putting to rest many fears surrounding genetic testing.

Plante also noted that Apple already has a team of biosensor experts in place, including an expert who has patented countless sensor technologies around patient monitoring. "One is called the Rainbow—a device you put on your fingertip to test blood hemoglobin and oxygen content that works by shining the light through your skin. It replaces tests that used to necessitate a blood draw."

This increase in personal and medical data is coincident with a topic that frequently floats to the surface these days, namely, end-of-life care. "It's what my peers talk about: our parents' horror show," Michael Wolff wrote in a highly publicized 2012 *New York* magazine cover story.[74] In 1990 there were around 3 million Americans over the age of eighty-five. Today that number has risen to 6 million. By 2050 the number of people eighty-five and older will reach 19 million, or nearly 5 percent of the population.[75] "The longer you live the longer it will take to die," Wolff writes. "The better you have lived the worse you may die. The healthier you are—through careful diet, diligent exercise, and attentive medical scrutiny—the harder it is to die. Part of the advance in life expectancy is that we have technologically inhibited the ultimate event. We have fought natural causes to almost a draw," he says, adding that we are living much longer but in conditions you would hesitate to call "healthy."[76]

In Western societies, contemporary medicine enables us to live nearly a decade longer than we did fifteen years ago. As medicine gets better at treating sickness, the number of people living long lives while ill is growing. According to Medicare

Would you rather live a short healthy life or a long one plagued by disease? #6G data, only a third of all patients die at home, surrounded by their family or friends. Fifty percent or more of us spend our last days in a hospital, typically in an ICU, leashed to machines and feeding tubes.[77] We die in pain, or in a blur of pain medicine. We die without remembering our names. One out of every four Medicare dollars is spent on medical care near the end of life, which costs American taxpayers around $125 billion dollars annually. As for the cost of treating the 5 million Americans with Alzheimer's today, it's around $200 billion and by 2050 will rise to $1 trillion.[78] Concludes Wolff, "Make no mistake, the purpose of long-term-care insurance is to help finance some of the greatest misery and suffering human beings have yet devised."[79]

Many of my contemporaries have little interest in surviving into their 90s or 100s, or at least they say so today. We all want to live good, long lives, just not in an eternally downward-facing spiral. We fear dementia. We fear pain. We fear burdening our children. Recently, the *New York Times* reported that with people living longer with illnesses, and with many wanting more participation and control over how (and where) they spend their last days and with what degree of life-sustaining treatment, private insurers have begun reimbursing doctors for "advance care planning" conversations, which more and more patients are requesting. "Far more significantly," the *Times* writes, "Medicare may begin covering end-of-life discussions . . . if it approves a recent request from the American Medical Association, the country's largest association of physicians and medical students." The *Times* adds that, "If Medicare covers end-of-life counseling, that could profoundly affect the American way of dying."[80]

"It's a very, very important conversation to have," says Daniel Kraft. "Medicine and science are often wed to the idea of stronger, faster, better. But just because we can support a patient on artificial kidneys doesn't mean we should. If you ask most people, they would tell you that they don't want life span—they want health span. Most of us would be happy to live to our nineties or older if we remained cognitively alert and able to get around and we weren't reliant on a lot of other people. As technology keeps moving forward, we need to be mindful of some of these elements."

Mickey McManus, the chairman of the board of design consultancy and technology research lab MAYA Design, observes that the healthcare profession has become extremely proficient at treating things at very high cost when it's too late to do anything else. He wonders aloud whether future technologies "can help us run right up to the edge of the cliff, and then fall off."

Talking about death is always a difficult conversation. Stronger even than the new relationship we have with our own bodies is the one we will have in the future with our own mortality. Historically, medicine and religion have always been blurred and intertwined. Centuries ago, God was synonymous with fate, and today, whether or not we believe in a God, many of us attribute a divinity-by-proxy to physicians and hospitals.

Which is why the profusion of health data will ultimately help each of us come up with our own individual definition of what it means to live a healthy life.

WHAT DOES THIS ENHANCED DATA, and this new relationship we have with our health and with the medical profession in general, mean for physicians and for hospitals? From my perspective, pooled data between patients and doctors will only improve communication. Not least, if and when our own "small data" is fed into a larger human pool, we will be able to receive a personalized diagnosis predicated on the medical histories and medical data of 5 billion other people. "What if someday you or I could actually *donate* our health data for a greater cause?" asks Amanda Mork, the cofounder of HealthTech Women and the director of communications for Scanadu, a portable biometric device that measures cuff-less blood pressure, temperature, heart rate, and other factors. "Maybe someday I might want to donate my data about my likelihood to develop breast cancer or my intestine data. There's a social-good element to donating my data for the good of the human race. I think that people are becoming more empathic to the fact that we're all human, and we all have bodies that transcend the world's social structures."

> "What if someday you or I could actually *donate* our health data for a greater cause?"
>
> *Cofounder of HealthTech Women and director of communications for Scanadu Amanda Mork*

Having all our medical data online inevitably leads to the subject of privacy. From my perspective, privacy is an archaic concept. In truth, privacy hasn't existed for years, since long before Google, Facebook, Edward Snowden, Julian Assange, and revelations of NSA spying. If we called a friend on our landline in the 1980s, the phone company tracked it. Back then, just as they do today, credit and debit card companies mark every deposit and withdrawal we make, along with our whereabouts. Of course, today, sophisticated consumer analytics make it possible for department and big-box stores to accumulate even more data on us, including our age, marital status, number of children, the distance we live relative to the store, our salary, our credit cards, and what websites we visit. If they want, they can also buy additional data about our ethnicity, marital and job histories, media habits, education, social media topics, politics, brand preferences, charitable giving, and the number of cars we own.

Is privacy dead? #6H

Once we make peace with the fact that privacy no longer exists, there's a strong argument to be made that humanity—and our overall health—is best served by us having no privacy at all. A controlled probe into enough health records could uncover a cure for cancer or for diabetes, but we would need to consolidate the data of millions of people. In 1986, for example, a specialist in Alzheimer's disease named Dr. David Snowdon carried out a research project involving 678 Roman Catholic Minnesota nuns who agreed to dedicate their brains to science. The sisters were ideal study subjects: a stable, homogenous group whose lifestyles precluded substance abuse or any physical changes connected to pregnancy or childbirth. As part of their admission to the convent, each nun had submitted a brief autobiographical essay. Snowdon and his team later discovered that early language ability—the length and density of their sisters' sentences and the complexity of their grammar—was linked to a decreased risk of Alzheimer's six decades later.[81]

"There's a Fortune 500 company I know of whose CEO wanted the best diabetes cure for his company," says Redg Snodgrass, the CEO of Wearable World. "Ten percent of the population has diabetes. But everyone in the company said no [to sharing their data], because they were afraid of being passed over, or punished for revealing their information." The data that can be used to help us can also be used to harm us when our ability to get good healthcare is predetermined by having good health. Healthcare qualification concerns, as well as fear and paranoia that our data might end up in the wrong hands, are privacy issues we must overcome if we are to make progress as a species.

Someday, we will be able to collect data passively on our mobile phones about our bodies and health. We will then upload this data into a diagnostic engine. Our physicians will be able to predict a condition early on, and choose the appropriate treatment. Someday, maybe, our doctor could text us a prescription for a genetically sequenced medication that we could upload into our home 3D printer. It would print out in seconds. Our pills would contain sensors that could passively track when we took our medicines, and whether or not our bodies were responding positively to it. This tracking could be done at home, too, via our mobile phones.

The future of health will be increasingly data driven, and right now, that data is captured and interpreted by our mobile phones. But who is to say that the interfaces we currently hold in our hands or wear on our wrists will remain the source and record of that data? We use iPhones and wearables today because there is no better way, but in time the technology measuring our health is likely to become invisible. It will be administered like medicine, and it won't be wearable, but rather embeddable and swallowable.

No matter the hardware, however, technology will never stop reminding us that we are a work, a brain and a body, still in progress.

7

politics: the new
two-way mirror

I N 2014, in an effort to explain the Affordable Health Care
Act to a younger, web-based demographic, President
Obama made an appearance on the Funny or Die internet
interview show *Between Two Ferns*. In addition to the subject
he'd shown up to discuss, Obama and host Zach Galifianakis
covered a wide range of subjects, including Kenya, pardoning
turkeys on Thanksgiving, Dennis Rodman, Bradley Cooper,
spider bites, Obama's birth certificate, and NSA surveillance.
Galifianakis called the president a nerd. Obama commented
that Galifianakis's latest *Hangover* sequel had done badly at
the box office. Aside from the expected partisan criticism,
most political observers and viewers considered the president's Funny or Die appearance to be a huge success.

More than just about any other politician, Obama is a
symbol of a government official at home and at ease with the
internet. The *New York Times* once noted that in the same way
Thomas Jefferson used the power of print media, Franklin

Roosevelt mastered radio, John F. Kennedy understood television, and former Vermont Governor Howard Dean pioneered internet fund-raising, Barack Obama has an intuitive understanding of how politicians "could use the web to lower the cost of building a political brand, create a sense of connection and engagement, and dispense with the command and control method of governing to allow people to self-organize to do all the work."[82]

To no one's surprise, the internet has reinvented the relationship voters have with the officials we elect into office. Historically, the relationship between voters and politicians has been at most a two- or four-year engagement analogous to an unsatisfying love affair. A politician was the person who contacted us once or twice every few years, asking if he could stop by and pay his respects. He asked about us, calling us by our names. He made pleasantly unreal plans and guarantees. Once we opened our doors, or our wallets, and gave him what he wanted, he moved on, efficiently, to the next person.

Today, thanks to technology, politics and politicians are in our lives and on our desktops and phones at all times. The relationship we have with our elected officials has evolved from a hasty encounter into an extended romance, with all the hero worship, frustration, pride, and disillusionment that accompanies any longstanding relationship. In an always-on Information Age, politicians today run for office every day of their lives. They (or their staffs) are on Twitter, Facebook, and Instagram, firing off messages up to a dozen times a day. Their every moment is captured, written about, filmed, and photographed. Everything they say or do is both a performance and an audition.

Do you think the increase in our access to politicians has any real impact on policy? #7A

To its users the internet has always held out the promise of access to power and the illusion of proximity to the people or organizations who run the world, make decisions, and keep the wheels of the earth turning. In this spirit, the internet has forged a new intimacy, and apparent twenty-four-hour availability, between voters and politicians. In an ideal world, politicians represent the people they serve. They are mirrors onto which we project an assortment of attributes. In our politicians we see men or women who are infallible but human, casual but masterful, accessible but formal. In a political climate dominated by social media, what does the new "human" politician look like? What do we want from him or her, and why and when do we want it?

This seemingly intimate new relationship has darker sides. If technology allows voters to feel as if they know politicians better than ever before, it also allows politicians to understand voters in ways that are new, unexpected, and slightly sinister. What happens when your senator or congresswoman knows more about you as a voter than you know about them? What if politicians could tailor their entreaties or advertisements to you on the basis of what they know about your tastes, background, and economic level? As it turns out, they can and they do.

"THE MINIMAL, DEFAULT TOOL KIT required of any contemporary politician is a website, a Facebook page, a Twitter stream, and a YouTube account," says Antonio Peronace, the cofounder of the Washington, DC, consultancy Apollo Political. Depending on the constituents they want to target, politicians might then move on

> "The minimal, default toolkit required of any contemporary politician is a website, a Facebook page, a Twitter stream, and a YouTube account."
>
> *Apollo Political cofounder Antonio Peronace*

to more nuanced, specialized platforms like Instagram and LinkedIn.

The contemporary path to electability is one that Mike Germano knows well. Germano, the chief digital office of VICE Media, as well as the CEO and cofounder of Carrot Creative, was one of the youngest elected officials in America when, during his senior year at Quinnipiac College in Connecticut in 2005, he was voted in as councilman of the 8th District in Hamden, Connecticut, against an opponent who, says Germano, won his first election before Germano was even born.

Still, in contrast to his opponent, Germano was a digital native who understood the internet in ways his rival didn't. Using MySpace, he was able to invite hundreds of new graduates of his alma mater to political events via email. By enlisting voters to visit his website, and closely tracking what they clicked on, Germano was better able to understand, and target, their concerns.

From a political standpoint, Germano tells me that the biggest advantage of social and digital data was the ongoing flow of information he was able to glean from voters. "I could be sitting at a council meeting with my campaign manager and chief of staff doing internet research, texting me real-time information on what voters wanted and the issues that mattered most to them." At the same time, Germano also recognized that voters could wield technology as ably as he could. With voters turning into amateur journalists equipped with cameras and palm-sized camcorders, he, and other politicians, needed to be vigilant in ways they never were before. As Peronace says, "We've moved very far away from the days of FDR in a wheelchair, when you could avoid public imagery."

One of the earliest victims of the internet's ability to define and memorialize a candidacy was former Vermont governor Howard Dean. In 2004, Dean, the Democratic front-runner in the presidential election, had just finished in third place behind John Kerry and John Edwards in the Iowa caucuses. The candidate was hoarse, exhausted, and emotional. After listing off the states he planned on winning, Dean let out an exultant, cracked-voiced, half-yell, half-scream.

In that moment, for all intents and purposes, the Dean campaign ended. The "Dean Scream" clip was broadcast any number of times as evidence that Dean, a Yale graduate and medical doctor, was unfit for office. It didn't matter what the former Vermont governor had said or done before Iowa. On YouTube alone the Dean Scream inspired a dance remix, a screaming goats remix, a scream mashup, a dubstep version, and a Dave Chappelle parody.

The Dean Scream, and countless examples of politicians saying the wrong thing, reversing their stances on issues, or snapping at reporters, illustrates how in an always-on era, a single moment or lapse of judgment can alter and even undo a campaign's trajectory. And with this expanded media comes expanded means of political sabotage in the hopes of creating a Dean Scream effect. Among the new players in today's political climate, for example, are "trackers"—men and women paid to attend town halls or seek out Congress people or candidates on the street and thrust camera phones in their faces while asking them leading or provocative questions. In 2012, for example, Republican Allen West, a Florida Tea Party–affiliated legislator, was asked by one town hall attendee what percentage of the American legislature he believed was made up of card-carrying Marxists or international socialists. Earnestly, West replied, "I believe there's about seventy-eight to eighty-one members of the Democrat Party that are members of the Communist Party."[83] Not surprisingly, the story was picked up nationally.

At the same time, a single defining moment can also benefit a politician, as the image of Barack and Michelle Obama dancing on Inauguration Night, 2012, a snapshot of physical intimacy that humanized the new president, attests. Instagram is especially eloquent when it captures politicians as they are about to go onstage before a speech, or as they come off a plane after a long day of negotiations. "No other medium today gives you that kind of human insight," says Peronace. "The best—and the worst—of those moments come from moments of vulnerability, when, say, a candidate is behind schedule. We are all human at the end of the day, even politicians."

IN ANCIENT GREECE, the original home of democracy, politically organized citizens assembled in town squares to discuss pertinent or pressing issues, with the square serving as the center or nexus for exchanging thoughts and opinions or for engaging in discourse. From a political perspective, more than Facebook, Twitter has taken the place of the town square, allowing politicians to communicate directly with voters without the need for a middleman. But this change in relationship between politician and voter is not the only way Twitter has impacted the political landscape. The prevalence of Twitter also has ramifications for how we as voters receive, and respond to, political and other news, and not least, for how we expect our officials to respond to threats and crises.

> "We still live in a representative democracy, but thanks to a tool like Twitter it's getting a little bit closer to direct democracy."
>
> *Twitter's director of political advertising Peter Greenberger*

According to Peter Greenberger, director of political advertising for Twitter, 98 percent of the House of Representatives, 100 percent of the Senate, and all fifty governors of all fifty states are active on Twitter. "We still live in a representative democracy,"

Greenberger says, "but thanks to a tool like Twitter it's getting a little bit closer to direct democracy."

Twitter has created a herd of political stars who use the site especially well. Barack Obama is by far the most followed political figure with his 46 million followers. Indonesian prime minister Narendra Modi has 6.13 million followers, and Susilo Bambang Yudhoyono, the chairman of the Democratic Party in Indonesia, has 5.37 million followers. Others on the top-performing Twitter list include first lady Michelle Obama, Abdullah Gül, the president of Turkey, Queen Rania of Jordan, UK prime minister David Cameron, and Mexican president Enrique Peña Nieto. Twitter is especially popular among politicians in Japan, which Greenberger believes is because 140 Japanese characters allows users to tell an extended story in a short format, in contrast to Germany, where thanks to the language's many portmanteaus users have a harder time simplifying their thoughts.

Political popularity on Twitter has its own rules. "The more provocative a politician is on Twitter, generally the more engaging his or her content will be," says Greenberger, adding, "If you are willing to go out and really express a strong opinion, you will get a stronger, more engaged reaction, with more clicks and retweets and favorites. In the sense of inspiring engagement, a case could be made that there are segments of the Republican Party who are perhaps even more provocative than their Democratic counterparts." In terms of generating crowd response, among those adept at "working" Twitter by design or by accident are New Jersey mayor Cory Booker, who often quotes scripture as well as inspirational quotes from figures including Malcolm X and Ralph Waldo Emerson, and eighty-year-old Republican Iowa

Do you think social media has made our government more of a direct democracy, rather than a representative one? #7B

Senator Chuck Grassley, known for tweets like, *Fred and I hit a deer on hiway [sic] 136 south of Dyersville. After I pulled fender rubbing on tire we continued to farm. Assume deer dead."*

Twitter excels at creating the illusion of access to power. You can tweet at Obama, but that doesn't mean he'll read it. That access is not so illusory, however, on more local levels, where Twitter can create real-time engagement and even solutions. Voters can tweet a city councilman about the pot-hole at the end of their road, or take issue with the fact that the garbage hasn't been picked up that day. In the Spanish town of Jun, outside Granada, Spain, the mayor requires that every single public office and employee have an official Twit-ter account, and that those accounts be clearly spelled out on all official vehicles, uniforms, and utility trucks. By integrat-ing Twitter handles and hashtags into city governance, Jun, Spain, has become, in effect, a Twitter-connected munici-pality. Every single citizen has a direct line of communica-tion to the mayor. They can tweet about whatever concerns them, and the mayor will publicly reply on Twitter about how and when the issue will be resolved. Last year, when one citizen tweeted about exposed wires, it took less than twenty-four hours for the mayor, and the town, to bury the wires. Greenberger believes that once one mayor responds to his constituents via Twitter, it's difficult to imagine the next mayor *not* doing it.

But above all else, says Kate Nocera, BuzzFeed's congres-sional reporter, Twitter, like Instagram, excels at chronicling unrehearsed, behind-the-scenes, "human" moments. During the government shutdown of 2013, during a late-night vote, "I kept smelling booze on all these members of Congress," Nocera recalled. "Understandably, it was late at night, and

Do you feel closer to politicians you connect with on social media?
#7C

most had gone to dinner and perhaps to a bar—but it was something I could tweet that you just wouldn't find on CNN or CSPAN."

Nocera acknowledges that Twitter's emphasis on speed can create mistakes and misunderstandings, and that the platform occasionally plays havoc with meaning. Last year, for example, former Arkansas governor Mike Huckabee said in a speech that "The Democrats want to insult the women of America by making them believe that they are helpless without Uncle Sugar coming in and providing them a prescription each month for birth control because they cannot control their libido or their reproductive system without the government." Huckabee's remarks were later scrambled across Twitter as, "Huckabee: Women 'helpless without Uncle Sugar coming in and providing them . . . birth control because they cannot control their libido,'" while failing to acknowledge that Huckabee was, in fact, taking aim against the Democratic Party.

"Things can backfire and get messy sometimes," Nocera says. "Unfortunately, once [a tweet] is out, it can be too late to change the narrative. But the good thing about Twitter is that as it evolves, reporters evolve, too."

A salient question for any politician on social media has to do with authenticity. Our politicians tweet and post on Facebook, but most of us recognize that it's not the politicians themselves spending time on social media, but their campaign staffers. The issue is especially noticeable with older politicians, who are understandably less acquainted with social media. Nocera believes that the issue of "authenticity" on Twitter depends on the politician in question. "If it's someone like [Missouri senator] Claire McCaskill engaging with their constituents, I think it's great. On the other hand, do I believe someone like [Utah senator] Orrin Hatch knows anything about Twitter? No, but when I see members of Congress on

Twitter and I know it's their staff tweeting press releases on their behalf, in my opinion it serves no purpose."

Twitter's Peter Greenberger believes that campaigns should do their best to get their politicians to write and tweet their own messages, and also to make clear when it is them, and not their staff, perhaps even by marking personal tweets with their initials, as Barack Obama does with his "-bo" tags.

While Twitter can be a net positive for public relations, and beneficial during campaigns, CNN's technology and media commentator Douglas Rushkoff says its effects have not yet proven to be enduring. "The problem with politics and social media is that people underestimate how short-term these tools tend to be," says Rushkoff. "Even the best social media–led political campaigns I've seen have been flash-in-the-pan. They're all about creating an immediate, knee-jerk response in voters. They have nothing whatsoever to do with long-term engagement, or with bigger projects or goals, or even, from a voter standpoint, with loyalty."

Perhaps this is why, the more engagement a politician has with voters via social media, the higher the chances are for voter disillusionment. "The problem with the Obama campaign is that it had no intention for that level of intimate engagement to continue," says Rushkoff. "From a practical policy standpoint, the Obama people used this media, and this network, to get elected. They didn't engage with them afterward, or invite them into the process of governing. Once he was elected, the president went back to the same old style of governing where you make decisions and engage with banks, and so forth."

Still, Rushkoff acknowledges the obvious fact that social media generally offers benefits, especially to up-and-coming political candidates who want to take up arms against the establishment or the system. Whether it's the Occupy Wall Street–style candidate fighting big business, or a Tea Party candidate battling the status quo, almost by definition social media has a grassroots, fighting-the-Man quality and spirit. "For politicians and for movements, the social media space is a metaphor for what 'the street' used to signify."

It could be argued that social media is also something that, so far, Democratic candidates have engaged with more effectively than Republican candidates, perhaps because the sorts of people who create, run, and operate social platforms are often liberals themselves. This might be changing, however—in 2012, the *New York Times* published a front-page article, "Republicans are Wooing the Wired," about that party's inability to match the Obama administration's sophisticated use of digital analytics during the last two presidential elections.[84] A Pew Research study showed that as the 2012 presidential election neared its culmination, Obama posted nearly four times as much as the Romney campaign, and made his presence known on nearly twice as many platforms.[85] In the wake of that election, the *Times* reported, Republicans were investing many millions of dollars "to match the interactive platforms, grass-roots databases, and sophisticated data analytics that allowed Democrats to identify voters, reach them with precision, and persuade them to vote."[86]

The worlds that voters inhabit online closely match the ones they inhabit offline. A recent Pew report concluded that the internet has further polarized American voters, and even diminished political participation. Why? Just as politically polarized viewers in the US watch Fox News or MSNBC, but not both, voters generally populate their Twitter feeds with voices, opinions, and pundits who share their opinions, while ignoring or bypassing news and users that offer conflicting views. Sites like Facebook and Twitter adjust their algorithms "to show us more content from people who are similar to us,"[87] and the Pew study found that the lack of diversity of opinion shown on social media made voters less likely to express their beliefs, especially when they suspect their opinions conflict with those of the people they interact with online. In other words, social media creates a political bubble that filters out other political world views. The study also found that social media users are "more reluctant to express dissenting views in the offline world."[88]

When it comes to political news in the Information Age, there is a larger problem than what individuals see and engage with via their social media feeds. The velocity of today's real-time news cycle can play havoc with what constitutes "news" in the first place. Nocera, who began her journalism career at Politico, notes that websites have had a strong influence on traditional television news organizations. "Today you see more people on television from political websites like The Hill and Roll Call—people who would have rarely appeared on television before, and who are reporting on breaking news in a way they would have previously in quick blog posts or newsletters." Echoes *Associated Press* political editor Liz Sidoti, "When everything is in 140 characters, it gives a skewed version of reality, and that impacts how editors think about what reporters should be covering, and it impacts what reporters think is important."[89]

The asynchronous nature of Twitter means a story about a threat of presidential impeachment can stand side by side with a story about the First Lady's wardrobe. Along with cable and television news networks, Twitter also creates the expectation that anything complex is also capable of simplification. If something cannot be summarized easily in 140 characters or less, it is beyond Twitter's understanding. One potent illustration of the limitations of social media was the

Do you express your political beliefs on social media? Do you like when other people express their political beliefs on social media?

#7D

historic overhaul of the American health system in 2010. Expecting a catchy sound bite, many citizens were confused by what the Patient Protection and Affordable Care Act really was—and by focusing on the government website going down, social media ended up distracting from something much more important: discussion of the Act itself. As Nocera reminds me, if transforming both the market and traditional payment systems were easy to place in bullet points, another president would have done it years ago. "You cannot explain the Affordable Health Care Act in 140 characters—*ever*." Far more enduring and emotionally "sticky" than the passage of the Affordable Care Act were any number of tweets like "How many more people have to die at the hands of Obama's death panels before someone trys [sic] to defund it?"

> "When everything is in 140 characters, that impacts how editors think about what reporters should be covering, and what reporters think is important."
>
> *AP political editor Liz Sidoti*

Then there is the problem of how Twitter exacerbates our expectations for how our elected politicians should respond to crisis. In 2014 the scandal surrounding the NSA spying program showed up on Twitter before the White House even had an opportunity to issue a formal statement. No organization, especially the White House, can be expected to move at the same pace as Twitter, unless it's willing to become entirely responsive and reactive. Nor is it the government's place to broadcast or respond to world events or emergencies via a Twitter stream. When Russia invaded Ukraine last year, the immediacy with which platforms like Twitter jumped on the story created a momentum and expectation that politicians, and even nations, should respond with the same impulsive assertion, and if they don't, they are weak, indecisive, or dithering.

What's more, the Twitter mob is frighteningly fast to pass judgment, not just on politicians but on average citizens. In 2014 Justine Sacco, a corporate communications head for the media firm IAC, was boarding a plane from New York to her hometown of Cape Town, South Africa, when she tweeted, "Going to Africa. Hope I don't get AIDS. Just kidding. I'm white!" At the time Sacco had fewer than 500 Twitter followers, but before her plane touched down in Cape Town, the Twittersphere had already convicted and sentenced her. Still in the air, Sacco had no idea any of this was happening, inspiring the hashtag #hasjustinelandedyet.

Once she landed in Cape Town, Sacco immediately deleted her Twitter, Facebook, and Instagram accounts, and issued a formal apology via a South African newspaper. Her employer dismissed her anyway. Sacco was young, and said something impulsive and unwise, and as a public relations executive she should have known better. But her story reminds us that, thanks to social media, there is now a rush to judgment, as well as a permanent record of all our mistakes and indiscretions. Above all, on social media, things move *fast*.

If nothing else, the velocity of today's environment shows that politicians may be better served by creating narratives more rapidly. As I wrote earlier in the chapter on language, today we have the tools and images to tell stories quickly and compellingly. Sometimes even a simple Instagram photograph will suffice. The only solution is to create faster, punchier narratives, using immediately recognizable visual cues and symbols. A simple photo of an ambassador, or the secretary of state, boarding a plane in the wake of a four-hour overseas meeting has the immediate effect or reassuring voters that elected officials are working tirelessly on their behalf, even if they aren't. Engagement shouldn't come to an end on election day. What if the president posted online a collage of the bills and issues he's focused on right now, or photos of the other world leaders with whom he's currently engaged?

The underlying problem is that many politicians in office today came of age in another era. Technology is different from any other medium. It's not television. It's not print. It's baffling why Twitter and Facebook aren't integral parts of the US government, or why most governments don't actively keep pace with the newest, latest technological innovations, or figure out a way to balance speed of communications with responsibility. I have never understood how a government believes it can legislate for a society that is being transformed by tech when it doesn't altogether understand that tech.

As it stands, ordinary citizens are smarter and shrewder about how technology influences politics than are many politicians or political parties. Among the most obvious examples of oversimplification and reduction—and instantaneous branding—in politics are the meme and the hashtag. If nothing else, they show how a lone image or sentence-fragment can be more influential and enduring than even decades of public service.

In 2012, for example, Hillary Clinton was photographed aboard a military plane, gazing down at her Blackberry from behind dark glasses. The photograph inspired a Tumblr account, "Texts from Hillary," created by Adam Smith and Stacy Lambe, that imagines Madam Secretary of State killing time by sending random texts to national and world leaders. (Sample: Tim Geithner texts Hillary, "The economy is going to sink," to which Hillary replies, "Sucks for You.") The meme Texts from Hillary launched as a joke, but when it went viral it turned into something else altogether. Most people can agree that Hillary Clinton is intelligent, competent, ambitious, and fierce, yet it took a lone unplanned meme to turn her into a badass.

Of course, political memes can also help undo a candidacy. The Dean Scream discussed earlier is just one example. In response to a question about equal pay for women during the second 2012 presidential debate, former Massachusetts governor Mitt Romney remarked ingenuously, "When I had the chance to pull together a cabinet, and all the applicants seemed to be men . . . I went to a number of women's groups and said, 'Can you help us find folks?' and they brought us whole binders full of women." It was, wrote the *Atlantic* afterwards, a comment custom-made for Tumblr, and in no time at all, "Binders Full of Women" became a crowd-sourced meme-generating project, garnered 242,000 likes on Facebook, and inspired any number of parodies.

Hashtags have also been used as a fast and easy way to promote, or support, a politician or cause. Wendy Davis is the Texas Democratic politician who in 2013 engaged in a filibuster against a bill that would place impossibly severe restrictions on women's health clinics across Texas, a story that garnered national news coverage. During an eleven-hour filibuster, Davis had to stand the whole time, as a result of archaic Texas state rules forbidding anyone in Davis's position to sit or even lean on a desk. Nor was Davis allowed to discuss any topic unrelated to the bill in question.

Almost immediately, the hashtag #Standwithwendy went viral, compressing the event in a shorthand that not only encompassed the fact of the filibuster, but threw support behind female reproductive rights in an overwhelmingly male-governed Republican state, creating a world of detailed meaning in a single oddball piece of punctuation.

WHERE DO MOBILE PHONES FIT in this new connected political ecosystem? According to an April 2014 Gallup Poll, only 23 percent of all Americans have used a smart phone for a "political interaction"—receiving electronic communications from political interest groups; posting opinions on Twitter, Facebook, or elsewhere; or making a donation using a phone or a tablet—suggesting that phones' impact is yet to be felt.[90] Despite the interactivity of social media, many voters still feel disengaged from the process of voting, and from politics itself. Voter levels during the 2012 presidential election were down from 2008 levels, which means that the 2012 presidential election was the first since 1996 in which fewer residents voted than during the election before.[91] In terms of actual numbers, this means that only around 61 percent of the American voter-eligible population bothered to vote in the last presidential election.

Eva Pascoe, who cofounded the digital think tank Cyber-salon, argues that the core problem of politics can be attributed to the disconnection between analog governments and digital voter bases. "The tension between the fast, instant and collaborative way of working that social media and other technological advances have inspired does not go hand in hand with the old world of government 1.0." Which is why eVOTZ, currently awaiting patent approval, may someday transform how we vote by turning mobile smart phones and tablets into secure, authenticated, location-based voting machines. The advantages for disabled and elderly voters are obvious, but far more intriguing is the platform's sheer convenience, as well as the possibilities for eliminating fraud.

"All voters, and not just younger ones, can benefit from improvements in the current and traditional voting process," says eVOTZ founder Elliott Klein. "After all, look at how mobilization has empowered citizens around the world to assemble, demand changes, and improve their lives." Thus

Have you ever interacted with a politician using your mobile phone? #7E far the biggest hurdles Klein has come up against are from people who don't trust the security of the internet, and who are especially concerned about future cyber attacks. For Klein, these issues are outweighed by the hope that eVOTZ may someday bring innovation into an archaic process long plagued by errors, inefficiency, and low turnout.

Today India, Estonia, and parts of the EU are exploring e-voting to save costs, increase turnout, and even help with sustainability. Electronic voting will eventually come to pass, but before then, an older generation will have to face down and overcome a few emotional barriers. Many of them bought their first computers in college during the 1980s, when computers crashed regularly and term papers and entire PhD theses vanished forever. No matter how much smaller, faster, and sophisticated computers have become, to an older generation technology will always be temperamental and untrustworthy, a craps game for idiots.

Earlier in this chapter, I wrote that the new intimacy voters have with politicians comes with an unseen price. Today, you and I can communicate with our senators, governors, state representatives, congresspeople, and even our president. We can fact-check their stances on the environment and marriage equality. We can discover in real time if they are telling the truth or flip-flopping. We can hunt down every piece of video they've ever appeared in on YouTube. We can scan their latest postings on Facebook and Twitter. But bear in mind that technology works both ways. Contemporary politicians know more about us as voters than ever before, and can adjust and splice their messaging to us depending on our age, our interests, our economic class, where we live, what we read, what sports we play, what television shows we watch, and even what cars we drive.

If you could, would you use your mobile phone to vote? #7F

In 2008, the Obama campaign targeted the youth vote by talking to younger voters about student loans and the high cost of college educations. The campaign bought commercial time on Comedy Central, VH1, and Spike. Browsers could access his website via Facebook, MySpace, YouTube, Flickr, and other social media sites. To reach African American voters, the Obama campaign ran ads on BlackPlanet, the largest African American community online, targeting members from all across the country, and even published a photo of himself visiting a barbershop in South Carolina.[92]

The degree to which technology has transformed data means that companies and organizations can now "buy" individuals, and even whole groups of people, as they need them. This idea originated in television advertising, where large companies historically bought advertising in categories known as "clusters." If you were a company eager to reach a demographic of eighteen- to thirty-four-year olds, you "bought" advertising across a "cluster" of television shows popular with that age group. Your next step would be to analyze those viewers to get a better sense of what they want and expect, and then to adjust the tone and imagery of the ads broadcast during the television shows in question. Naturally, the commercials that showed up on action sports channels were different from those that appeared on, say, the Cooking Channel.

When the internet came along, it effectively supercharged the advertising industry. Today, companies have cookie-level data that tells them about every single website you and I visited and everything we did or didn't do on that same website. Advertisers today have the ability to target, or "buy," say, males between the ages of forty-five and fifty years old, with blond hair, who subscribe to *New York Times*, visit the Lexus website, watch *Dating Naked*, listen to Nas, and buy their clothes online at Jack Threads. They can "buy" young women between the ages sixteen and twenty who shop at Sephora and Forever 21 and are fans of Beyoncé and Lil Wayne and the television show *Pretty Little Liars*. In short, today businesses can fine-tune their advertisements to individuals who match a specific computer profile. When those businesses also import data culled from mobile phones, their messaging becomes, if possible, even more precise.

Not surprisingly, politics is making the shrewdest possible use of this same data. What if you could find out what a female voter was thinking at that very moment, and give her an immediate solution to that problem? A canny politician would appear to be reading her mind, because, with the help of data, this is precisely what he's doing. In 2012, voters who accessed the Re-Elect Obama website were asked to join one of eighteen different constituency groups, including Latinos, African Americans, LGBT, and young Americans. The request felt personal, flattering even, as though the campaign wanted to get to know us more deeply and increase our level of engagement with others like us. But the campaign then redirected that data for the purpose of targeting us with messages tailored to our self-selected identity, orientation, background, occupation, interests, and tastes—a practice known as "segmented messaging."

It's not that politicians in most cases are evil, or manipulative, only that today they can now leverage the most sophisticated data imaginable—including data that, unlike in the example above, we aren't aware we're relaying. Let's say the president asked everyone to check in at Foursquare during a State of the Union speech, and his social media team then extracted the data from those visits, and in the process identified four characteristics Foursquare voters have in common. This information could then transform how the campaign, or even the political party, targets its political messaging to those individual demographics.

Segmented messaging is nothing more than the price of doing business today. Everyone does it, for the simple reason that they can, and that includes both the Republican and Democratic parties. Politicians, who rely heavily on the collection and analysis of data, can now adjust a message to appeal to each constituent in each district or part of the country, with each message claiming to be genuine and representative of the candidate's beliefs. But if politicians can adjust their messaging on the basis of their demographics' education, color, social, or economic class, then what's the whole truth? Is there one? A millennial living in Brooklyn will get one message, a conservative military wife from San Antonio, Texas, will get a second, and an elderly widow living in Northern California will get a third. Same candidate, same information, but the words, the tone, and occasionally even the images will vary.

A recent study by Princeton Survey Research Associates International of 1,500 internet users in the US age eighteen or older revealed that 87 percent of respondents said they would be angry if political campaigns used customized messages on Facebook, based on users' interests. That's a lot of infuriated Americans, and obviously, very few of them know the extent to which segmented messaging has now become everyday practice in politics. It won't be long, either, before politicians begin using so-called "unstructured data," including Facebook and Twitter conversations, to analyze voters and trends, make decisions, and amass voter insights. It is only a matter before a political team is able to receive an alert when a conversation spike is beginning to happen, allowing them to address it in real time.

One final issue that intrigues me is transparency. From now on, every single member of our society will have come of age on social media. Every promise or mistake we have ever made will be captured, memorialized, and replayed. The internet asks politicians for a purity and straightforwardness we demand of few others in public life. Are we really ready for the "human" politician? Do we, in fact, even want our politicians to be "human"?

What do we see today when we glance into the mirror of our elected officials' online lives? We see tweets delivered in 140 characters or less, delivered by the men and women we elected, or the staffers who work for them. We see Facebook posts devoted to our politicians' latest speeches, accomplishments, and appearances. We see carefully curated Instagram photos of our politicians at work, or on a plane, or seated at their desks, signing their names to legislation, or YouTube videos addressing special-interest groups or town hall assemblages. In return, what do politicians themselves see when they look into the same mirror at us, the voters? They see a bearded millennial who listens to the Antlers. They see a conservative Hispanic voter. They see a military mother. They see a senior citizen. They see geographically based clusters of interests, attributes, and economic backgrounds. In short, distortion exists on both sides.

Still, illusion is what matters, and today, as Antonio Peronace reminds me, the internet serves to preserve politicians' authority while also giving voters a feeling of intimacy and companionship with their leaders. "A great example is a Twitter town hall, where you and I can participate via our mobile phones, or while we're sitting in our car. We can tweet something or send in a question. With just a few clicks, all of us are now able to have a conversation with someone we might not ever cross paths with in a physical room. After all, what's the point of the digital age if it's not able to create a broader conversation?"

Is it a good thing to know more about our politicians? #7G

8

the second screen:
boyhood, girlhood, and us

I N A SPEECH HE DELIVERED LAST YEAR in St. Peter's Square in Rome, the current pontiff, Pope Francis, told a crowd of 50,000 to beware squandering their lives on their phones. "Time is a gift from God," the pope said. "Perhaps many young people waste too much time in useless things . . . the products of technology that should simplify and improve the quality of life, but sometimes take attention away from what is really important."[93]

It was an interesting statement coming from Pope Francis and the Vatican, considering that the papacy was the subject of a pair of iconic compare-and-contrast photos that went viral in 2013. In the first, taken in 2005 as Pope Benedict was being announced as the new pope, the crowd packing St. Peter's Square was attentive and phone-free. In contrast, the

Do you think technology sometimes takes attention away from what is really important? What do you do to try to prevent that? #8A second photo from 2013, taken when the new pope, Francis, made an appearance on a Vatican balcony, looked more like a rock concert singalong, except rather than matches or lighters, almost every member of the crowd held his or her phone up high in the air, taping the event for posterity, whatever posterity means in a digital era.

Perhaps we shouldn't express frustration, or alarm, or outrage about the contemporary phenomenon of photographing, videotaping, posting, and chatting about every small and large event, get-together, celebration, and vacation in our lives. It may be time to let go of the idea that in the process of recording our lives, we are missing out on them, and instead acknowledge instead that by using our phones, many of us are doing everything in our power to wrest control of time back from life itself.

"Second Screen" is the catch-all industry term given to the suite of new viewing habits and rituals created by, and in some ways designed to complement, the new relationship between viewers and the companies and advertisers that deliver us shows, movies, and commercials. But it has a deeper meaning in most people's lives than social media or any companion device or app. Mobile phones, and the habits and rituals we have developed around them, are transforming our relationship to life itself. They are altering how we track, chronicle, and diarize who we are and where we've been.

IN ORDER TO EXPLORE THE MEANING of Second Screen as the term is used most commonly in my industry, it's worth first taking our minds back to a few years before the internet exploded into common use. At that time, Ross Perot was running for the American presidency against Bill Clinton and the incumbent George Herbert Walker Bush. Euro Disney opened its doors outside Paris. Pearl Jam was in rotation on the radio. *Home Alone 2: Lost in New York* was playing in theaters. Country singer Billy Ray Cyrus and his wife became new parents to a baby girl, Miley.

At various times in the morning, bedside alarm clocks all around the country went off, and we reached over to silence them. We got up, made and drank coffee, showered, brushed our teeth, shaved, put on makeup. We may have turned on a television morning show, or the radio, to get a summation of the latest news, weather, and traffic.

If you or I were at all susceptible to advertising, mornings were the perfect time for companies to sell us things. A clear thread connected the television commercials we were exposed to from 7 AM to 9 AM to what we bought that day, week, or month, and businesses spent a lot of money analyzing and segmenting human habits and patterns. In 2007, an advertising agency even released an extensive study, "The Ritual Masters," analyzing the roles and occasions that ritual plays in our lives. These included "Preparing for Battle" (showering, eating breakfast, getting ready for work); "Feasting" (sharing meals, reuniting with our "tribes," e.g., our friends and colleagues); "Returning to Camp" (coming home at night, reading the mail, relaxing, fixing a drink; making dinner); "Sexing Up" (transitioning from our everyday selves to our public, more glamorous selves); and "Protecting Ourselves for the Future" (lowering the thermostat, checking in on sleeping children, programing the coffee machine, turning on the burglar alarm, shutting off the lights).

The Ritual Masters was published the same year the first iPhone came to market. It is still a fascinating study, but it goes without saying that since then the outlines of our mornings have been reimagined and re-choreographed by our mobile phones.

Most of us in the Western world awaken today to a preinstalled ringtone melody or sound effect like "Silk," "Stargaze," "Bamboo," or "Popcorn" or a song hand-cut from our iTunes library using the Ringtone Designer app. Eight out of ten of us keep our mobile devices on, and recharging, by our bedsides. Our phones were the last physical objects most of us held and gazed at before we fell asleep, just as they are the first objects we reach for when we wake up.

Our collective first impulse is to discover what happened, and what we missed out on, while we were sleeping. Who emailed or texted us, and with what level of affection, intimacy, or urgency? Who didn't? Depending on our age, we proceed to check off various boxes, ranging from the morning's news headlines to Facebook to Twitter to Pinterest to Instagram. An hour later we're showered, dressed, ready for the day. If we've turned on a television morning show, we watch it while also looking at a tablet or a mobile device. Our phones are so all-encompassing they block out the voices of the anchorpeople and the audio from the commercials. If we commute by car, AM/FM radio is mostly irrelevant. Instead we listen to podcasts, a streaming music station, or the artists and songs topping our personal music libraries. During the day, we juggle a multitude of screens. If we're anything like the average user, we check our phones anywhere from 110 to 150 times a day, or around nine times an hour, with peak usage occurring between 5 PM and 8 PM, which also happens to coincide with peak television-viewing hours.[94] From 7 PM onward, if we watch the nightly news, a television program, an awards show, or a sporting event, we do it while texting, emailing, tweeting, or Facebooking our friends.

In short, thanks to phones and tablets, the relationship we had once with the networks and advertisers who provide us media has been turned around, with the advantage today, it seems, going to you and me. Twenty years ago, if our favorite

Do you check your phone as soon as you wake up in the morning? What app or website do you check first? #8B television show came on at, say, 10 PM, we were at the mercy of broadcasters' timetables. We had no choice but to stay at home and wait for the show to begin. Today, of course, with some exceptions, a network's evening lineup feels naïve and presumptuous—who do they think they are, and why do they bother? It's an accepted fact that you and I now watch programs when we want to watch them, often an entire season's worth in a single inhalation, and very rarely on our actual television sets. Just as we saw with music, television and movie-watching has become a private affair between us and our headphones. As *Forbes* magazine has noted, "If Netflix were a channel, the 87 minutes per day that the average subscriber spends streaming the service would make it one of the most-watched cable networks."[95] If and when we do watch television in real time, we do it amid a murmuring of shares, likes, updates, comments, tweets, and retweets, transforming television-watching into a ritual that is simultaneously private and collaborative. The average American still watches approximately five hours of television a day, but "in many ways television shouldn't even be called television anymore," *Forbes* once wrote. "'Video' would prove more apt."[96]

Similar to the dynamics we saw in impulse buying, today you and I find ourselves wielding a new, almost inadvertent power: the power to *not* see what we were once obliged to see—in the case of television, because we no longer fear missing out. But as you'll see, networks and advertisers are fighting back, and their secret weapon, it turns out, is us, the viewing audience.

EVERY SPRING, I attend what's known in the marketing industry as "Upfronts," an annual meeting made up of television network executives and advertisers. The mission of Upfronts is twofold: Networks roll out their upcoming fall schedules, and marketers from major companies commit to their advertising for the upcoming year. Everyone knows how consumers digest media today, which is why I'm always surprised when I hear network executives referring to programming lineups on, say, a Tuesday or a Thursday, or a Saturday night. Don't they realize that time, and timing, are no longer in their control? Whenever I give speeches around the world, I often ask how many members of the audience watch television as it's happening. Few hands go up. Some of my friends and colleagues' teenage children, who are in the habit of watching entire seasons of a show on their laptops, seem to have no idea that television shows were designed to be interrupted and supported by thirty-second-long commercial breaks.

Equipped with mobile phones, you and I have abducted and scattered the absolute power once held by media companies. Which is why television networks, programmers, and advertisers are doing whatever they can to reengage us, via our phones. According to one study, 84 percent of smart phone owners and 86 percent of tablet owners confess to using one or both devices while watching television "at least once during a thirty-day period" and "nearly half of those tablet owners said they visited a social-networking site during a program."[97] To capitalize on this new behavior, networks have developed a category of apps known as "companion content." For example, last year the *Wall Street Journal* ran a story about the cast of the AMC television series *The Killing*. The show's actors were on location in Vancouver, but the footage being shot, including photos, clips, games, and trivia pertinent to the series, was designed exclusively for the show's downloadable companion app. A similar app for *Breaking Bad* offered teasers, cast biographies, and previews of upcoming episodes. Both apps were designed to be used in real time, in conjunction with the actual shows. "By offering so-called second-screen content synchronized with the broadcast," the *Wall Street Journal* wrote, "the networks hope they can persuade viewers to watch programming live, instead of on a digital video recorder several days after their initial broadcasts are recorded."[98] Why? For the simple reason that you and I are more liable to be exposed to advertising when we watch a television show as it's happening.

Breaking Bad and *The Killing* aren't the only shows that have gotten into Second Screen companion-content. The accompanying app to *The Vampire Diaries* tries to keep fans engaged via poll-taking, trivia, photos, and flashbacks, as well as a feature allowing at-home viewers to compose and share their own captions to assorted screenshots. The HBO Go app provides extra content around *Game of Thrones*, including, mercifully, a breakdown of each noble house. Conan O'Brien has his Team Coco app. Even Shazam, with its 375 million users, has gotten in on the act, broadening its music-tagging capacities to give both program and cast information for individual television shows. Shazam has also partnered with *Jimmy Kimmel Live* to allow viewers to unlock a free downloadable musical track as they watch bands performing live on the show.

A popular mobile phone app known as Secret, created by two former Google employees as a platform allowing users to anonymously post their blackest thoughts, has even created an inadvertent Second Screen experience for at-home television viewers. "We definitely saw a lot of Second Screen usage on Secret during *House of Cards*," says Secret CEO Chrys Bader-Wechseler. Viewers, he says, weren't just remarking on what was happening onscreen, but confessing things like, "I'm watching *House of Cards* instead of having dinner with my girlfriend." Some users, adds Bader-Wechseler, go so far as to use the Secret app to divulge plot spoilers.

· · ·

Have you ever used a television network app to access additional content while watching television? #8C

Second Screen behavior has also transformed television news broadcasts. More and more, anchorpeople urge us to "Go check us out on Facebook" or "Continue this conversation on Twitter." The future model of broadcasting may, in fact, be made up of ordinary citizens across the country engaging with an app that allows them to report on, or post photos and videos about, newsworthy events in their cities and towns. If a newsworthy event takes place where they live—a tornado, a fire, a thrilling sports victory—they may someday be able to submit and sell content to a local or national news station. (I actually recently invested in an app, called Centric, that hopes to be able to tackle this problem.)

But Second Screen isn't just about trying to recapture a rebellious audience who can now watch what they want when they want to watch it. Nor it is really about deepening engagement with popular shows. According to Ian Wolfman, an expert on social media strategies, "It's really all about getting social."

Which brings me to an important point about Second Screen and its role in our lives now and in the foreseeable future. Much more than any app, the most powerful Second Screen influencer—the ingredient that can make or break a television show—is the at-home television-watching audience. We no longer live in a world where we can see, or touch, the media we love and consume. Video-rental and music stores have vanished. Without a physical representation of a CD or a DVD to hold, or scan, or read, or make decisions about, we become all the more dependent on the tastes, choices, opinions, and recommendations of friends and strangers. In the splintered, multiscreen era we inhabit, it may be hard to believe that television is as powerful as it has ever been, but it is. In combination with Facebook and especially Twitter, television has gained measurably in influence, thanks in large part to the smart phone–wielding, social media–using audience. For example, during its fourth season premiere in 2013, *The Walking Dead* drew in around 16 million viewers, with the show's finale attracting roughly the same number. These figures are impressive, but they are dwarfed by the 100 million people who talked about or referenced *The Walking Dead* on Twitter that season. Even more interesting, 90 percent of those Twitter users hadn't seen the actual show.

Welcome to another, more shadowy definition of Second Screen, where you and I serve as influencers and cheerleaders, as unpaid brand ambassadors, for a television series, an awards show, or a sports event. If the first screen is television, the Second Screen refers to our newfound desire to share our every thought and glancing impression with an unseen army of friends and strangers. No one is asking us to do this. No one is paying us to do this, either. But thanks to our participation in social media, a premiere or final episode of a show becomes a word-of-mouth spectacle, one that's simultaneously private and public. Thanks to Second Screen, television has evolved into a national hearth once again, as it was back in the days of Walter Cronkite and the moon landing.

> "As people watch TV nowadays, the conversations about what they're watching are conducted on Twitter."
>
> *Twitter COO Adam Bain*

"The reality is that as people watch TV nowadays, the conversations about what they're watching are conducted on Twitter," confirms Twitter COO Adam Bain. "Our mobile devices— and specifically Twitter, whether it's installed on your phone or on your tablet—has become the Second Screen for whatever we're watching."

It's a fact today that most if not all of humanity's greatest and most baleful moments take place in real time on Twitter, and alongside the music we listen to, Twitter has become the soundtrack of our lives. To an even greater extent than Facebook's—which, like a DVR of our life, is less dependent on timeliness and urgency—Twitter's power derives from the in-stream engagement of its users. After all, when you think about it, we do only a few things when we're watching television. We go onto Facebook. We Google a name, a fact, a date. Or we tweet.

Bain tells me that Twitter has, in fact, helped drive us all back to the days of pre-DVR television watching, encouraging real-time participation. As social creatures, no one wants to be excluded from a larger conversation. Almost incidentally, our phones have eliminated the need for "water cooler" conversations—those chatty, next-day conversations about an awards show or sports event. Thanks to social media, those conversations now take place in real time. Bain has even heard of people holding Super Bowl parties alongside a screen featuring a real-time Twitter feed.

Is there a kind of show that inspires Facebook or Twitter use more than another? Award shows, it turns out, are huge, and so are shows that have captured the public imagination, including the aforementioned *Game of Thrones* and *Breaking Bad*. Even if we live in a fragmented world, we still need the illusion of belonging to something greater than ourselves.

The ability of Twitter to provide that has also influenced how television shows are produced, according to Bain. "In particular, reality shows like *The Voice* are definitely rethinking how they can integrate Twitter into their programming early on, as opposed to it being an afterthought."

Companies, too, are constantly considering how they might be able to use Twitter in the future as a platform for encouraging television viewers to buy on impulse. In 2014, the *New York Times* reported that with 87 percent of all Americans now watching TV while using smart phones, the department store Target planned to feature an assortment of products, including baskets, pillows, and photo frames, on a future episode of the television show *Cougar Town*, to be simulcast online. The moment a pillow or a basket shows up on the TV screen, you and I would be encouraged to buy it on our phones or tablets at Target.com.[99]

Right now, at least, whatever influence Twitter has on what you and I buy typically comes about as the result of our feeds, in which, for example, a friend tells us she has just bought a new pair of shoes or headphones, which in turn inspires us to go out and get a pair ourselves. At the same time, advertisers are most certainly aware that peak television-watching time coincides with our peak mobile phone usage. Marketers today now target us from 5 PM to 8 PM not only with commercials, but also with Vines, tweets, and Facebook messages.

The only issue that Twitter faces, one that annoys a lot of viewers, is the same one that Secret app users face, namely, that many people breathlessly give away crucial plot twists, thereby destroying the experience for others. Still, this seems like a small price to pay for the Second Screen experience.

AWARD SHOWS AND PRESTIGE TELEVISION are not the only large drivers of Second Screen use. So are huge national sports events like the Super Bowl, the NBA Finals, the World Series, NASCAR, and the World Cup. In common with television programs, the sports industry has invested heavily in Second Screen apps. In 2014, for example, viewers watching the NFL Network's coverage of the National Football League draft could augment their viewing experience by downloading an app offering video interviews with first-round selections.[100] Given what we know of patterns of Second Screen use, it isn't surprising you and I are using our phones while watching games on television at home. But what is our relationship with our phones when we attend a game in person?

By their very nature, live sports events are inclusive and participatory. The experience of being a sports fan centers around looking up, not down. If fans prefer gazing down at their phones instead of watching what is taking place on a field or auditorium right in front of them, they are better off watching the game at home, where, among other things, the audio and video are better. But as anyone who has recently been in the audience at any public event knows, or scanned a random selection of YouTube videos, millions of YouTube videos are uploaded from rock concerts and sports events every day.

"If you ask every single member of an audience whether he or she has an addiction, ninety-nine percent would tell you no," says Peter Guber, the chairman and CEO of Mandalay Entertainment and co-owner of the Golden State Warriors (basketball) and the Los Angeles Dodgers (baseball). "But they're not telling the truth. Eighty-five percent of the people who come into a sports arena or movie theater have their smart phones with them."

Guber reminds me that the three core components of any kind of entertainment are, first, living through the experience; second, capturing it; and third, sharing it with others. Into this traditional equation come mobile phones, which, along with everything else, allow us to take photographs and play back video instantaneously. "Our devices provide an extraordinary platform to enable people—not just fans, but their friends and their colleagues at work the following day—to join the party, join the team, join in the spirit of the team. In some ways they allow us all to pay the experience of being a fan forward."

> "Eighty-five percent of the people who come into a sports arena or movie theater have their smart phones with them."
>
> *Chairman and CEO of Mandalay Entertainment and co-owner of the Golden State Warriors and the Los Angeles Dodgers Peter Guber*

Guber notes that most sports fans believe they themselves make a difference in the outcome of a sports contest or competition. Being a fan is an inherently emotional experience. So how do you merge that emotionality of being a sports fan with a mobile device?

We are nearing the day when, at a sports event, we will be given the opportunity to vote in real time for the game's most valuable player, or the best shot, or the best play. Perhaps our tweets could be selected to appear on a stadium or ballpark scoreboard. And someday, our Second Screen experience will commence days or even weeks before the game, at the moment we buy our tickets online.

Imagine: As game day nears, our phones will send us team lineups, background stats, and other data in both video and audio formats. If we're true believers who like to dress up or paint ourselves in team colors or insignias, we will be directed to a merchandise store that will deliver our T-shirt or cap to our house or apartment, to our cars upon arrival at the stadium, or even to our seats. Once we're at the stadium, rather than waiting in line or trying to get the attention of the food and drink vendors, our phones will allow us to get our hot dogs and sodas hand-delivered to us in our seats. We'll be able to sign up to receive an alert from the arena that superior seats are available for a few bucks more. A crowd-sourcing app will determine if we have any friends or acquaintances near us, and, if we feel like it, let us reveal our identities in return.

As the game gets underway, data such as player stats and player profiles are delivered continuously to our phones. Video of great plays, dunks, touchdowns, or home runs will appear in our hands as if by magic and via Twitter or Facebook, we can retweet or post them to our friend networks. Someday, uniforms may even be embedded with sophisticated chips, so fans will know at all times where their favorite players are on the floor, the field, the dugout, or the sidelines. And once the game is over, our phones will send us a highlights reel that we can share with friends and family at home or at work.

In other words, rather than being distractive or interruptive, the Second Screen experience will seamlessly integrate into the game. "In short," concludes Guber, "you and I are continually using a device as a means of making the game and the event even more compelling and unique than it is already."

BUT SECOND SCREEN, as we've defined it so far, has less to do with the relationship between television and our devices and more to do with how mobile phones change our relationship to the daily moments of our lives. The comedian Louis C.K. once performed a stand-up routine about his daughter's dance recital in middle school. He sat in a high school auditorium as all the other moms and dads raised their smart phones or tablets into the air to videotape the performance taking place only thirty feet away. No one in the audience was actually looking at their kids. They were too busy filming them. It was a safe guess, too, that none of them would ever rewatch the videos they were shooting. They would download them instead to their computers and forget about them, or transfer them onto a CD and then lose or break that CD. They were commemorating a memory in real time, while skipping over the basic step of experiencing it first. To put it another way: Fearful of missing out on a magic moment in their kids' lives, they were missing out on a magic moment in their kids' lives.

Just about all of us have been witness to moments like this, or have done it ourselves. Parents on sidelines at children's soccer or football games with their cell phones set to record. Birthday parties where no sooner is the cake brought in and the song sung than both are captured and uploaded onto Facebook. Weddings, anniversary toasts, high school and college graduations, sunrises, sunsets, sleeping dogs, cats, birds, rabbits, all of them photographed, videotaped, uploaded, towed by cursor into a desktop file. Critics of the Information Age argue that our mobile devices have kidnapped our souls, that they're blinding us to what's taking place in front of us. They say we are no longer able to live in the moment, to *be*, even though shooting a video of a touchdown, or of Jay Z sauntering onstage, feels to those of us holding our phones aloft as though we are focused on that moment more than we would be if we'd left our phones at home. Finally, critics say that using our phones as mediating devices between us and our lives puts everyone at risk of missing out.

Why do we do it, then? What is life for, in the end, if not to see, hear, experience, taste, touch, and feel all that's good, bad, and in between? Do we really need a palm-sized technological device to interpret, and replace, what only ten years ago our own senses gave us? Are we tech-drunk, simply not thinking, or both? Or is there something going on that's bigger than that?

Last year, the English singer Kate Bush, returning to performing live after thirty-five years, issued a statement asking her fans to leave their hardware at home. "We have purposefully chosen an intimate theater setting rather than a large venue or stadium," says the singer's note, posted, ironically, on www.katebush.com. "I very much want to have contact with you as an audience, not with iPhones, iPads, or cameras."[101] Kate Bush may be fighting not only against technology, but against something more primitive and profound. When we buy a mobile phone, we're not just buying a communication device, we're buying a witness, a testifier, a mirror, a collaborator, and a *daemon*. In a way, we're buying control over our lives, our experiences—the ability to capture and keep them

Why do you think people record moments instead of just experiencing them? #8D forever. It is a desire that is intimately related to how we feel about our own memory. We can't trust our brain's ability to remember the way we can trust the more stable silicon.

Consider that the first Kodak, and the first movie cameras, came to market in the late nineteenth century. A century or so later, a lot of us owned a camcorder, which we stored in our hall closets. In contrast to our phones, camcorders were neither intuitive nor unconscious. They were bulky, cumbersome, and almost never within reach when we needed them most. If something great or memorable was happening, we had to run and find the camcorder and load it with a tape. By the time it was set up and running, often the moment we had hoped to capture was gone.

Recently, the recorded life has been touched on in film. In 2014, Richard Linklater's nearly three-hour movie, *Boyhood*, chronicling the coming-of-age of a Texas boy from age six through age eighteen, came out. With *Boyhood*, Linklater had made a film no other director until then had had the time or patience to create. Filming took place over the course of twelve years, so the characters' (and the actors') development was actual. The closest analogy is perhaps the British filmmaker Michael Apted's ongoing *Up* documentary series, beginning with *7-Up*, in which the director has followed and filmed a group of British schoolchildren every seven years since 1964, when they were in elementary school. Lightly scripted, *Boyhood* was, in its own way, a documentary. Viewers could watch life as it took place under the fixed stare of a camera. The boy got older; his parents and sister got older; the actors playing them got older; and technology matured, too. One reviewer said that *Boyhood* "charts a life lived on camera." Another wrote, "*Boyhood* is a stunt, an epic, a home video, and a benediction," while according to a third, *Boyhood* "reminds us of what movies could be and—far more impor-tant—what life actually is."

Not much happens in *Boyhood*, but it's never boring. Many critics mentioned wanting to see it a few times, probably because as soon as the movie was over, they found it dif-ficult to remember, mysterious, elusive. In that sense, how different is *Boyhood* from your, my, or anybody's life, with its friends, meals, work, love, vacations, births, deaths, wed-dings, celebrations, vacations, family, parents, children, and pets? Significant things happen in our lives, but not *that* much happens either, and looking back, a sense of the whole can be slippery to grasp. *Boyhood* made the impression it did not only because it illuminated something about the everydayness of life, but because it also captured something we can't easily see as it happens in real time, namely, the people closest to us—ourselves included—changing, getting older, shooting up, broadening, moving forward. It allowed us to just watch the highlights.

Thanks to our phones, however, we can now film and capture our own highlight-driven versions of *Boyhood* or *7-Up*. Our phones provide evidence we were here. They prove we loved, ate well, married great people, surrounded ourselves with friends, celebrated birthdays, laughed, watched our chil-dren dance at school, went on bike rides. They show we visited our parents, went sailing and zip-lining, traveled to Africa and Mexico, taught our dog to play catch, opened the pool for the summer, learned French.

It's a deep human need to know who we are, where we've been, and where we're going. We want to make an impact on others. We seek validation and approval. We want to know we did something, or meant something, during our lifetimes.

· · ·

Do you think capturing moments on our mobile phones makes us remember them differently? #8E

Today, the first thing many newborn infants see when they come out of their mother's womb is a phone held aloft by a strange man, their father. How could this embedded vision not set a precedent and a tone for an entire life? "Marketing the self and receiving recognition for it is an American tradition, and the rest of the world has followed suit," Redg Snodgrass tells me. "When you think about it, we spend nine months connected to our mothers, and then spend the rest of our lives trying to reattach, and to feel that connection again." He adds, "To me, the Second Screen is the reattachment to that first nine months of our life—and an extension of human validation."

> "Marketing the self and receiving recognition for it is an American tradition."
>
> *CEO of ReadWrite and Wearable World Redg Snodgrass*

Nothing, not even life itself, takes a back seat to our phones. We sleep with our phones under our pillows. We go to work with our phones in our jacket pockets, right next to our hearts. Rather than criticize an entire world for being on their devices all the time, it might make more sense to cherish the vulnerability inherent in the sight, as when the new pope was announced, of hundreds or thousands of mobile devices raised high in the air. Armed with our phones, we are engaged, fecklessly, with trying to take back life and dictate its terms, contain its force and flood in iPhoto "moments," whether we are in a middle school auditorium or standing shoulder to shoulder with jubilant strangers in St. Peter's Square. We know that it's never going to work, that life always wins, but what moves me is the fact that we are persevering nonetheless.

Still, by taking a two-against-one approach to life in concert with our mobile phones, are we missing out on life as it's happening right in front of us? No, says Adam Bain, who recently saw, on Twitter of course, two side-by-side photographs showing commuters awaiting a bus. In the first, taken in 2014, everyone was looking down at their screens. The caption read, "Cell phones are making people not see the world around them." But that wasn't the payoff. It was the second photo, from the 1920s, which showed of a bunch of tall-hatted men and women on a curb biding time. Literally everyone had his or her face buried in a newspaper. Says Bain, "I would argue that our mobile devices help us participate in life, and have a great time, and then document and share that experience."

The question remains: What will most of us end up doing with all our photographic and video footage? To date, no one has come up with ways to take advantage of these random, continuous moments that we now and in the future will spend our lives accumulating. Someday, when picture frames throughout our living spaces become connected, and we can walk through the rooms of our homes to see our lives turning and revolving in ways that link together the past and the present, it will alter how we think about life and even narrative itself.

Last year, Facebook celebrated its ten-year anniversary by creating a tool that allows users to curate and reassemble our histories from our timelines in video format. Every photo and video we post and every considered or off-handed comment we make becomes fodder for a slideshow retrospective to share with family and friends. Soon the market will be flooded with platforms allowing us to assemble all the visual and oral evidence we have accumulated. With them, we will be able to transform a child's tenth birthday into a celebration of his or her first decade on earth. We will be able to recall, vividly, the joyous blur that was our wedding day, the first word our baby spoke, our twenty-fifth anniversary. We will be able to see how we looked and what our voices sounded like and the color of our hair at thirty, forty, fifty, sixty, seventy, eighty. We will be able to say, to someone, anyone, "I was here." As ever, mobile phones will be the driver, for the simple reason that they are almost always in our hands and pockets. Greater than the fear of missing out on our lives, it seems, is the opportunity we all have today to *not* miss out. One question remains, however, as we are so busy capturing our lives: Will we ever have time to watch them back?

9

the future of memory

N 2012, Michael Bloomberg, then the mayor of New York City, challenged the city's leading architectural firms to submit designs for the construction of an apartment building made up entirely of "micro-units"—living spaces measuring anywhere from 250 to 400 square feet. It's a construction trend that's caught on in other popular urban destinations like San Francisco, Seattle, Boston, Washington, DC, and Vancouver. Micro-units make sense for a city like New York, which has always been able to attract, retain, and monopolize most of the country's high-profile industries and whose population is expected to grow to 9.1 million people by 2030.[102]

The concept of micro-living began in Asia, which has wrestled for a long time with problems caused by overpopulation. With 130 million people crowded into a nation the size of Montana, Japan was a pioneer of the "capsule hotel" idea, where guests angle their bodies inside a plastic or fiberglass block that looks to the Western eye like a long-term fMRI or a very deep clothes dryer. In addition to housing the long-term unemployed, capsule hotels in high-density cities like Tokyo and Osaka offer a place for office workers who are too tired to commute home to check in for the night.

If nothing else, New York's micro-apartments are a timely idea. Statistics show that more and more people are living alone. New York rents are high, and rents for micro-units, while not cheap, are still within reach for college graduates with well-paying jobs. Plus, the mayor reasoned, retaining a younger demographic who would otherwise be priced out of New York could help inject some energy into a city many believe has become an amusement park for the rich.

In ways that might not be immediately apparent, micro-units are a near relative of another variety of construction, the self-storage unit. For the last four decades, according to industry estimates, self-storage has been the fastest-growing, most recession-proof category in the commercial real estate industry.[103] Storage units are everywhere, spread across large and small cities and towns, typically imposing their squat featurelessness across once-pretty fields and pastures. With their corrugated, padlocked slider doors, most of them look like minimum-security military barracks. Open up any unit and you'll find tables, chairs, lamps, vases, rugs, photo albums, record albums, boxes of cassettes, books, skis, bikes, scooters, skateboards, sleds, snowshoes, and tennis racquets. There's a lot of outmoded technology—old turntables and chunky speakers, VHS and DVD players, Karaoke machines with Sing-Along-With-Destiny's-Child CDs—that the owners have held onto in the hope a child or grandchild might want it someday or, if not, that it might have value on eBay. In short, most storage units are the displaced crazy clutter of many people's attics, basements, and storerooms.

There's a reason I think about self-storage in conjunction with the contemporary trend of micro-apartment construction. The storage unit of today and the American micro-apartment of the future both speak to the discomfort and lack of certainty we feel about what it means to own physical objects in a digital world, about the destiny of our stuff when we're no longer around to keep an eye on it, about whether our belongings were ever ours to begin with, and whether they, or we, will endure in any old-fashioned lasting form. A self-storage unit is a freeze-frame of an increasingly obsolete way of life—history, warmth, spill, chaos—whereas micro-apartments coolly mirror the realities of a digital world that is gradually reinventing our relationship with physical objects.

Micro-units are designed with millennials in mind—new college graduates, generally, whose best accumulating days lie ahead of them. At the moment, they're people who store their books and magazines on e-readers, their photographs in the cloud, and their music, television shows, movies, home movies, address books, maps, white noise machines, flash-lights, alarm clocks, video games, card games, kitchen tim-ers, kitchen recipes, tape recorders, newspapers, magazines, calendars, and to-do lists on their tablets and smart phones. Urban density, high rents, and the need for younger blood are all viable explanations behind the twenty-first-century boom in building small, but a hidden enabler of micro-units is tech-nology. With things that used to take up space on shelves and in drawers and closets and cabinets stashed instead on hand-held portable devices, the only thing micro-renters really need are clothes, food, pots and pans, and a few pieces of reversible furniture that allow a dining room table to collapse into an armchair or an ottoman to double as a shirt wardrobe.

As far as our physical objects are concerned, right now a lot of us have a foot in two conflicting times: the *then* of the pre-internet era, and the *now* of today and the future. What does it mean anymore to "own" something, to have a personal relationship with our stuff? Overnight many of our physical objects have taken on the look of, if not antiques, then objects that have outlasted their moment in history. Our loose-leaf photographs strewn in stained boxes look and feel color-drained and hectic. The stack of old thick magazines we're holding onto—*why* hold onto them? High school year-books are starting to look like a black-and-white ad for Amana fridges in a 1950s magazine, and the desk we're holding onto for a phantom future grandchild appears to have been built for a generation that has already passed, one whose school-work required more than just a screen. Our belongings, our things, the *stuff* we carry with us through the years, is a loud-mouthed insult to the clean, lit, trim computer surfaces that function, among other things, as password-protected digital safes into warrens containing our pasts.

If memory is linked to the human need to matter, to leave behind something of value in a world whose future now consists of traveling light, what do the mementos and accouter-ments of our lives mean anymore, and did they ever mean what we thought they meant in the first place? What will they look like twenty years from now?

Technology, then, has upset our relationship to our stuff, and to the past. As I wrote in the chapter on Second Screen, our phones can now capture the flow of life and time. It turns out they can also vacuum up our basements and attics. As a result, the physical things we own have lost whatever power they once had over us.

Our physical stuff may no longer be as lasting, but our dig-ital stuff is more lasting than ever. In an article that appeared in 2010, the *New York Times* noted that, "The web means the end of forgetting," adding, in case no one had noticed, that, "The Internet records everything and forgets nothing."[104] Nothing in this case means every email, text, snapshot, phone call, property record, tax lien, police arrest, charitable donation, byline, accidental mention, friend, almost-friend,

Do you still print photographs for display? #9A

employer, Facebook post, tweet, and Foursquare check-in—in short, every imaginable public or private mention or cameo appearance we've ever deliberately made or had, for whatever reason, to endure. In 2013 it was even reported that Facebook keeps records of what users were about to post, comment on, or like before they thought better of it. The internet, with its capacity to petrify everything we do well and do badly during our lives, may mean the end of forgetting, but its permanence may come at the expense of our own memories.

PEOPLE ASK ME SOMETIMES WHAT I REMEMBER about growing up, and my response is to point to all the photos perching on every surface of my apartment. Having a dad who was not only a jazz musician but a special effects photographer means that almost every moment of your life ends up in a frame, especially when you're a first child. Literally thousands of images of me as a kid exist—playing the piano, squirming in my dad's lap, wearing my first pair of shoes, swinging on a rope in a city park, taking fencing lessons, poking around with a toy computer, at a science fair, piecing together an astronaut jigsaw puzzle, wearing powder-blue Superman pajamas, looking delirious, almost crazed, as I rip open a birthday box of Legos.

I grew up in a 5,000-square-foot studio in the East Village section of Manhattan. It was a space crowded with drafting tables and photo set-ups in progress, camera equipment balanced on stands, lights, scrims, props, sandbags. My dad was both a technician and a magician, bending light, angling and lopping images to call forth moments and images of beauty and strangeness. Using a miter saw and a glue gun, together we assembled a Plexiglas fish tank, the soap bubbles and gel-colored lights making a psychedelic undersea effect. He could fix anything, and he taught me every tip and trick he knew. We ripped things apart just to see if we could bend them back to life, replaced door locks, soldered circuit boards, stripped copper-vein wires to repair worn plugs. In his off-hours, he was always by my side, helping me operate my first remote-control balsa-wood airplanes, my first racecars.

Outside the studio, we roamed around the city as he and his camera went about nailing the squalls and blue notes of pavement life. He taught me composition, and the zone system, a technique that gives photographers a systematic way of matching the visions in their heads with the pictures they want to capture. Where others saw rudeness, rudderlessness, or nothing, he pointed me toward order and magnificence.

My mom was just as big an influence on me. Instead of soap bubbles and gel lights, she handed me puzzles, taught me math, and toted home as many pounds of Lego as she could afford, not to mention countless train sets, space crafts, and medieval fortresses. She schooled me in her profession, accounting, and when I was older, in graphic design. It didn't take long for Legos to evolve into a kind of magic my brain and my fingers couldn't live without. Years before the company went electronic, I was using my toy-airplane remote control to jerk the mechanical working arms on my Lego structures or to open and close drawbridges against the invaders.

It was a gift from my mother, in fact, an Apple Mac 512K, that changed the direction of my life. With my new graphic design savvy, I created my own magazine, known as *WHAT*, short for *Washington Heights Action Teens*, which was later adapted by the local board of regents across area public schools. One of the photos I prize and love from that time shows me dressed in a gray suit and silk tie, an attaché case in one hand, glancing down at my wristwatch as if to say, *Hmm, train's late*, or *I wonder why Sandra is late for our meeting*. I was ten. Just as some parents groom their kids to be ballplayers or beauty pageant queens, my parents primed me to be an executive.

Yes, today I still have an old drafting table of my dad's, folded up, not-used, smaller and narrower than I remember; his much-loved atmospheric clock; and the wall unit where our family's record player once sat. I wish I had enough space in my apartment to show them off, but keeping them close by me is enough. Still, no physical stuff could ever compare to my photographs and the good memories they stir up: Home. Family. Trips I've been on. People who mean the most to me.

Things that can't be digitized are at risk of being orphaned to the same limbo as my dad's natty drafting table. We can scan and upload packs of old love letters into the cloud, but aren't old love letters more than words? Don't they have, for lack of a better word, a soul, a heart? Don't the smell and the texture of the paper, the ink, bring back how old we were when we wrote or read them, the beautiful not-knowing that permeates being in love for the first or second time? If it is true, as digital strategist Brad Behrens has said, "Everything that can be digitized will be digitized," what becomes of the original objects, and what happens to the physical evidence any of us were ever here?

> "Everything that can be digitized will be digitized."
>
> *Digital strategist*
> *Brad Behrens*

I first came up against this question when I was transforming a few of my dad's old LPs into MP3s. Afterward, I was left with a bunch of record albums, and the decision of whether to hold onto them, give them away, or toss them. They had been an important part of his life. Some had his signature or initials on them. Old LPs, I knew, had recently found new life on teenagers' bedroom walls. But I was no longer an adolescent and had just scraped the music from them like a pickpocket. Was there any reason to keep them around in physical form?

Old books, old letters, old record albums: I know I'm not alone in believing that these physical objects have enormous significance. We want to hold on to them without necessarily being able to say why; however, I also recognize how suddenly and strangely bereft of meaning they have become, too. In the end I gently settled my dad's old records in the hallway closet, telling myself I'd deal with them later.

The billion-dollar self-storage industry, and thousands of acres of landfill space, are making money from this kind of indecision and procrastination. On the one hand, most of us are surrounded by objects and memories we no longer have any idea what to do with, and that no longer complement the digital world we, our children, and our grandchildren will inhabit. On the other hand, we're spending a lot of money accumulating possessions that have no future value to anyone, especially our children.

I'm talking about tech. When I look down inside the drawers of my desk only to find a greasy black shallow-end swamp of defunct hardware, I don't know what to say. There are unlabeled cords that attach to machines no one makes anymore, hard drives, floppy discs, zip drives, two- and three-pronged adapters built to accessorize technologies that disappeared from the market in the early 2000s, first-generation cell phones, clamshell phones, and Ziploc baggies crowded with black and orange earbuds in all sizes made to pad expensive earphones I left by mistake on a transatlantic flight seven years ago.

Over the years I and everyone else have spent thousands of dollars on the latest, greatest technology, only to crater it for the newest stuff. A year from now, no one will want to have anything to do with our old technology. Old tech isn't like a scuffed, jaundiced baseball signed by the 1938 Yankees or Marilyn Monroe's dress from *The Seven Year Itch*. Aside from its value to museums, it has no use, no value, no nostalgia, no provenance, no beauty, not even any charm. The bumper-to-bumper slowness of a five-year-old MacBook Pro can be appreciated only in the context of the speed of today's microprocessors. Defunct tech reminds us how far and fast we've come, but without the accompanying sentimentality of, say, a World War II–era Victrola music player and a stack of 78 RPM records, or your mom's Woodstock-era jeans, which you could imagine your daughter wearing at a '60s-themed middle school dance. In contrast to the inherited objects that remind us of who we were and are, the Everglades of entangled cords and add-ons choking up our desk drawers is both ugly and pointless.

In a digital world, what we own is a growing pile of outdated hardware and accessories—and a growing collection of digital media. However, when it comes to those media, in some cases we don't even own what we think we own. According to a story originally run in the Sunday section of the *New York Times*,[105] the actor Bruce Willis was planning to take legal action against Apple. The gist of the article was that Willis had parsed the small print on his iTunes licensing agreement, only to discover that the music, movies, and television shows he'd bought on iTunes still belonged to Apple, which meant that he was legally prohibited from bequeathing his huge music and movie library to his children. It later turned out the story was false,[106] having been floated by someone who wanted to publicize how Apple defined "buying," but that didn't matter. Everybody now knew what was in the small print no one reads.

It's worth repeating: None of us "own" the music or the televisions shows or the movies we "buy" from the Apple iTunes Store, and neither do we "own" the digital books we've "bought" from Amazon or the Barnes & Noble website depicted on our e-readers. Via the terms of these contracts, "buy" means only that we've bought a license for private "use" of the song, book, television show, or movie. We basically buy a license to listen rather than an object. The stuff we buy is supposed to expire when we do.

The internet takes what was once implicit about being human and makes it explicit. In this case, the idea of listening to music and watching television shows and movies under a kind of land-lease arrangement can't help but turn into an existential issue, reminding us that we all have only a short time on earth. So think about it: Most if not all of what we own has no place in the lives of our children and grandchildren. Most of the technology we buy becomes irrelevant six months to a year later. In a digital environment, what happens to memory in general and to our own memories in particular? In short, we subcontract them to the internet and to our smart phones.

GROWING UP BEFORE THE DIGITAL AGE, the two most essential things a child could memorize were his home phone number and his street address. Today, when someone asks me for my cell phone number, it takes me a few moments to stutter it out. It's not that I don't want people to call me. It's more that those ten digits today have to share finite brain storage space with other digital forms of ID, from my home and work emails to my Twitter handle to my Facebook log-in to a dozen other usernames, each one faintly, obnoxiously different from the others.

My and everyone else's memory—both short-term and long-term—have been shredded. A friend of mine calls this phenomenon the "Tsunami-Katrina Problem." When Hurricane Katrina leveled New Orleans in 2005, he told me that along with all the other emotions he was feeling, Katrina

Are you less likely to buy digital files from iTunes and Amazon, knowing that you won't "own" them? #9B reminded him that he had already completely forgotten about the tsunami that leveled Thailand just a year before, and the earthquake in Japan only two weeks before. He is a decent and compassionate man, but for the life of him he couldn't recall the details of those earlier tragedies, which made him feel uncaring, despite being anything but that. The capacity of our brains now is such that we can only really remember the things that are of immediate importance to us.

Remember, if you still can: It hasn't always been like this. As recently as a decade ago, a new movie might have opened nationwide, and good or bad reviews notwithstanding, it would have played in theaters for anywhere from six weeks to three months before moving on and then reappearing on DVD after a long wait engineered by the studio to maximize anticipation. The same kind of longevity was true of a big news story, or a sports victory, or someone who'd made a difference in the world: notable media, events, and people rooted themselves in the long-lasting shade of the collective imagination.

Today, though, a movie opens to an out-breath of over-saturation and in many cases a week to two weeks later has left the cineplex with no more resonance than a soft knock at the door you're unsure you even heard. A news story lands heavily, explodes across media outlets, then atomizes. The death of a great artist, or actor, or writer, or political figure, elicits not much more than a universal "Noted." The news cycle, with its cresting EKG-like spikes of short-lived emotion-ality, feels like a tide, a relentless waterborne current whose knob is now turned permanently to "High." What's more, instead of actually seeing a movie or reading a book, we can easily find others online, including major news outlets, who

Do you think owning a smart phone has made your memory worse?

#9C

will summarize and bullet-point it for us. Our memories have become so scattered and benumbed that today we inevitably recall a link to a piece of information—or the device on which we first read it—rather than the details themselves. Most everything else trickles and sparkles through memory's sieve.

After all, why bother to recall directions to someone's house when Waze or Google Maps can take you there? Why remember the title of a new film or book, or the museum where an exhibit just opened that you wanted to see, when you can just look it up online? Why recall anyone's anniversary or birthday when your calendar can issue a reminder? Why remember your passwords when your phone or laptop will do it for you? Most of us now depend on our computers and smart phones to keep the facts and figures of our lives straight. Even when we have only half-assed pieces of information, or have trouble articulating what we want to say, Google will complete our unfinished sentences for us like some precocious kid with his hand always up in the air. Conduct an online search for "museum with rodins boulevard st. whatever, paris" and in response you'll not only get the name of the museum, you'll also be informed of the unoriginality of your request, as this exact semi-query has clearly been Googled a zillion times before, which reinforces how Google is partly responsible for compromising your memory in the first place. If our computers and smart phones are our ever-evolving links to our memories, the bookmarks we add to our browsers become dog-ears, memory-tags—a to-do list we might someday get around to addressing.

There are downsides to the reliability of the internet's memory, of course. Physical objects are short-lived because they're human—they collapse, lose a wheel, fall apart, get outmoded—but the virtual world is immortal. There is a minibiography of each of us online forever. Nor do any of us have any say or control over what the internet decides to remember. I once heard about a well-known business-world figure who hit and killed someone while driving drunk. Within twenty-four hours, he had hired an internet reputation-control company. The company's tech whizzes used an arsenal of methods and techniques to adjust Google's search rankings so that the story of what the man did ended up buried in Google's sub-depths, the digital equivalent of a rusted spoon resting alongside the *Titanic*. Who among us has the time, patience, or inclination to flip to page thirty of a Google search, or even page two? But they couldn't erase the story permanently. For a searcher committed enough, the information is there.

The problem of an internet that never forgets has found its way into the courts as well. In June 2013, the European Union's top court passed a ruling giving people the right to "request removal of results that turn up in internet searches for their own names."[107] The ruling gives individuals what some began calling "the right to be forgotten." Google even installed a "removals team" to assess individually the roughly 91,000 delisting requests it had received, most of them, according to the *Washington Post*, from French and German citizens.[108] "As of this writing, the new law has affected more than fifty links and web pages on Wikipedia," the *Post* writes.[109] Yahoo and Microsoft's search engines in the European Union plan to follow suit, and the ruling is also prompting other nations, including Canada and Japan, to reconsider what privacy means.

Free speech advocates and legal scholars weren't happy. "This is a form of censorship, one that would most likely be unconstitutional if attempted in the United States,"[110] wrote Jonathan Zittrain, a professor of law and computer science at Harvard University, in a 2014 *New York Times* op-ed. He added that, "In Europe, search engine users will no doubt cultivate the same internet workarounds that Chinese citizens use to see what their government doesn't want them to see."[111] Today, the EU version of Google appends a statement to redacted searches that, "Some results may have been removed under data protection law in Europe."

Elsewhere online, though, our reputations, our lives, anything that has ever been written or thought or speculated about us, now live on indefinitely, even after we die. One of the strangest examples of this I've heard took place when the father of a close female friend of mine died a few years back. At the time of his death, the father and his daughter were playing Scrabble on Facebook. In the days and weeks that followed, Scrabble kept asking my friend to remind her dad it was his turn to play.

Like every other example of authority we've seen in this book, death, too, has become flattened, democratized, lowercased. Twenty years ago, we would have most likely heard about a good friend's death via a phone call. Today we're more likely to learn about the deaths of people we love most via the same channels where we learn about the new Pitbull video or a sighting of the Loch Ness monster.

In 2015, a brief media controversy exploded around a thirty-seven-year-old Connecticut mother of three named Lisa Bonchek Adams, a patient at Memorial Sloan Kettering Hospital in New York who had been tweeting and blogging about her stage 4 breast cancer. Adams was far from the first cancer patient to do this. In 2011, a tech culture journalist, Xeni Jardin, live-blogged her first mammogram, where she discovered she had breast cancer, and in 2013 NPR's Scott Simon live-tweeted his mother's cancer and eventual death, a decision many found distasteful, too personal and just . . . why would he do that?

Writing in the *Guardian* and the *New York Times*, respectively, journalist Emma Gilbey Keller and her husband, Bill Keller, the former executive editor of the *Times*, wrote pieces days apart on the phenomenon of a cancer patient tweeting the day-by-day trials of living with breast cancer. "Are her tweets a grim equivalent of deathbed selfies, one step further than funeral selfies?" Emma Keller wondered aloud. She found the whole thing riveting, but was this a case of Too Much Information?

A few days later, Bill Keller weighed in. His *New York Times* op-ed referenced his father-in-law's relatively peaceful, unheralded cancer death in the United Kingdom, and "the expensive misery of death in America." Both pieces had points to make around issues of medicine and privacy, but despite claiming to be about Lisa Bonchek Adams, a reader couldn't help but be left with the subtext that dying is profound, private, and solitary, whereas social media is trivial, and the two don't belong together. And that the so-called controversy around Adams's profligate tweets had less to do with the issue of public exposure during a miserable period of her life than with the nature and definition of celebrity in the twenty-first century. The unspoken question both Kellers seemed to be asking was: How had an internet blogger, a nonprofessional writer, captured this much media attention? In contrast to most "famous" people, she had done little other than get sick and defy convention by blogging and tweeting about it. Was this really what "fame" was in the early twenty-first century?

A week later—in case we needed additional reminder of the nature of our memories—the story was forgotten, washed out to sea.

Yes, today, in our digital age, Lisa Bonchek Adams and millions of other people have their own platforms and their own tribes of followers, or believers, or parishioners, or rubberneckers, and once-private things such as illness, dying, and death are now public in ways they never have been before. But I'd add that no one seems to be the worse for it.

Grieving online has even sparked a new word, "thanato-sensitivity," to describe websites' and mail servers' engagement with issues surrounding death. Legacy.com is a website that posts online obituaries collated from hundreds of national newspapers. It allows friends and acquaintances who weren't able to physically attend a funeral or memorial service to leave online remarks, memories, or condolences. Unlike a newspaper-based obituary that most of us clip, file away, and forget about, online obituaries are now permanently online.

When a Facebook user dies, a family member or relative must submit proof of that death to Facebook. From that point on only already-confirmed friends are able to access that Facebook page. Facebook also disables the site's birthday reminders as well as other automatic notifications. The dead person's home page immediately turns into a memorial site, where friends can "talk to the dead" for as long as they want to, and family members can delete remarks they find strange or unbecoming.

It's worth reminding ourselves that, at twenty-two years old, the internet is still a young medium. Humans are a young species. No wonder, then, that amid the prevailing climate of newness, innovation, and disruption, we have focused less on endings, or on the death of things, than we have on beginnings. But this lack of attention on death has presented opportunities of which enterprising tech companies have begun to take advantage. Among the weirder ways to ensure we live on via social media is the Facebook app "If I Die," which allows Facebook users to upload a final message onto their wall once they're gone. First, three friends designated by the user as "trustees" have to confirm that the person has in fact died, at which point a message, a series of messages, or even a video shows up on the wall. Users can even pre-compose a series of messages timed to appear at different dates, like ghostly skywriting, such as on their children's birthdays. It's a new variation of social media lastingness, in which users can keep on posting otherworldly remarks for years and even decades after they're gone. "If I Die" currently has around 100,000 subscribers. As the site's cofounder and CEO, Eran Alfonta, put it, "We all have things to say and don't necessarily have the audience with the patience to hear us."[112]

Other websites and apps have stepped in to help survivors understand and take control of life after death. Entrustet, Legacy Locker, and My WebWill enable account holders to pass down their digital data to hand-selected heirs, including passwords, blogs, emails, websites, Tumblrs, LinkedIn accounts, and online financial information.

We live on after death in public ways we wouldn't have before the internet. The Interactive Vietnam Veterans Memorial, for example, is devoted to tales and remembrances of soldiers who served in but didn't survive Vietnam, and there's even a website that lists the names of deceased MySpace members. But no matter who we are, how high we have or haven't climbed, no matter what we have done or not done in our lives, no matter where we live, or how many or how few friends we have, no matter if we have created something, or nothing, or made money, or no money, today we all have a footnote of a legacy that lives on, buried and sub-buried in a stream of numeric code.

OUR DIGITAL SELVES MAY LAST FOREVER, but as the fake Bruce Willis story from earlier reminds us, our digital possessions do not. When it comes to physical objects, too, we inhabit an increasingly rentable culture. Perhaps emulating the timeshares model that took hold in the US in the early seventies, our contemporary "pay-per-use" economy makes me wonder sometimes if the only things we won't lend out to strangers

Would you want your Facebook page to remain up if you died? #9D are our food, booze, and smart phones. Almost everything else is swappable, barter-able, or lease-able—short-term or long-term. Millennials really embrace this "sharing economy," presumably in part because it is about instant gratification. They want things now, and cheaply, too. In an era of fast evolution and obsolescence, why spend money on something they'll have no use for twelve months from now? Thanks to the sharing economy, they don't have to work for years to afford the luxury penthouse—they can just rent it for a day.

The best known of today's rental-economy businesses, Airbnb, allows homeowners and apartment dwellers to lease their spaces to guests. What else can human beings rent? Many other companies have answered with a number of shrewd, strange business ventures: If you own a car, Relay-Rides and Sidecar will help you rent it out to strangers. Via TaskRabbit, you can hire an assistant to shop for groceries, clean your house, do yard-work, and even plan your next vacation. Other markets allow people old-school enough to own a driveway, a rake, or a snow-blower they're not using to make money off them. If you live in an area where crowds congregate for high school graduations, music concerts, football games, or beach access, Parking Panda allows you to rent out the unused last twenty feet of your driveway. Instead of sending your dog to a kennel when you go away, Dogvacay lets you stow your golden retriever with a nearby dog-lover. If you have an unused power washer in your garage, lend it to someone on Simplist, or use Spinlister to lease your old bike to a tourist on vacation. Poshmark allows women to take photographs of their clothes, upload them, and sell them to other women who are looking to spruce up their wardrobes. In 2013, the *New York Times* even profiled Rent-a-Chicken, a service where, for $350, a husband and wife team "will deliver to customers a pair of egg-laying hens, a coop, a supply of food and a water dish for a rental period typically lasting from May through November."[113]

As humans we were always just renting, not buying, anyway. Even when we buy a house and "put down roots," we can always sell that house a month later, making the distinction between permanence and impermanence moot. As the internet increasingly reminds us, the illusion of lastingness was always just that—an illusion.

THE HARVARD-TRAINED NEUROLOGIST Eben Alexander writes in his 2013 bestseller, *Proof of Heaven,* that scientists today believe that human consciousness is made up of digital information similar to what computers use. A single memory, say, of a sunset, or a beautiful piece of music, is in fact quantitatively the same as any other memory, no different from any of the other unnumbered flecks and motes of information our brains compose and then shelve. "Our brains model outside reality by taking the information that comes in through our senses and transforming it into a rich digital tapestry," Alexander writes. "But our perceptions are just a model—not reality itself."

Our memories, in other words, are emotion and meaning infused into more or less neutral neurons. And our neurons are just another example of physical *stuff.*

When my parents are both gone, it won't be any physical objects of theirs I use to remember them. It won't be their slanted handwriting or a stack of record albums or a magazine from 1990 or a vase or a lamp. It will be an automatically curated digital video of the times I spent with them. I care less about physical objects than I do about my photo collections. My idea of heaven is sitting back and watching my Apple TV scroll through pictures of the vacations, places, and people I love, which I and others have snapped over the years.

Recently, I rang up my dad and asked him: What do you want me to remember? In lieu of physical objects, or pure stuff, what do you think is worth holding onto?

My dad, Martin Luther Bough, was born in 1927 in Evanston, a suburb of Chicago best known for Northwestern University and the Women's Christian Temperance Union. His childhood is family legend. His parents didn't have much of an education. His older brother, Powell, was considered the smart one of the two, and expectations were lower for my father. Dad was given his first saxophone—"a gold-plated alto sax, a Buescher," he remembers—by his grandfather, who worked as a butler for a wealthy businessman who lived on the shores of Lake Michigan and had been storing the sax in his attic. Dad went onto become a jazz musician, a photographer, and a college professor.

At eighty-six, my dad is willowy, slender, with an elegant face, long-boned with freckles and age marks on both cheeks, and a strip of white hair that sits on top of his head like a crown he's pushed up and away from his eyes. He still moves like an adolescent, all bones and sinews. No one who meets him doesn't comment on his stylish-looking glasses, two brown steely protruding rectangles that make him look like a captain of bebop, though in fact they're specially designed to magnify his eyesight.

My mom got my name, Brant Bonin Bough, from a tree, a bird, and an archipelago of islands off Japan. "I wanted to have a kid," my dad says, "especially a boy." The only time he remembers doing anything with his own father was one afternoon when the two of them went to the circus. "The whole time, he didn't say anything to me. Not even 'Do you want some popcorn, Martin?' There was no connection between us, no interaction whatsoever. So when you were born, Bonin, all that weighed on me because I knew I wasn't going to do it that way. It was important for me to have a boy because I felt no one had understood me when I was younger. I wanted the chance to do it over again, but this time give a boy what he needs."

One of the first things he did when I was born was go out and buy a sling and a baby backpack. "That way, you could be close to me at all times. Whatever I did, and wherever I was going, I did my best to take you along with me, so that you and I could be together." My dad falls momentarily silent. "So I hope that you have all of those things to remember."

He's not done. "You remember the time you and I went to Chicago, Bonin? I remember saying to you, 'Let's go see my mother's grave out in Skokie.' I found the stone—it was so small. Her name was spelled wrong, too. The graveyard was spooky, and we got out of there fast. But it's when I look at photographs of her that I remember her. Mostly good things, too."

"I wish I'd known your mother," I said. My grandmother died in 1977.

"It's like after a hurricane, Bonin, when people have lost everything, and they burrow through the mess to find their photographs. Everything around them might be destroyed, but people still dig through the mess and the mud to find their photos. Photos, Bonin, are an extension of your memory, of your mind. The body will always fall apart—it's just like an old car that goes to the junkyard. But a photograph is an incredibly valuable thing."

In my twenties, my dad began giving me boxes of old photos. On the phone, he tells me, "Bonin, you're busy all the time. I wish I could spend more time with you. But the photographs I gave you will bring back the times that are valuable to both you and me. Those times are gone. So anything that brings back to your mind the good times we had is important. I always taught my photography students that they should use their cameras as a means of communication, that once they figure out the technical stuff, they need to marry those cameras to their hearts."

Then, because he's my dad, he embarrasses me. He was once at a newspaper kiosk in his neighborhood, he tells me, when he spied a headline article about me in *Fast Company*. "I told the newsman and he shouted out, 'This is the guy's father. You're Bonin's father!' Someone else came up to me and said, 'You can now die a happy man.' Another person came up to me and said, 'I want to shake your hand because you clearly did a magnificent job.'"

"Dad, let's move on," I said.

"No! In the black community, where the issue of fathers being around for their kids is so important, I am so incredibly proud. I'm proud of myself and I'm proud of you. Proud, too, that I had a chance to redo what I felt I missed out on a kid. And prouder still watching you go forward with all the love and support coming from me and your mother."

The digitization of memory feels as strange as it does because it's new, but I consider it to be a profound act and habit of remembering, a reinvention of the memory work that, in the past, we have done through print photography. One reason I love Instagram is because it encourages an entire generation to capture themselves in the moment, to document a thousand instants of their daily lives. Not only Instagram, but every Facebook timeline entry, every Foursquare check-in, every tweet, and every online scratch help us assemble a fabric of faces and places and words that in new ways tell the story of who we were and are. From now on, parents and kids coming of age today no longer have to rely on their own memories to evoke a person, or a time, or even themselves. Instead, they can relive them as often as they want.

One of these days I'll hire someone to digitize my dad's entire photo collection. That way I can display individual pictures on rotating digital frames all around my apartment.

My fantasy is that I'll be walking past ever-evolving frames, beautifully surprised by the sight of a person or a life experience or a younger version of myself I'd forgotten about, and then I'll remember.

What about the old, undigitized photos themselves, the ones overstuffing our shelves, attics, basements, and storage units? What about the love letters, the ribbons we got at camp for good citizenship, the diplomas handed to us in high school or in college, the bits and pieces of our lives that sit around today in boxes, plastic Staples tubs, or storage units along the sides of country roads?

Physical objects have soul, and maybe a mystery even greater than that, but in most cases we've been assassinating that soul. When do we take out old photos from their places in the shadows? How often do we read old love letters? Once a year? Twice a year? Ever? No, our oldest, most loved, most precious stuff tends to live in the dark—under mattresses, in drawers, in the boot-laden backs of closets. It's unseen, disregarded, and disrespected. It's already dead. If someone wanted to find a photo of my mom, Monica, I'd rather bring up that photo from the internet for them in ten seconds than spend half the morning searching for it in some damp dark cubicle.

If you want your things to live on forever, if you want to establish a thread that will connect you to your children, and their children, then put them online. For his seventy-sixth birthday, my dad and I flew to Chicago. It was the first time he had been back home in thirty years. Outside Evanston we paid a visit to his cousin, who at some point brought out a family photo album containing shots of my father and his brother. A second album held other photos dating back to his great-great-great-grandmother. Two albums' worth—that was all he had. Imagine, I kept thinking, if Facebook had existed back then.

What will I pass down to my own children someday? It won't be a drawer full of defunct cell phones, or a tangle of wandering wires. Instead I'll give them what my father and mother gave me. When the time comes, I will buy a sling and a baby backpack. I will teach that boy or that girl how to rewire a plug, replace a broken lock, see life through a photographer's eyes. I will teach them accounting and graphic design and math. I will hum or sing the old Lester Young tune, "DB Blues," my dad's favorite song. Those are the legacies that matter. With the exception of the old, folded-up table in one corner of my apartment, I don't have much from when I was growing up. I don't keep a storage unit. But when I look back on my childhood, it isn't the objects I remember anyway, it's the memories they evoke.

The tradition of physical objects and inheritance may be gone forever. It's at least at risk. Technology has permanently transformed our relationship to objects and to space. And I wouldn't trade what we've gained.

In 2012 my dad and I took a trip to Mayan ruins in Mexico to celebrate his eighty-fifth birthday. At some point we pulled out the video camera, and I spoke to him directly. "Dad, you did good," I said. "First things first: You chose my mom. Second thing is you've had a profound impact on my life. You've taken the job of father so seriously, and been positive and supportive to allow me to blossom and grow." He would never really die, I said. "You are in me. You will always be in me."

It was my dad's turn. He looked straight into the camera, too. He said he hoped he'd instilled in me, his son, a strong sense of right and wrong, and that he knew he had raised a son who wasn't covetous, or hateful, a man who reached out

Are your most valued possessions physical or digital? If your house were on fire (and your loved ones were already safe), what one thing would you save? #9E to other people. "I think I have left my son a legacy of love," my dad said. "I feel like I've done the right thing and that he's on the right track, and that when I die, I can die happy."

When that time comes, and I hope it's not for a long time, believe me when I say I'll watch that video over and over again. Have physical things ever mattered, or has it always been the memories they evoke that make us feel good? By loosening our tight grip on objects and putting as many of them as we can online, we might be sacrificing their souls, but in return we're giving them back their life. When a webpage refreshes, isn't the nearest analogy the intake and outtake of breath? More than any pocket watch, record album, or drafting table, I'd rather be able to access a thousand family photographs, or watch a movie of my dad relaxing and chatting, the cuffs of his pants rolled up, his feet soaking in the Gulf of Mexico surf.

10

the world linked in

THE PRIVILEGE OF OUR LIVES IN THE WEST risks hobbling our future innovation. Anyone who has ever spent time overseas, especially in a developing country, generally comes back home humbled by the relative luxury of our day-to-day concerns. In the West, we choose between the retina display and the regular iPad; the 13-inch and the 15-inch; Pandora and Spotify; Skype and Facetime; Candy Crush and NFL Quarterback15; Hightail and WeTransfer; the Kindle and the Nook; the iPhone and the Android; Waze and Mapquest; Map My Ride and BikeBrain: our choices are infinite. We welcome Uber and Lyft as disruptive options to hailing a cab, when in many parts of the world people lack transportation entirely. We complain about logy Wi-Fi connections, when many don't have access to the internet at all. We forget that, across India, Brazil, and Africa where the infrastructure is crippled and overburdened, a simple technological fix that seems unsophisticated or makeshift to the Western eye has the power not only to make peoples' lives better but to give them life, period.

In places like these, innovation, driven by occasionally enormous urgency, flows naturally toward the most pressing social needs, whether it's access to education or healthcare for pregnant women. In Africa, an app was created that gives farmers a way to access the market prices for their commodities. In Russia, government repression and surveillance were behind the recent launch of what is possibly the most secure text-messaging app ever developed.

Earlier, I mentioned that a big part of my job involves traveling overseas. As my company's chief media and e-commerce officer, I'm in other countries at least one, sometimes two weeks a month, and occasionally for even longer stretches than that. In spite of juggling multiple time zones, by far the best part of visiting and working abroad is the opportunity I get to observe firsthand what's happening in both the digital and mobile spheres. Which is never *not* surprising, never what I thought or assumed beforehand. Often it's inspiring and even electrifying. Especially in countries less developed than ours, there is always something to learn and bring back home.

I SPENT A PORTION OF LAST YEAR working out of our offices in Shanghai. Every morning out my window, Chinese boys and girls practiced tai chi in sun-speckled schoolyards. Afterward, they filed back indoors to study math and engineering. Knowing that the future of the global economy is data and technology, the Chinese government is fiercely preparing its citizens to participate within it. One night during my stay there, a local girl picked up my iPhone and tweaked my settings so that she and Siri could converse in Chinese. Another Chinese friend told me that one day he saw and heard his four-year-old daughter banging away at the family's baby grand piano. She had downloaded an app that instructed her what piano keys to play, and in what sequence, too.

There are roughly 600 million internet users in China out of an overall population of 1.2 billion people. That's 44 percent of the overall Chinese population, giving China more internet users than any other nation on earth. Around 80 percent of Chinese users access the web from their mobile devices, compared to 63 percent of American users. The Chinese actively communicate on the web, too, with more than three-quarters regularly contributing online content, compared to only a quarter of all Americans.[114]

These are intriguing statistics in light of Chinese internet censorship. Authorities and internet regulators there blockade and monitor websites we take for granted in the US, including Facebook, Twitter, and YouTube, and replace them with heavily edited Chinese versions that exist alongside home-grown sites that have no American equivalent, including 9158.com and yy.com, where Asian users "can sing for or with other people."[115] Few experiences are stranger to me when I arrive in Beijing than typing in "YouTube," and waiting as nothing pops up. The Chinese government also tracks individual usage. Still, given the sameness of much of Chinese TV programming, for many Chinese people the internet is an informative, entertaining way to explore national events and goings-on, and to watch American-made TV shows. Twenty-four hours after *The Walking Dead* airs in the US, you can find it on the Chinese internet if you know where to look.

Mobile phone ubiquity in China can be traced to any number of local phenomena. More so even than Americans, Chinese citizens relocate long distances from family and friends, and email and texting enable them to maintain far-away ties. In underpopulated rural areas, where few options exist to meet other people for either friendship or romance,

Does your mobile phone make you feel more connected? Too connected? #10A the internet holds the possibility of company, sociability, and more. There's also China's one-child policy. For children with no siblings, the internet serves as close friend, game console, time-waster, news source, and babysitter.

From the standpoint of innovation, no discussion of China would be complete without taking note of the country's lax intellectual property (IP) laws, which create a landscape of technological innovation and competition at a scale most Westerners can't imagine. China may be technologically lawless, but that's why it's so exhilarating. IP copyright violations take place regularly, especially in the automotive and technology sectors, with companies engaged in an ongoing battle to outmaneuver and outflank one another. In the US, large companies typically buy smaller ones, while also buying up rival patents, meaning that these parent companies are able to dictate and determine the speed of all innovation across their industries, and so innovation moves more slowly than it otherwise could. Moral and criminal considerations aside, the Wild West landscape of China ignites and drives a speed and intensity of innovation I've seen nowhere else in the world.

In the West, instead of welcoming the latest technological disruptions, we are more likely to legislate against them. Uber is one of the most revolutionary start-ups of recent memory, but in New York City and other cities across the world, it faces legal cases from traditional taxi owners and city councils.

Still, no legislation can stop an American business like TechShop, a chain of member-based workshops that describes itself as "Part fabrication and prototyping studio, part hackerspace and part learning center." TechShop members, who pay a yearly fee, are given unlimited use of laser cutters, plastics and electronics labs, a machine shop, a wood shop, a metal working shop, a textiles department, welding stations, and a water-jet cutter. They also have open access to design software, huge project areas, and large worktables. Square, the mobile payments company, was born in a TechShop. Why there and not somewhere else? Jim McKelvey, who along with Jack Dorsey founded Square, couldn't convince any venture capitalists to write him a check until the company produced a physical prototype. After building three of them at TechShop, McKelvey raised 10 million dollars, and today Square is worth a billion dollars.

In terms of social policy, in contrast to the US, China is a "closed" society. But considering that most of Asia engages with and encourages new technology, which society seems more closed and forbidding? Square's success speaks to the general lethargy and entrenched thinking of the Western business world, and the failure of the financial industry in particular. Why didn't Visa, Mastercard, or American Express see Square coming? Where was their willingness to experiment? "I have a mantra," said TechShop CEO Mark Hatch when he and I spoke. "Make something and then launch your product, it doesn't matter where—China, South Africa. Get feedback from customers, incorporate it, and keep rolling. Be an early adopter." It's good advice.

As I mentioned in the chapter on parenting, China is also home to WeChat, the world's biggest, most state-of-the-art mobile text-messaging app, today owned by China media conglomerate Tencent. Launched in 2011, the app has already reshaped Asian industries including video-calling, taxi booking, and video game distribution. Via WeChat, you can not only track down the nearest McDonalds but also use it to buy your meal and send tea gift certificates to your friends. If you're visiting Club Med, WeChat will book your plane tickets on China Southern Airlines, and help you check in or change your seat assignment. Once you arrive, WeChat provides maps, a Club Med staff roster, and a list of local beaches and museums. No Western-made text-messaging app service comes even close.

It hasn't yet happened, but I believe we'll soon see an "Asia-out" phenomenon—the full-scale migration of Asian technology to the rest of the world. In 2014, the giant Chinese e-commerce company Alibaba, described by one analyst as Amazon, eBay, and PayPal rolled into one, announced its plans for an American IPO, which, the *New York Times* pointed out, was expected to be "the biggest American IPO since Facebook's $16 billion offering in May 2012," adding, "Last year, the value of all merchandise sold on Alibaba exceeded $248 billion, more than the volume on eBay and Amazon combined [with] nearly 20 percent of those purchases . . . made through mobile phones in the last three months of last year."[116]

Perhaps someday China will also import its emphasis on gender equality, one reason why it is such an innovative force in technology. When it comes to education, China treats its boys and girls the same. Contrast this to the subtle gender socialization within US elementary and high schools. Early on, girls in the US get the message that an interest in math, science, or technology is at odds with femininity. A former high school girlfriend of mine found herself the only woman in her engineering class at Tulane. When I used to visit my best friend Peter Caputo at Carnegie Mellon, there were more robots than there were women on campus. In New York City I've met more women from Asia working in technology than I have American women in the same industry.

China is moving faster than the US because it has to, and it wants to. Is there a lesson there?

ANOTHER NATION THAT IS MOVING QUICKLY because it has no alternative is India. We hear about Indian entrepreneurs in America all the time—four out of the thirteen members of Google's current management team are of Indian heritage, for starters—so what's the state of mobile and digital across India itself?

As far as internet adoption is concerned, India is still in its early stages, with slow-moving, unreliable Wi-Fi across most major cities. Only 16 percent of India's overall population of 1.2 billion people has access, but that's still 243 million people, or around ten times the population of Australia. This figure also means that India has now officially surpassed the US as the world's largest internet base, with China coming in third. India also offers some of the least expensive handsets and data plans in the world. Of the 900 million telecom subscriptions in India, around 97 percent are mobile connections. Close to 600 million Indians use mobile phones, with usage divided equally across rural districts and urban centers. Most users are male, with the highest penetration in the nineteen- to twenty-four-year-old age group.[117]

"One of the first things you notice in India is the huge generational divide based on mobility," notes Alex Johnston, a partner at Fleming Media. "In a traditional Indian family in a large metropolis, you might have three generations living in the same house. What separates the seventeen-year-old from the twenty-two-year-old from the twenty-eight-year-old are their phones. Dad might have an old black Nokia and he's fine with that—but the youngest son may have the latest smart phone and as a result, an access to the world his own father will never have."

> "One of the first things you notice in India is the huge generational divide based on mobility. Dad might have an old black Nokia and he's fine with that—but the youngest son may have the latest smart phone and as a result, an access to the world his own father will never have."
>
> *Partner at Fleming Media*
> *Alex Johnston*

Indians use the internet primarily for email, though the country's eighty-two million Facebook users make it the site's second-largest market. Indian developers are busy creating apps, features, and businesses for the first and ultimately only media device many Indians will have or hold: the mobile phone. My friend, Mumbai-based entrepreneur Mahesh Murphy, agrees that internet growth in his country will happen on the mobile phone and not the desktop, "and in languages other than English."

Innovation in India has always fascinated me. India's president has dubbed the next ten years the "Decade of Innovation," but notwithstanding the country's explosive economic growth, R&D expenditure amounts to less than 1 percent of the country's GDP.[118] That statistic is key to what is so amazing about India, a movement known as "frugal innovation," or *jugaad*, as it's known in Hindi: innovation that's born of scarcity and a lack of capital. Frugal innovation transforms material, financial, geographical, and institutional limitations into advantages. In India, as in parts of Brazil, where citizens and entrepreneurs have to make do with outdated technology, locals have developed the mind-set of making things work on a grassroots level, or, as the Brazilian saying goes, "changing the tires while driving."

India, for example, is the birthplace of the Tatu Nano, which at $2,500 is the world's least expensive family car. How did someone even get the idea of making it? Necessity. Many Indians can't afford high-priced vehicles. Why are mobile phones and data plans in India so cheap? Because incomes are much lower there than they are in the West. In India someone has connected a diesel engine to a cart to make a truck, motorbikes power crop sprayers, wind drives irrigation systems, and one entrepreneur created a refrigerator out of clay that keeps working during the nation's frequent power outages. In India, "It's not just about making things cheaper, but better, more appropriate, and scalable," wrote researchers Kirsten Bound and Ian Thornton in one study by UK innovation foundation Nesta. "It involves leveraging available resources in new ways, reducing or re-using waste, or even re-thinking an entire system around a product or service."[119]

Thanks to its density, India also has complex logistical issues that have impacted the course of innovation. E-commerce has bypassed the country entirely. There is no organized modern retail—no Target, no Marks & Spencer, no Barnes & Noble. "Typical Indian shoppers don't want to buy at a big-box store," says Alex Johnston. "They want to go down the street to a store they know, and haggle for a bargain." Johnston foresees a future explosion in India not of e-commerce (it's too late for that), but of mobile commerce. India, he notes, is not a credit card culture. There are cows on the roads. Most parts of the country are shockingly poor. The population is mostly unbanked, and people don't trust one another. Flipcart, the closest thing to an Amazon.com that exists in India, is a company where consumers pay for the goods they've ordered only when the object they've ordered shows up at their door and has not only been opened up in front of them but also has passed muster.

From India the rest of the world can learn that there are better and more cost-effective ways to use the materials and processes we already have.

MOVING ACROSS THE PACIFIC TO BRAZIL, the world's sixth-largest economy, we find a byzantine nation for any media to penetrate. With a landmass larger than India, Australia, or the contiguous US, Brazil is home to 200 million people, a huge, dissociated sprawl of races, cultures, and ethnicities spread across 3.3 million square miles and twenty-six states, split into five regions. The country divides itself further into five distinct, economically based classes ranging from A to E, each with its own unofficial music, tastes, foods, and levels of products and goods. This means that, thanks to its size and diversity, while citizens may be evolving toward digitally-based media in one region of Brazil, elsewhere others are only beginning to digest print media.

Of the five classes that make up Brazilian society, as of January 2015 the middle class represented over 70 percent of all households, and controls 60 percent of all consumption and e-commerce sales.[120] Class A, the highest class, buys the biggest number of mobile devices, but the middle class is rising quickly, with more than a third owning smart phones.[121] In a nation where class is defined by financial means, poorer Brazilians would sooner spend their money on status symbols like high-tech gadgets than on basic goods and services. "We have many more cell phones in Brazil than there are people, meaning that some people have more than one," reports my Brazilian colleague Natacha Volpini, adding that the biggest barriers to mobile penetration are the high prices of electronics—a new iPhone can cost over US$1,000, while an iPad is a relative bargain at $950—and an archaic mobile infrastructure that hasn't kept pace with consumer adaptation. (The World Economic Forum ranks Brazil 107th among 144 countries in infrastructure, which puts the country well behind its BRIC peers.)

That said, Brazil's is a mostly urban, youthful population, with an average age of around thirty, compared to thirty-seven in the US and forty in the UK. Brazil is ranked fourth in mobile connections globally, and consumers of all classes embrace social networking. Nearly eight out of ten Brazilians on the internet use social networks, a figure expected to jump to nine in ten by 2017.[122] The nation has around 90 million Facebook users[123] and is also home to Google's Orkut; while Facebook has unseated Orkut as Brazil's largest social network, Orkut still has millions of users. As of January 2014, Brazil also had the third-largest Twitter user base in the world.

Well-known retailers and services are entering the Brazilian market, too. Yelp and eBay recently made their local debuts, Amazon recently launched a Brazilian Kindle store, and Spotify has Brazil in its sights also. There's some exciting innovation, as well. In 2013, Fiat Brazil added a feature to its Punto cars allowing drivers to hear text-to-speech updates from their closest friends while driving; Budweiser Brazil released the Buddy Cup, a tech-enabled beer glass that allows two beer drinkers to become Facebook friends simply by clinking their mugs together; and Brazilian clothier C&A features "likable" hangers that track in real time the number of Facebook likes "earned" by a shirt or pair of pants. Not least, thanks to governmental corruption and an omnipresent danger of street robbery, especially in large cities like Rio de Janeiro and São Paulo, Brazil is today an incubator for highly sophisticated security protection and tracking and facial recognition software. The reasons why may not be pleasant, but the results are cutting-edge and world-class.

ALONE AMONG THE SEVEN CONTINENTS ACROSS THE GLOBE, Africa is generally considered to be a "mobile-first" and even "mobile-only" culture, for the simple reason that it has no other option. Africa's poor infrastructure—1.5 billion Africans lack access even to basic electricity—means that mobile phones are neither a luxury nor a convenience, but a practical, essential tool. On a continent that features nine out of the ten highest total fertility rates, the world's lowest life expectancies, and the highest rates of HIV and AIDS,[124] mobile phones are making crucial differences in people's lives, socially and professionally.

In your life, do you think of smartphones as a luxury, a convenience, or an essential tool? #10B

In 2014 I sat on a panel at the Milken Conference in Los Angeles, where I met Akon, the songwriter and hip-hop artist. Born in St. Louis, Missouri, Akon's early childhood was split between the US and Senegal until his family returned permanently to the US when he was seven. A superstar in America, Akon is by far the most popular singer in Africa and has also sold more ringtones than any artist in history. Akon told me that the lack of access to electricity in many rural areas and even in urban centers is a huge obstacle to the growth and sustainability of Africa's government and economy. To that end, in early 2014 he launched the "Lighting Africa Project," with the goal of using mobile phone infrastructure to bring electricity to a million African households.

During our conversation Akon told me that mobile phones in Africa are poised to generate entirely new industries. For example, if you send a letter from the post office in most African countries, most likely it will never get there, given the absence of infrastructure and in some cases even roads. But thanks to the GPS feature in SIM cards, which can be embedded in, say, the solar panels of roofs, and which don't require an internet connection, postal service drivers can now determine the precise coordinates where packages are supposed to go.

Recently, two English journalists affiliated with a major UK newspaper conglomerate exported the idea of citizen journalism to Africa. They brought a mobile phone into a tiny village and gave it to the most responsible woman there. "This is the emergency phone," they told her. "When something good or bad happens, we want you to call us with the story." A single mobile phone has the ability to unlock the flow of information from a whole town.

Understand that Africa's fifty-four independent countries boast an overall population of more than a billion people, which is expected to grow to 2.3 billion people by 2050.[125]

Hundreds of millions of Africans will come of age without ever owning a landline, a desktop computer, a laptop, or a tablet. Most will access the internet for the first time on a two-and-a-half-inch mobile phone screen. This is why, in part, it has taken only a decade for Africa to become the second-most connected region of the world in terms of mobile subscriptions, trailing only behind Asia-Pacific. By 2015, led by Nigeria, Egypt, and South Africa, Africa will be able to claim one billion mobile subscriptions. As the *Guardian* has noted, "Africa's claim to be the 'mobile continent' is even stronger than previously thought, with researchers predicting internet use on mobile phones will increase 20-fold in the next five years—double the rate of growth in the rest of the world."[126]

Understand, too, that across sub-Saharan Africa, only one out of five adults has a bank account, and fewer still qualify for credit. Even if that weren't the case, around 60 percent of African's population lives in remote rural locations where the nearest bank branch is miles away. Which is why the mobile phone service M-Pesa—*Pesa* is Swahili for "money"—has had such a transformative effect on African life, culture, and economies. Launched in 2007 with the humble goal of helping beneficiaries of microfinance payments repay their loans, M-Pesa has evolved into a service handling all varieties of banking transactions, allowing anyone with a national ID card or a passport to deposit, withdraw, and transfer funds across the continent. Using SMS technology, Africans can pay bills, buy goods and services, redeem deposits for cash, transfer money, and purchase airtime. With 18 million users in Kenya alone, M-Pesa is considered to the most successful mobile phone financial service in the developing world and a model for other countries. Today M-Pesa handles $20

If the first time you accessed the internet was via mobile phone, what would you do first? #10C million a day in transactions, with the mobile money industry in Africa projected to become a $617 billion industry by 2016. According to a survey by the Gates Foundation and the World Bank, more than half of all adults in Kenya, Sudan, and Gabon use mobile money.[127]

M-Pesa has been extraordinarily influential across all industries and walks of life in ways that may not be immediately obvious. Across Africa, small farmers make up 65 percent of the workforce. Thanks to M-Pesa, and mobile phone apps like MFarm, farmers can access crucial weather information, check daily market prices for the commodities they're selling, buy goods directly from manufacturers, and connect with potential buyers without a middleman. For farmers, there's even a mobile app, iCow, self-dubbed "the world's first mobile phone cow calendar," which helps farmers oversee their cows' gestation periods, while providing breeding and nutritional tips. Elsewhere, using M-Pesa, parents can pay their children's school fees, and families can budget and stockpile funds. Not least, by linking younger consumers who live far away from urban centers to the goods sold there, M-Pesa is helping to transform Africa's retail industry.

In a 2013 TED Talk, South African journalist Toby Shapshak gestured to a map of the world. Africa was in shadow, while the rest of the world flickered with light. "It's easy to see where innovation is going on," Shapshak said, before giving the answer: "In all the places with lots of electricity it *isn't*, and the reason it isn't is that everybody is watching television and playing Angry Birds." In Africa, he said, innovation is born from the desire to solve vital social, environmental, educational, and healthcare problems. One African entrepreneur has created

> "It's easy to see where innovation is going on: in all the places with lots of electricity it isn't."
>
> *South African journalist Toby Shapshak*

a platform that helps parents find missing children, while another launched an app that reroutes motorists from Nairobi's clogged roads and highways. Settlement camps across the continent have created databases where refugees can document their personal details and track down friends and family members with whom they have lost touch. Frugal innovation has also driven the creation of online education in Kenya and a mobile job-matching app in Ghana.

Mobile technology across Africa is even helping save lives. The infant mortality rates in some African countries are among the highest in the world—in South Africa alone, 75,000 children die before their fifth birthday—but a SMS card can connect pregnant African mothers with midwives and physicians and give a disadvantaged rural population data about pregnancy, nutrition, and childcare. Mimba Bora, for example, is a mobile phone app targeted at pregnant women in rural areas who would otherwise lack any information about pregnancy and childbirth. Once a pregnant woman downloads the app, she is connected to the nearest local clinic. Throughout her pregnancy, she gets pregnancy tips and information about Lamaze classes, counseling, nursing, and legal services. Another app, MedAfrica, gives users basic data and counsel about health and medicine. Then there is mPedigree, whose goal is to safeguard consumers against the dangers of counterfeit drugs, including antimalarial vaccines, which is a huge ongoing problem in Africa. Users input a serial number from a prescription bottle and are alerted via text message whether the medicine is authentic.

According to Stephen Ozoigbo, the CEO of the African Technology Foundation, a Silicon Valley–based organization dedicated to globalizing African technologies, African tech

What do you think drives more innovation: necessity, or access to resources? #10D innovation has also benefited and empowered women. Across Africa, as is true around the globe, women juggle simultaneous roles as mothers, household heads, bill-payers, and small-business owners. The independence and time-savings created by mobile banking allows them to focus more on their entrepreneurial ventures.

Entertainment is also huge across Africa, with mobile phones allowing Africans to tweet, vote for contestants on reality shows, download songs and ringtones, and share videos and audio. As a result of Africa's status as largely mobile-only, media companies and brands such as Coca-Cola are directly targeting phone users, and one app, AfriNolly, even delivers African movies directly onto users' phones.[128]

Finally, there is Ushahidi, Swahili for "testimony," an internet mapping tool created in Kenya in the wake of that country's disputed 2008 presidential elections. Ushahidi allows people to anonymously report acts of violence, rioting, and criminality, which are then plotted on a map. During the 2010 earthquake in Haiti, the country was able to use Ushahidi to field thousands of reports of trapped victims, the huge majority of which originated on mobile phones via an emergency texting number advertised on national radio. Outside Boston, the local Haitian American diaspora translated the messages, and volunteers sent text messages to the US Coast Guard based in Haiti, telling them where to search. Since then, Ushahidi has been deployed in the Democratic Republic of Congo and in Gaza to monitor violence, and worldwide to help gather reports about the recent swine flu outbreak. As the *New York Times* commented, "Ushahidi suggests a new paradigm in humanitarian work. The old paradigm was one-to-many: foreign journalists and aid workers jet in, report on a calamity, and dispense aid with whatever data they have. The new paradigm is many-to-many-to-many: victims supply on-the-ground data; a self-organizing mob of global volunteers translates text messages and helps to orchestrate relief; journalists and aid workers use the data to target the response."[129]

SO WHAT HAVE WE SEEN SO FAR? That thanks to government deregulation, China is making huge gains on the US. Hardship born of necessity is responsible for creating flashes of innovation across India, Brazil, and Africa. In Russia, however, it is geographic distance, loneliness, and a lack of access to conventional media that have driven the creation of something pioneering, in the form of that country's biggest social network.

As the world's largest nation, whose almost six thousand square miles border countries ranging from Norway to Poland to China, the former Soviet Union is also geographically decentralized, and divided into numerous republics, provinces, territories, and districts. In a country this fragmented, the idea of "belonging" to a social media site—or to anything—takes on a bigger meaning. Russia's natives are by far the most active and engaged social network users in the world. They spend more time on social media sites than any other country, but with a few fascinating local differences. Websites popular across the world, including Google and Facebook, are also-rans in Russia. The top Russian search engine, with a roughly 60 percent market share,[130] is Yandex, and Russia has its own version of Mark Zuckerberg in the guise of entrepreneur Pavel Durov. Born in 1986 in St. Petersberg, he founded Russia's leading social network site, VKontakte.com, or VK, in 2007. Today, VKontakte, which means "in touch," has around 110 million users, compared to Facebook's 10 million or so, and after Yandex is the second-most visited website in Russia.[131]

In large Russian cities mobile phone usage is up to 30 percent, but in less populated regions, it can drop to as low as 13 percent.[132] As is true in many other developing nations, cheaper "feature phones" are more prevalent than smart phones. But recently, according to Alexander Kryglov, the head of client services at VK, the social media site recently celebrated an important milestone: nearly 50 percent of its users accessed the site from a mobile device.

Upon its launch, VK had a number of advantages in its favor. First, VK had the home-court advantage at a time when Facebook was unclear about its plans for Russia, and lacked even a Russian interface. Second, Kryglov told me, few Russians have international connections, or have traveled widely if at all outside their own country. They didn't need a global platform.

Still, the biggest reason why VK is the top social network in many Eastern European countries comes down to two distinguishing features. The first thing you or I would likely notice about VK is how much it resembles Facebook in both design and layout. Like Facebook, it offers users private messaging, status updates, and photo sharing as well. But VK also serves as a dating and matchmaking site. Users can customize their searches for women or men who match their criteria. Second, VK makes an enormous catalog of high-definition, illegally acquired music and movies available for easy download or streaming. Russia is several years behind Europe and the United States as far as the legal regulation of content consumption is concerned; piracy is epidemic and unchecked, in large part because media is unavailable in any other way.

Privacy, and the fear of censorship, is also a longstanding and ongoing issue in Russia. In 2014, President Putin signed a law requiring all internet operators to store their user data in centers within Russia by the year 2016. Companies that refuse to comply, he announced, would simply be removed from the web. This means that since data will be stored on Russian servers, "it will be subjected to Russian laws, putting it at risk for censorship."[133] Other legislation passed by Putin requires blogs with a reader base of over 3,000 daily views to register officially as "media," thus subjecting them to monitoring. It's little wonder that, in response to possible online government surveillance, VK's Durov founded a text-messaging app, Telegram, largely "to build a means of communication that can't be accessed by the Russian security agencies," as he later told TechCrunch.[134] Telegram's "Secret Chat" feature offers users end-to-end encryptions and leaves no evidence on company servers. Like Snapchat, Telegram users can activate self-destruct timers on messages, ranging from two seconds to one week. Today, it's the top free app in forty-six countries. Even in the US, Telegram is the most popular app in social networking categories, ahead of Facebook, WhatsApp, Kik, and others.[135]

In the wake of the recent political conflicts in Ukraine, Durov made headlines in 2013 by publicly refusing to hand over information about Ukrainian protesters to Russian security agencies, and he also declined to block the VK page dedicated to the anticorruption foe and outspoken Putin-critic Alexey Navalny, who in 2011 famously denounced Russia's ruling party as "a party of crooks and thieves." Instead, Durov posted the government's orders on his VK home page.

His brave decision had consequences. In April 2014, Durov was dismissed as the company CEO. A longtime proponent of freedom of expression, Durov later made it clear that his company had been effectively colonized by the Russian government. He has since left Russia, publicly stating he has no plans to return, adding, "Unfortunately, the country is incompatible with internet business at the moment."

IT'S HARD TO IMAGINE SILICON VALLEY PRODUCING many of the innovations that I've described above. We wouldn't want to emulate the environments or conditions that drove these innovations, but we can build, have built, and no doubt will continue building on the technologies engendered by that those needs. Chinese mobile phones, for example, have had fingerprint sensors for many years. During last year's Apple convention, Tim Cook rolled out a feature in the new iOS8 to make credit card payments on a mobile phone, which is, of course, very old news for Africa.

What I see in looking at innovation across the globe is the way that our privilege can get in our way. It doesn't prevent innovation, of course, but it can blind us to ideas and technologies that take into account the fundamental needs of those across the world less fortunate than we are. As I mentioned earlier, many concepts hatched overseas aren't about improving a cumbrous old way of doing things. They're about creating a way of doing things in the first place. Need drives risk, intensity, and speed, and unless we look to other countries for inspiration, and stop legislating against the future in our own nation, we are at serious risk of falling behind. The Roman Republic was only the Roman Republic, after all, until one day it wasn't.

Have you ever made a credit card payment using your mobile phone? #10E

conclusion

I N AN ARTICLE ENTITLED "The Death of Adulthood in American Culture" for the *New York Times* in 2014, critic A.O. Scott
concluded that unlike in any other era in recent memory,
contemporary adults and children are intertwined as never
before, thanks, in part, to a cultural breakdown of authority.
Focusing on television shows like *Mad Men*, *The Sopranos*, and
Breaking Bad, and the popularity of figures from Huck Finn
to Louis C.K. and Lena Dunham, Scott wonders whether
this cultural flattening has done away with the notion of a
"grown-up." "A crisis of authority is not for the faint of heart,"
Scott writes. "It can be scary and weird and ambiguous. But it
can be a lot of fun, too."[136] He never used the word "technology," but he just as easily might have been writing about it.

　　*Digital is 100 percent good, and for that reason, everything that
came before it isn't*, I've heard people say, or *Digital disrupts
things that needed to be disrupted*. In my experience, neither of
these two statements is true. As we've seen throughout this
book, technology has a habit of creating problems that it then
steps in to patch, whether it's parental controls to discourage

porn watching, or meditation apps designed to address the distractibility that technology has helped create. But a lot of the solutions to problems created by technology are to be found not online, not via a digital fix, but offline. Life isn't always supposed to be easy, time-saving, instantaneous, or a hack of some kind.

As I hope this book illustrates, every single longstanding relationship you and I have is in play, whether it's personal, professional, or in between, including many I haven't named. Even in these very early days of tech, the changes we've seen so far will be with us forever, or at least until today's children become tomorrow's parents and leaders and begin redefining what authority means to their own generation.

Throughout these pages, I've used the words "equality," "flattening," and "democratization." But if everything is horizontal, does this mean that power and authority no longer matter? Of course not. For many of us, what equality we gain via the internet ends when we go offline. The world today is more economically asymmetrical than ever. Hierarchy, status, and social divisions are a part of life. Misogyny and racism are as strong as they've ever been—if anything, the internet reveals the gruesome extent of the problem— as is every other cultural, social, and economic imbalance that existed before the internet came along. The internet and our smart phones equalize *use*, *access*, and *opportunity*—what they don't do, it seems, is transform the way people treat one another. Formal titles such as *father*, *boss*, *doctor*, *judge*, and *president* aren't going anywhere.

More than those formal titles themselves, new, perhaps, are the definitions we give them, because if nothing else, technology makes us ponder some interesting questions: Who

Do you think mobile phones have broken down social hierarchies?
#CA

ever said that a parent, or a politician, or a musician, had to be remote, or unavailable? How much or how little should parents communicate with their children? Should consumers offer to pay for music, even if they don't have to? What does it mean to take control of one's own health?

Even the best minds in the digital space don't yet have the answers as to what the future will bring, other than that it will be even faster and more connected. What we do know is that as a species we will make mistakes. We will learn things the hard way. We will experiment, fail, and try again. Right now, no one has any more wisdom, experience, or perspective than anyone else. Across the world, we all share in the same enchanted, disorienting learning experience we call technology. Like fairy-tale protagonists, we inch our way forward in the dark, guided only by the light of our phones and the connectivity we have all been granted, like an answer to prayers we don't remember saying.

I WROTE THIS BOOK FIRST AND FOREMOST to highlight the ongoing changes in relationships we see across every aspect in our lives. But to be frank, the impulse came out of the frustration I still feel, as a person who has spent a large part of his life working inside large organizations, when I observe the gulf that exists between society and the business world. Everyone I work alongside relies on his or her mobile phone. Why, then, do most institutions still insist on traditional and—to me, at least—archaic ways of doing business? What keeps them from acknowledging the changes taking place outside their walls and inside, too, among their own employees?

Maybe their resistance shouldn't come as a surprise. Any new technology can feel short-lived to people who've watched countless other technologies come and go—cassettes and CDs, Palm Pilots and Blackberries, Walkmans and iPods, zip drives, MySpace, Second Life, fax machines, phone answering machines, Betamax and VHS. The United States is both an innovative culture and a puritan one, and some of the things the internet carries off can feel suspiciously easy to us, as though technology has cut the line and defrauded a perfectly adequate system that hurt no one. What's more, almost none of us who love our phones can nonetheless be said to be entirely happy about how they make us behave.

Still, considering that mobile phone use will only get more widespread, I worry whether schools and colleges are preparing students properly not just for the digital revolution, but for future volatility and disruption. Every research and market trend report tells us that information technology will continue to be the hottest sector of the global economy. By 2020, the most in-demand jobs will be in computer systems analysis, software development, medical science, and biomedical engineering. Yet compared to students in twenty-seven other industrialized nations, the US ranks twenty-fifth in mathematics, seventeenth in science.[137] With coding poised to become the next blue-collar profession, how much sense does it make for our vocational schools to overstock their curriculums with courses in collision repair, cabinetmaking, cosmetology, and electrical? Are we preparing our students for today's and tomorrow's technological landscape? If not, why aren't we?

I never attended business school, but the last time I looked, the prefix "digital" showed up in roughly 1 percent of all business school course descriptions. This suggests that in the future, new MBA graduates will be unequipped to spark or

Are you happy with the amount of time you spend on your mobile phone? If you could stop one behavior of yours around mobile phone usage, what would it be? #CB propel any sort of meaningful innovation inside the companies where they work. Instead they will enter fiefdoms constructed by past generations with a mission to fortify and preserve the kingdom gates. Almost every job for which our top business schools prepare their graduates will bear no resemblance to real-world jobs in an all-out digital landscape, which means that organizations, societies, and countries will be obliged to spend countless millions of dollars retraining entire workforces. At the same time, organizations persist in asking people who came of age in earlier media environments to do their jobs in a landscape where a generation is no longer defined by ten or twenty years but by two. "The MBA students I speak to today are avid users of mobile," my boss, Dana Anderson, confirms. "They swim in that pool, but whether they're prepared for the workplace, I don't know."

> "The MBA students I speak to today are avid users of mobile. They swim in that pool, but whether they're prepared for the workplace, I don't know."
>
> *Mondelēz International's senior VP and chief marketing officer Dana Anderson*

With only 2 percent of America's education budget allotted to high tech, it's no wonder that the US continues losing ground to other nations. The White House has taken notice, too. In 2013, the Obama administration committed $3.1 billion to improve STEM education by training educators and driving new programs, curriculums, and methodologies. Western parents, and teachers and professors in middle school, high school, and college, need to awaken to the importance of math, science, and engineering, whether for the janitor whose broom will someday be connected invisibly to the internet,

> Do you think schools are properly preparing students for the digital revolution? How should schools integrate mobile in the classroom? #CC

the mother whose children's schedules can be adjusted with a tap on a screen, or the owners and employees of any and all small and large businesses. In today's tech environment, where the barriers to entry are malleable and the laws of hierarchy are in flux, everyone has the opportunity to get in on the ground floor, and end up a superstar.

How many generations are lucky enough to know that they are living *in* an era as they're living *through* it? I wrote earlier that one of the stranger attributes of being human is our inability to see ourselves changing as we are, in fact, changing. Today, we can see ourselves doing just that, and in real time, too. From the plow to the wheel to the light bulb to the automobile to satellite computing and everything in between, it's technology's job to challenge, disrupt, and disorient the reigning order. By taking a look at how technology is affecting relationships, just maybe, in the end, this book is about how technology is changing the relationship we have with ourselves.

endnotes

introduction

1. "Mobile Technology Fact Sheet," Pew Research Center, last modified October 2014, http://www.pewinternet.org /fact-sheets/mobile-technology-fact-sheet/.

chapter 1

2. Tesco Mobile (@tescomobile), Twitter post, October 6, 2013, 4:23 AM, https://twitter.com/tescomobile/status /386783638097915905.
3. Elizabeth Weingarten, "Forget Journalism School and Enroll in Groupon Academy," *The Atlantic*, last modified December 20, 2010, http://www.theatlantic.com/technology /archive/2010/12/forget-journalism-school-and-enroll-in -groupon-academy/68257/.
4. Christina Sterbenz, "So This Is Why Everyone Starts Sentences With 'So' These Days," *Slate*, May 1, 2014, http://www .slate.com/blogs/business_insider/2014/05/13/mark _zuckerberg_s_frequent_use_of_so_might_be_a_trend _especially_in_silicon.html.
5. "A Brief History of Customer Relationship Management," *CRMSwitch*, September 12, 2013, http://www.crmswitch .com/crm-industry/crm-industry-history/.
6. Ben Crair, "The Period Is Pissed," *New Republic*, last modified November 25, 2013, http://www.newrepublic.com /article/115726/period-our-simplest-punctuation-mark-has -become-sign-anger.

7. Albert Mehrabian, "Silent Messages: A Wealth of Information About Nonverbal Communication," 1981, http://www.kaaj .com/psych/smorder.html.

8. Lee Rainie, Kathryn Zickuhr, Kristen Purcell, Mary Madden, and Joanna Brenner, "The Rise of E-Reading," April 4, 2012, http://libraries.pewinternet.org/2012/04/04/the -rise-of-e-reading/.

chapter 2

9. Brandy Shaul, "WildTangent: 80 Percent of Moms Play Mobile Games at Least Once a Week," *AdWeek*, December 2, 2014, http://www.adweek.com/socialtimes/wildtangent -80-percent-moms-play-mobile-games-least-week/554272.

10. Parmy Olson, "Teenagers Say Goodbye to Facebook and Hello to Messenger Apps," *Guardian* (UK), last modified November 9, 2013, http://www.theguardian.com/technology/2013/nov /10/teenagers-messenger-apps-facebook-exodus.

11. Deepa Seetharaman, "Survey Finds Teens Prefer Instagram, Twitter, Snapchat for Social Networks," October 16, 2015, http://blogs.wsj.com/digits/2015/10/16/survey-finds-teens -prefer-instagram-snapchat-among-social-networks/.

12. Jenna Wortham, "WhatsApp Deal Bets on a Few Fewer 'Friends'," *New York Times*, last modified February 21, 2014, http ://www.nytimes.com/2014/02/22/technology/whatsapp -deal-bets-on-a-few-fewer-friends.html?_r=0.

13. Ferris Jabr, "Steven Pinker: Humans Are Less Violent Than Ever," *New Scientist* October 12, 2011, https://www. newscientist.com/article/mg21228340-100-steven-pinker -humans-are-less-violent-than-ever/.

14. Brooke Donatone, "Why Millennials Can't Grow Up," *Slate*, last modified December 2, 2013, http://www.slate.com /articles/health_and_science/medical_examiner/2013/12 /millennial_narcissism_helicopter_parents_are_college _students_bigger_problem.html.

chapter 3

15. Jordan Crook, "Who Runs the (Social Media) World? Girls." Techcrunch.com, last modified March 6, 2014, http ://techcrunch.com/2014/03/06/who-runs-the-social-media -world-girls/.

16. Diuk, Carlos Greg, "The Formation of Love," February 14, 2014, https://www.facebook.com/notes/facebook-data-science /the-formation-of-love/10152064609253859.

17. Valeriya Safronova, "Exes Explain Ghosting, the Ultimate Silent Treatment," *The New York Times*, June 26, 2015, http://www .nytimes.com/2015/06/26/fashion/exes-explain-ghosting -the-ultimate-silent-treatment.html.

18. Aaron Smith and Maeve Duggan, "Online Dating & Rela- tionships," October 21, 2013, http://www.pewinternet.org /2013/10/21/online-dating-relationships/.

19. Kate Knibbs, "Man-Ranking App LuLu Has a New Worst Enemy: The Brazilian Legal System, *Daily Dot*, last modified January 9, 2014, http://www.dailydot.com/lifestyle/brazil -axes-lulu/.

20. Maureen O'Connor, "The Nice Girls of Lulu, So-Called 'Yelp for Men'," *New York Magazine*, last modified November 13, 2013, http://nymag.com/thecut/2013/11/nice-girls-of-lulu -so-called-yelp-for-men.html.

21. Deborah Schoeneman, "What's He Really Like? Check the Lulu App," *New York Times*, last modified November 20, 2013, http://www.nytimes.com/2013/11/21/fashion/social -networking-App-allows-women-to-rate-men.html.

22. Nick Bilton, "Tinder, the Fast-Growing Dating App, Taps an Age-Old Truth," *The New York Times*, October 29, 2014, http://www.nytimes.com/2014/10/30/fashion/tinder-the -fast-growing-dating-app-taps-an-age-old-truth.html.

23. Elizabeth Segran, "Beyond Tinder: Can Anyone Create a Female-Friendly Online Dating Platform?" *Fast Company*, last modified September 10, 2014, http://www.fastcompany .com/3035471/strong-female-lead/beyond-tinder-can -anyone-create-a-female-friendly-online-dating-platform.

24. Ann Friedman, "Overwhelmed and Creeped Out," *New Yorker*, last modified February 26, 2013, http://www.newyorker.com/culture/culture-desk/overwhelmed-and-creeped-out.

25. Isaac Abel, "Did Porn Warp Me Forever?" Salon.com, last modified January 12, 2013, http://www.salon.com/2013/01/13/did_porn_warp_me_forever/.

26. Siobhan Rosen, "Dinner, Movie, and a Dirty Sanchez," *GQ Magazine*, January 27, 2012, http://www.gq.com/story/real-life-porn-sex-youporn-facial.

27. Ibid.

28. Gladys M. Martinez, PhD, and Joyce C. Abma, PhD, "Sexual Activity, Contraceptive Use, and Childbearing of Teenagers Aged 15–19 in the United States," Centers for Disease Control and Prevention, NCHS Data Brief, Number 209, last modified July 2015, http://www.cdc.gov/nchs/data/databriefs/db209.htm.

chapter 4

29. Candice Choi, "Gum Sales Have Been Mysteriously Tumbling for Years," March 20, 2014, http://www.businessinsider.com/gum-sales-are-tumbling-2014-3.

30. "Snack Attack: What Consumers Are Reaching For Around the World," *Nielsen*, September 2014, http://www.nielsen.com/content/dam/nielsenglobal/kr/docs/global-report/2014/Nielsen%20Global%20Snacking%20Report%20September%202014.pdf.

31. Mondelēz International CAGNY Conference, slideshow, February 18, 2014, http://files.shareholder.com/downloads/AMDA-1A8CT3/1415176841x0x726479/F6AEEF3E-70CD-4423-A11D-C7022FA2DE0C/CAGNY%202014.pdf.

32. The National Agricultural Library, "Basic Report: 19163, Chewing gum," National Nutrient Database for Standard Reference, Release 28, http://ndb.nal.usda.gov/ndb/foods/show/6193.

33. Mondelēz International CAGNY Conference.

34. Huget, "Be It Resolved: Embracing Mindful Snacking for the New Year."

35. Olga Kharif, "Shoppers' 'Mobile Blinders' Force Checkout-Aisle Changes," *Bloomberg*, March 21, 2013, http://www.bloomberg.com/news/articles/2013-03-21/shoppers-mobile-blinders-force-checkout-aisle-changes.

36. Richard Finnie, "Time is Money! The Impact of Customer 'Dwell Time' on Retail Sales," August 7, 2014, https://www.linkedin.com/pulse/20140807162720-258558574-time-is-money-the-impact-of-customer-dwell-time-on-retail-sales.

37. Katie Evans, "Mobile Devices Can Help Drive Store Sales," November 14, 2013, https://www.internetretailer.com/2013/11/14/mobile-devices-can-help-drive-store-sales.

38. Helen Leggatt, "IBM: Showrooming No Longer Top Threat to Brick and Mortar Stores," BizReport.com, last modified January 14, 2014, http://www.bizreport.com/2014/01/ibm-showrooming-no-longer-a-top-threat.html.

39. Emily Adler, "'Reverse Showrooming': Bricks-and-Mortar Retailers Fight Back," *Business Insider*, last modified July 13, 2014, http://www.businessinsider.com/reverse-showrooming-bricks-and-mortar-retailers-fight-back-2-2014-2.

40. Andrew Perrin, "One-Fifth of Americans Report Going Online 'Almost Constantly,'" December 8, 2015, http://www.pewresearch.org/fact-tank/2015/12/08/one-fifth-of-americans-report-going-online-almost-constantly/.

41. "Gartner Predicts Over 70 Percent of Global 200 Organisations Will Have at Least One Gamified Application by 2014," *Gartner*, last modified November 9, 2011, http://www.gartner.com/newsroom/id/1844115.

42. Lauren Johnson, "Mondelēz Prioritizes Hyperlocal Engagements Over Branding in Year-Two Tests," February 20, 2014, http://www.mobilemarketer.com/cms/news/strategy/17217.html.

43. Andrew Solomon, "Honey Maid and the Business of Love," *New Yorker*, last modified April 5, 2014, http://www.newyorker.com/business/currency/honey-maid-and-the-business-of-love.

44. Ibid.

45. Michelle Bertino, "Facebook vs. Twitter—How Does Engagement Differ on Each?," *The Official Klout Blog*, May 9, 2014, http://blog.klout.com/2014/05/topics-that-get-a-reaction/.

46. "Retail Divisions," *Walmart*, http://corporate.walmart.com/_news_/news-archive/2005/01/07/our-retail-divisions.

chapter 5

47. "The Heist 1 Year Anniversary. A Look Back on the Year that Changed Everything," *Macklemore.com*, accessed December 3, 2015, http://macklemore.com/post/63746955005/the-heist-1-year-anniversary-a-look-back-on-the-year.

48. Ibid.

49. "A Stream of Music, Not Revenue," http://www.nytimes.com/2013/12/13/business/media/a-stream-of-music-not-revenue.html?pagewanted=2&_r=0&hp.

50. "Concert Ticket Sales in North America from 1990 to 2014," *Statista*, http://www.statista.com/statistics/306065/concert-ticket-sales-revenue-in-north-america/.

51. Tom Cheshire, "BioBeats App Generates Custom Music from Your Heartrate," March 14, 2013, http://www.wired.co.uk/magazine/archive/2013/03/play/your-heart-is-a-dj%20.

52. Georg Szalai, "Spotify's Daniel Ek Zings Dr. Dre's Beats Music," *Hollywood Reporter*, January 22, 2014, http://www.hollywoodreporter.com/print/672509.

53. "Shazam Surpasses 100 Million Mobile Monthly Active Users," *Shazam*, http://news.shazam.com/pressreleases/shazam-surpasses-100-million-mobile-monthly-active-users-1042187.

54. "Shazam Predicts 2014 Grammy Winners," Business Wire, last modified January 20, 2014, http://www.businesswire.com/news/home/20140120005499/en/Shazam-Predicts-2014-Grammy-Winners.

55. Stuart Dredge, "Streaming Music Payments: How Much Do Artists Really Receive?, *Guardian* (UK), last modified August 19, 2013, http://www.theguardian.com/technology/2013/aug/19/zoe-keating-spotify-streaming-royalties.

56. Lewis Randy, "Music Industry Revenue in 2013 Stayed Flat at $7 Billion, RIAA says," *Los Angeles Times*, March 18, 2014.

57. "An industry of growing digital revenues and multiple income streams internationally," *IFPI*, http://www.ifpi.org /facts-and-stats.php.

58. Randy, "Music Industry Revenue."

59. Michael Calore, "Why Neil Young Hates MP3—And What You Can Do About It," *Wired*, February 2, 2012, http://www .wired.com/gadgetlab/2012/02/why-neil-young-hates-mp3 -and-what-you-can-do-about-it/.

60. "Neil Young Hates MP3 Quality, Says We're Missing 95% of the Sound, *98.7 KLUV,* January 26, 2012, http://kluv.cbslocal .com/2012/01/26/neil-young-hates-mp3-quality-says-were -missing-95-of-the-sound/.

61. Mary Kaye Schilling, "Get Busy: Pharrell's Productivity Secrets," *Fast Company*, last modified November 18, 2013, http://www.fastcompany.com/3021377/pharrell-get-busy.

chapter 6

62. "America's Health Disadvantage," *New York Times*, January 10, 2013, http://www.nytimes.com/2013/01/11/opinion /americas-health-disadvantage.html.

63. "Ambulatory Care Use and Physician Office Visits," *Centers for Disease Control and Prevention*, http://www.cdc.gov/nchs /fastats/physician-visits.htm.

64. Sandeep Jaurar, *Doctored: The Disillusionment of an American Physician* (New York: Farrar, Straus & Giroux, 2014), 13.

65. Albert Sun, "The Monitored Man," *New York Times*, March 10, 2014, http://well.blogs.nytimes.com/2014/03/10/the -monitored-man/.

66. Conn, Joseph, "No Longer a Novelty, Medical Apps Are Increasingly Valuable to Clinicians and Patients," *Modern Healthcare*, December 14, 2013.

67. Angela McIntyre and Jessica Ekholm, "Market Trends: Enter the Wearable Electronics Market with Products for the Quantified Self," *Gartner*, last modified, July 1,

2013, https://www.gartner.com/doc/2537715/market-trends-enter-wearable-electronics.

68. Arwa Mahdawi, "The Unhealthy Side of Wearable Fitness Devices," *Guardian* (UK), last modified January 3, 2014, http://www.theguardian.com/commentisfree/2014/jan/03/unhealthy-wearable-fitness-devices-calories-eating-disorders-nike-fuelband.

69. Ibid.

70. Harry McCracken, "Jawbone's UP Fitness App Will Support Apple's Hardware—and Everybody Else's, Too," *Fast Company*, last modified September 8, 2014, http://www.fastcompany.com/3035462/jawbones-up-fitness-app-will-support-apples-hardware-and-everybody-elses-too.

71. Ibid.

72. Denise Grady, Tara Parker-Pope, and Pam Belluck, "Jolie's Disclosure of Preventive Mastectomy Highlights Dilemma," *New York Times*, last modified May 14, 2013, http://www.nytimes.com/2013/05/15/health/angelina-jolies-disclosure-highlights-a-breast-cancer-dilemma.html?pagewanted=all.

73. Angelina Jolie, "My Medical Choice," *New York Times*, last modified May 14, 2013, http://www.nytimes.com/2013/05/14/opinion/my-medical-choice.html.

74. Michael Wolff, "A Life Worth Ending," *New York Magazine*, last modified May 20, 2012, http://nymag.com/news/features/parent-health-care-2012-5/.

75. Grayson K. Vincent and Victoria A. Velkoff, "The Next Four Decades: The Older Population in the United States: 2010 to 2015," *Census.gov*, May 2010, https://www.census.gov/prod/2010pubs/p25-1138.pdf.

76. Ibid.

77. Howard Gleckman, "More People Are Dying at Home and in Hospice, But They Are Also Getting More Intense Hospital Care," *Forbes*, February 6, 2013, http://www.forbes.com/sites/howardgleckman/2013/02/06/more-people-are-dying-at-home-and-in-hospice-but-they-are-also-getting-more-intense-hospital-care/.

78. "2015 Alzheimer's Disease Facts and Figures," *Alzheimer's Association*, http://www.alz.org/facts/.

79. Ibid.

80. Pam Belluck, "Coverage for End-of-Life Talks Gaining Ground," *New York Times*, last modified August 30, 2014, http://www.nytimes.com/2014/08/31/health/end-of-life -talks-may-finally-overcome-politics.html.
81. Deborah D. Danner, David A. Snowdon, and Wallace V. Friesen, "Positive Emotions in Early Life and Longevity: Findings from the Nun Study," *American Psychological Association*, October 2010, https://www.apa.org/pubs/journals /releases/psp805804.pdf.

chapter 7

82. David Carr, "How Obama Tapped Into Social Networks' Power," *New York Times*, last modified November 9, 2008, http://www .nytimes.com/2008/11/10/business/media/10carr.html.
83. Martin Kaste, "When Politicians Slip, Video Trackers Are There," NPR.org, last modified April 23, 2012, http://www.npr.org/2012/04/23/151060718/behind-the -scene-to-the-next-debacles-video-trackers.
84. Matt Richtel and Nicholas Confessore, "Republicans Are Wooing the Wired," *New York Times*, last modified February 8, 2014, http://www.nytimes.com/2014/02/09/technology /republicans-are-wooing-the-wired.html.
85. "How the Presidential Candidates Use the Web and Social Media," Pew Research Center, last modified August 15, 2012, http://www.journalism.org/2012/08/15/how-presidential -candidates-use-web-and-social-media/.
86. Matt Richtel and Nicholas Confessore, "Republicans are Wooing the Wired."
87. Ibid.
88. Claire Cain Miller, "How Social Media Silences Debate," *New York Times*, last modified August 26, 2014, http://www .nytimes.com/2014/08/27/upshot/how-social-media-silences -debate.html.
89. Chris Cillizza, "How Twitter Has Changed Politics— and Political Journalism," *Washington Post*, last modified November 7, 2013, http://www.washingtonpost.com/blogs /the-fix/wp/2013/11/07/how-twitter-has-changed-politics -and-political-journalism/.

90. Frank Newport, "Mobile Technology in Politics More Potential than Reality," Gallup.com, last modified April 29, 2014, http://www.gallup.com/poll/168767/mobile-technology-politics-potential-reality.aspx.

91. Sean Sullivan, "Presidential Election Turnout Ticked Down from 2008," *Washington Post*, last modified November 8, 2012, https://www.washingtonpost.com/news/the-fix/wp/2012/11/08/presidential-election-turnout-ticked-down-from-2008-estimate-shows/.

92. Rashimi Athlekar, "Strategic Review of Obama's Segmenting and Targetting [sic] Strategies," slideshow, last modified on November 30, 2008, http://www.slideshare.net/rascorpion/segmenting-targetting-for-obama-campaign-presentation.

chapter 8

93. Cindy Wooden, "Pope: Young People Shouldn't Waste Their Time on Mobile Phones," CatholicHerald.co.uk, last modified August 6, 2014, http://www.catholicherald.co.uk/news/2014/08/06/pope-young-people-shouldnt-waste-their-time-on-mobile-phones/.

94. Victoria Woollaston, "How Often Do You Check Your Phone?" *Daily Mail* (UK), last modified October 8, 2013, http://www.dailymail.co.uk/sciencetech/article-2449632/How-check-phone-The-average-person-does-110-times-DAY-6-seconds-evening.html.

95. Jeff Bercovici, "Can Twitter Save TV? (And Can TV Save Twitter?)," *Forbes*, last modified October 28, 2013, http://www.forbes.com/sites/jeffbercovici/2013/10/07/can-twitter-save-tv-and-can-tv-save-twitter/.

96. Ibid.

97. Suzanne Vranica, "MTV Aims for Multitasker," *Wall Street Journal*, last modified September 5, 2012, http://www.wsj.com/articles/SB10000872396390443589304577633664201676608.

98. Amol Sharma, "TV Networks Play to 'Second Screen'," *Wall Street Journal*, last modified June 1, 2013, http://www.wsj.com/articles/SB10001424127887324682204578515630138741200.

99. Andrew Adam Newman, "Like That Vase on the TV? Click Your Phone to Buy It," *New York Times*, last modified March 17, 2014, http://www.nytimes.com/2014/03/18/business/media /like-that-vase-on-the-tv-click-your-phone-to-buy-it.html.

100. Ibid.

101. Melena Ryzik, "An Encore 35 Years in the Making," *New York Times*, last modified August 22, 2014, http://www .nytimes.com/2014/08/23/arts/music/kate-bush-fans-travel -to-see-rare-concerts-in-london.html.

chapter 9

102. New York City Department of City Planning, "New York City Population Projections by Age/Sex & Borough, 2010– 2040," *New York City.gov*, last modified December 2013, http://www.nyc.gov/html/dcp/pdf/census/projections _report_2010_2040.pdf.

103. Self Storage Industry Fact Sheet, *Self Storage Associaton*, last accessed October 3, 2015, http://www.selfstorage.org/ssa /content/navigationmenu/aboutssa/factsheet/.

104. Jeffrey Rosen, "The Web Means the End of Forgetting," *New York Times*, last modified July 21, 2010, http://www.nytimes .com/2010/07/25/magazine/25privacy-t2.html.

105. John Harlow and Robin Henry, "It's iHard as Willis Fights Apple,' *The Sunday Times*, last modified September 2, 2012, http://www.thesundaytimes.co.uk/sto/news/uk_news/Tech /article1117103.ece.

106. Charles Arthur, "No, Bruce Willis Isn't Suing Apple over iTunes Rights," *The Guardian*, last modified September 3, 2012, http://www.theguardian.com/technology/blog/2012 /sep/03/no-apple-bruce-willis.

107. Sam Schechner, "Google Starts Removing Search Results Under Europe's 'Right to Be Forgotten'," *Wall Street Journal*, last modified June 26, 2014, http://www.wsj.com/articles /google-starts-removing-search-results-under-europes-right -to-be-forgotten-1403774023.

108. Brian Fung, "Google Has Scrubbed Fifty Links to Wikipedia, Thanks to the 'Right to Be Forgotten' Law," *Washington Post*, last modified August 6, 2014, https://www.washingtonpost

.com/news/the-switch/wp/2014/08/06/the-folks-behind
-wikipedia-have-issued-their-first-transparency-report
-heres-whats-in-it/.

109. Ibid.

110. Jonathan Zittrain, "Don't Force Google to 'Forget'," *New
York Times*, last modified May 14, 2014, http://www.nytimes
.com/2014/05/15/opinion/dont-force-google-to-forget.html.

111. Ibid.

112. Zachary Sniderman, "If I Die: Facebook App Lets You Leave
Sweet Last Words," *Mashable*, last modified January 6, 2012,
http://mashable.com/2012/01/06/if-i-die-facebook-app/.

113. Claire Martin, "Rentals That Let You Fly the Coop," *New York
Times*, last modified October 26, 2013, http://www.nytimes
.com/2013/10/27/business/rentals-that-let-you-fly-the-coop
.html.

chapter 10

114. Misiek Piskorski, "Why China Loves the Internet," *Harvard
Business Review*, last modified December 2, 2013, https://hbr
.org/2013/12/why-china-loves-the-internet/.

115. Ibid.

116. Vindu Goel, Michael J. De La Merced, and Neil Gough,
"Chinese Giant Alibaba Will Go Public, Listing in the US,"
New York Times, last modified May 6, 2014, http://
mobile.nytimes.com/blogs/dealbook/2014/05/06/alibaba
-files-to-go-public-in-the-u-s/.

117. "India Census: Half of Homes Have Phones but No Toilets,"
BBC, last modified March 14, 2012, http://www.bbc.co.uk
/news/world-asia-india-17362837.

118. "Research and Development Expenditure (% of GDP) in
India," *Trading Economics*, http://www.tradingeconomics
.com/india/research-and-development-expenditure-percent
-of-gdp-wb-data.html.

119. Kirsten Bound and Ian Thorton, "Our Frugal Future: Lessons
from India's Innovation System," *Nesta*, last modified July

2012, http://www.nesta.org.uk/sites/default/files/our
_frugal_future.pdf.

120. "Fernanda Hoefel, Dikran Kiulhitzan, Julia Broide, and
Marina Mazzarolo, "Mapping the Mindset of Brazil's Not-
So-New Middle Class Consumers," *McKinsey & Company
Marketing*, last modified January 2014, http://www
.mckinseyonmarketingandsales.com/sites/default/files/pdf
/CSI_Brazil%20middle%20class.pdf.

121. "Global Wealth Databook 2013," *Credit Suisse Research Insti-
tute*, last modified October 2013, http://usagainstgreed.org
/GlobalWealthDatabook2013.pdf.

122. Claire Charron, Cullen Schiele, Victoria Cana, and Evann
Clingan, "Global Twitter Trends: Brazil," *360i*, July 2014,
http://www.360i.co.uk/reports/global-twitter-trends-brazil/.

123. "Leading Countries Based on Number of Facebook Users as of
May 2014," *Statista*, http://www.statista.com/statistics/268136
/top-15-countries-based-on-number-of-facebook-users/.

124. "11 Facts About HIV in Africa," *DoSomething.org*, https://www
.dosomething.org/facts/11-facts-about-hiv-africa.

125. "World Population to Exceed 9 Billion By 2015," *United Nations*,
press release, last modified March 11, 2009, http://www.un
.org/esa/population/publications/wpp2008/pressrelease.pdf.

126. David Smith, "Internet Use on Mobile Phones in Africa Predicted to Increase Twenty-Fold," *Guardian* (UK), last modified June 5, 2014, http://www.theguardian.com/world/2014
/jun/05/internet-use-mobile-phones-africa-predicted
-increase-20-fold.

127. Toby Shapshak, "Africa Not Just a Mobile-First Continent—It's Mobile Only," *CNN*, last modified October 4,
2012, http://edition.cnn.com/2012/10/04/tech/mobile/africa
-mobile-opinion/.

128. Jay Moye, "Coca-Cola Named 2014 Mobile Marketer of
the Year, *Coca-Cola Company*, last modified January 14,
2015, http://www.coca-colacompany.com/stories/coke
-named-2014-mobile-marketer-of-the-year/.

129. Anand Giridharadas, "Africa's Gift to Silicon Valley: How
to Track a Crisis," *New York Times*, last modified March 13,

2010, http://www.nytimes.com/2010/03/14/weekinreview/14giridharadas.html.

130. "Yandex: Google's Russian Rival," *Ignition One*, last modified January 16, 2014, http://www.ignitionone.com/yandex-googles-russian-rival/.

131. "Russian Social Media," *Translate Media*, https://www.translatemedia.com/translation-services/social-media/russian-social-media/.

132. "The Mobile Consumer: A Global Snapchat," *Nielsen*, February 2013, http://www.nielsen.com/content/dam/corporate/uk/en/documents/Mobile-Consumer-Report-2013.pdf.

133. Kari Paul, "Putin Signs Law with Potential to Censor Facebook and Twitter in Russia," Mashable.com, last modified July 23, 2014, http://mashable.com/2014/07/23/putin-signs-low-that-could-block-social-media/.

134. Alexia Tsotsis, "Telegram Saw 8M Downloads After Whats App Got Acquired," *Tech Crunch*, February 24, 2014, http://techcrunch.com/2014/02/24/telegram-saw-8m-downloads-after-whatsapp-got-acquired/.

135. David Rowan, "Messaging Apps Shouldn't Make Money," *Wired UK*, last modified January 12, 2015, http://www.wired.co.uk/magazine/archive/2015/03/features/messaging-apps.

conclusion

136. A. O. Scott, "The Death of Adulthood in American Culture," *New York Times*, September 11, 2014, http://www.nytimes.com/2014/09/14/magazine/the-death-of-adulthood-in-american-culture.html.

137. "Programme for International Student Assessment (PISA) 2012," OECD, http://www.oecd.org/pisa/keyfindings/pisa-2012-results.htm.

index

about the author

B. BONIN BOUGH is Chief Media and e-Commerce Officer at Mondelēz International. He has been active in transforming large organizations, having lead some of the industry's largest and most innovative global media investments across mobile, digital, television, print, and outdoors. He is unique in his commitment to forging partnerships with the industry's largest players—including Facebook, Twitter, YouTube, Sony, Paramount, and ABC—making him a force to be reckoned with.

Found consistently at the forefront of thinking and execution in mobile, Bonin is recognized as one of business' hottest rising stars and one of the industry's top mobile marketers. He was recently inducted into the American Advertising Federation's Advertising Hall of Achievement. He can also be found in lists such as *Fortune*'s 40 under 40, *Fast Company*'s 100 Most Creative People in Business, *Ebony*'s Power 100, and *The Internationalist*'s Internationalists of the Year.

As a driving force behind numerous first-of-their-kind initiatives and brand reinventions, Bonin is recognized as a leader in diversified talent, partnering startups with brands and executing the first-ever branded campaigns with Instagram, Foursquare, Tinder, Snapchat, and countless others. More recently, Bonin has championed talent as the pivotal transforming agent over the next decade, including the need for established companies to invest in their employees in order to better compete in the marketplace and move their businesses into the future.

Prior to joining Mondelēz International, Bonin spent over three years at PepsiCo, where he oversaw digital strategy globally and drove the implementation of countless digital marketing campaigns. Bonin was instrumental in integrating digital media into PepsiCo's overall brand vision and growth strategy, securing them a spot on *Fast Company*'s Most Innovative Companies list.

Bonin's passion for the new and nascent as well as his expertise in mobile led to the launch of some of the first-of-their-kind corporate mobile accelerators, PepsiCo10 and Mobile Futures.

Bonin attended Hartwick College, earning degrees in physics and political science. He also taught for five years at NYU's Center for Publishing, leading courses on the principles and applications of online publishing. Bonin is the co-author of the 2010 book *Perspectives on Social Media Marketing* and is a board member of the Mobile Marketing Association's Executive Marketer Advisory Board, the Digital Collective, and the Social Media Advisory Council.

Bonin's achievements in the world of mobile marketing have won him numerous awards, including a Cannes Lions Grand Prix, Webby, Stevie, Golden Pencil, SABRE, Big Apple, Communication Arts magazine, and SXSW People's Choice for MrPicassoHead.com.